MARCHING
WITH
WELLINGTON

by the same author

The Inniskilling Diaries 1899–1903

(Leo Cooper, 2001)

MARCHING WITH WELLINGTON 1808–1815

The 27th (Inniskilling) Foot
from the Peninsula to Waterloo

by

MARTIN CASSIDY

with a Foreword by

BRIGADIER W.J. HILES CBE

LEO COOPER

First published in Great Britain in 2003 by
LEO COOPER
an imprint of Pen & Sword Books,
47 Church Street, Barnsley, S. Yorks, S70 2AS

ISBN 0 85052 981 6

A CIP record for this book is available from the British Library.

Typeset in 11/13pt Sabon by
Phoenix Typesetting, Burley-in-Wharfedale, West Yorkshire

Printed by
CPI UK

Dedication

For my son and friend Steven,
(B.Sc. Hons. Dip. I. S.)
a remarkably brave young man
without whom the world is a much sadder place.
Also my wife Penny
and children Simon, Ruth and Stephanie.

Contents

Foreword		ix
Acknowledgements		xi
Introduction		xiii
One	3rd Battalion the 27th Inniskilling Fusiliers 1807–1811	1
Two	1812, The 3rd Battalion	7
Three	1813	13
Four	Lieutenant Charles Crowe	19
Five	1814	64
Six	The Battle of Toulouse	102
Seven	Across the Atlantic	132
Eight	Arrival in Belgium	141
Nine	Waterloo	148
Ten	The 27th Square	156
Eleven	Napoleon's Last Throw	164
Twelve	A Raw Deal	171
Thirteen	The 6th Inniskilling Dragoon Guards	176
Appendix I	Officers killed and wounded in the Peninsula	180
Appendix II	Roll of Officers, 27th Foot (Inniskilling Fusiliers) 25 March – 24 June 1815	187
Appendix III	Roll of Non-Commissioned Officers & Other Ranks who served with the 27th Foot 25 March – 24 June 1815	190
Bibliography		199
Notes		201
Index		213

FOREWORD

Wellington's campaigns in the Iberian Peninsula and at Waterloo have been well documented over the years by numerous authors, mostly concentrating on the higher levels of command and, in particular, the actions of the great man himself. Few have dwelt on the lower levels and even fewer have been able to colour their narrative with detailed contemporary observations. Martin Cassidy has skilfully achieved this by weaving together the relevant parts of the history of The Royal Inniskilling Fusiliers and the contemporary diaries of Lieutenant Charles Crowe of the 27th Inniskillings held in the archive of the regimental museum in Enniskillen. He paints a fascinating picture of regimental life on campaign in the early 19th Century as observed by a participant, a picture which allows us a simultaneous glimpse of the military history and the social background of the period. There are many lessons in Mr Cassidy's book for the serious student of military and social history. Among the most interesting is the all-embracing influence of the regiment in determining the character and performance of its officers and men when put to the test.

The terms "Regiment" and "Battalion" are frequently confused, and perhaps understandably so. A regiment is infinitely expandable and can comprise any number of battalions. The 27th Inniskillings, for example, rose to three battalions during the Peninsular War, each of which could (and did) feed off the others to adjust strengths if necessary. Where there is but a single battalion of a regiment, the terms are interchangeable. However, it is the regiment that is the foundation stone on which all else is built and from which springs the esprit de corps that is so important to the maintenance of morale in hard times. It is built up over many years and involves the differences that make each individual regiment feel it is 'special'. The 27th took pride in being one of the six "Old Corps" allowed its regimental badge (the castle of Enniskillen with St George's flag flying) from 1751, whilst others had to use the royal cipher. These, and the many other such distinctions accumulated along the way, contribute to the corporate pride which, in turn, leads to high standards of morale and conduct such as those portrayed in this book.

Lieutenant Crowe's diaries contain a wealth of information, revealing in some detail the organization and management of the lines of communication, the efficient functioning of which was essential to the success of Wellington's front-line operations. Billeting, the provision of rations and the re-supply of both men and material are all well covered, as are disciplinary matters and the medical system. The latter was particularly well tested by Crowe whose writings betray near obsession with his own state of health, though he does, occasionally, poke fun at his own concerns. The reader is also given an insight into the relationship between officers and enlisted men and the status of wives and families within the army. Operational matters are also well covered, as we follow the travels of the 27th in a number of theatres. A critical look is taken at the professional ability of commanders at the regimental, brigade and divisional levels in relation to operations in which the 27th took part and there is no doubt that some were found wanting, illustrating the dangers of the prevailing system of promotion by purchase, allied to the preferment often given by senior officers to relatives and friends. Promotion thus gained was not always matched by ability and often the soldiers were the losers.

Martin Cassidy's narrative culminates in that epic, final clash between those two giants of military endeavour, Wellington and Napoleon, at Waterloo, one of the few occasions on which the two regiments raised in Enniskillen in 1689 fought on the same battlefield. The operations of the 27th Inniskillings and the 6th Inniskilling Dragoons are both chronicled. We read of the 1st Battalion of the 27th Inniskillings, a battalion of young, inexperienced soldiers, holding a key position and enduring horrendous casualties with fortitude and tenacity that stirs the pride and admiration of their successors to this day. There could be no more dramatic an ending to a thoroughly enthralling story. Martin Cassidy's second foray into the archives of The Royal Inniskilling Fusiliers has brought to life a colourful period of the regiment's history in yet another masterly work, of which he can be justifiably proud.

Brigadier W.J. Hiles, CBE
Chairman of Trustees
The Royal Inniskilling Fusiliers

ACKNOWLEDGEMENTS

Writing a book can never be a solo undertaking; by its very nature it is an amalgam of numerous peoples and institutions. It is for this reason that I wish to acknowledge the following individuals and organizations who have helped me bring this project to fruition.

First and foremost I would like to thank my wife Penny and children Simon, Ruth and Stephanie for their constant support and encouragement throughout this undertaking. A very special debt of thanks is owed to my late son and friend Steven, a graduate in Applied Computing at the University of Ulster. Although sadly no longer with us, it was his inspiration, example and perseverance which drove me to complete the task. I am also indebted to my son Simon, a computer whiz and graphic artist, without whose expertise this book would never have been possible. I would also like to thank my daughter Ruth, an A Level history student, for aiding my research, and my daughter Stephanie for her keen knowledge of photography and scanning. Without them there is no doubt my task would have been all the more difficult.

I would also like to thank Mr David Hall of Enniskillen, a trustee of the Royal Inniskilling Fusilier Regimental Museum, who realized the true importance of my work and encouraged me to continue.

I would like to express my sincere thanks to Brigadier W.J. Hiles CBE for taking the time to read my MS and write the Foreword. Also the Trustees of the Royal Inniskilling Fusiliers for their support and permission to use Lieutenant Charles Crowe's diary/memoirs of which the museum holds the copyright. I would also like to extend my thanks to the Curator of the Royal Inniskilling Regimental Museum, Enniskillen Castle, and his staff, for their assistance.

I also thank Mr David Truesdale for his help in furnishing me with details relating to a number of the casualties sustained during the Peninsular campaign.

However, undoubtedly the bulk of my appreciation must fall to Lieutenant Charles Crowe. Without his invaluable insight into the period, the attitudes, bias and customs, this book would have been much the poorer. Unpretentious, his diary/memoir does not attempt to analyse any aspect of the war in detail. Instead he records the day-to-day events as they occurred in relation to his own movements. His graphic account of nineteenth century Portugal and Spain gives us a privileged glimpse into the more social aspect of military history.

Throughout the book I have kept to Crowe's personal script in its entirety. To interfere with this would be to alter the reader's perception of the writer. However, it has been necessary to clarify certain points such as place names and those of individuals in an attempt to bring his script up to a more readable twenty-first century standard. Nevertheless in doing so it has lost none of its original character.

Finally no acknowledgement would be complete without a debt of thanks being extended to my publisher Pen & Sword Books/Leo Cooper, especially Brigadier Henry Wilson for his patience and understanding. His guidance and encouragement both in this present endeavour and my previous publication *The Inniskilling Diaries 1899–1903* has been invaluable.

INTRODUCTION

In recent years the highly enjoyable novels of Bernard Cornwell and the exploits of his fictional character, Major Richard Sharpe, have brought the Peninsular War and the Battle of Waterloo to the forefront of the public mind. Adapted for television, these stories have been tailored for the small screen in such an entertaining fashion that they have created a whole new appreciation of the period, albeit one which views the Peninsular War as entertainment rather than fact. Nevertheless, though fictional, they have helped create a healthy interest in the Napoleonic Wars and the early nineteenth century by bringing the period alive to thousands not normally conversant with that era.

History, I believe, is not a random or even consecutive accumulation of facts, figures or statistics. True history is life. It is an accumulation of lives, lived and lost. To truly appreciate history, it must be enjoyed. Above all, history is people, an acknowledgement of those who have gone before. Life is neither dispassionate nor remote, therefore neither should history. As with all aspects of life, history and the writing thereof should be enjoyed and made entertaining, rather than being portrayed as simply a dry regurgitation of facts and dates which numb the senses and alienate the reader.

Nevertheless it is, in all probability, safe to assume that the Battle of Waterloo is possibly one of the most thoroughly researched, most extensively commented upon battles of the nineteenth century, if not *the* most. As the culmination of Wellington's encounters with Bonaparte, it surpasses the battles of the Peninsula in importance and significance. The memory of that fateful day, 18 June 1815, has over the centuries been further enhanced by the mystique which surrounds its two main protagonists, those two great leaders of men, Sir Arthur Wellesley, Duke of Wellington, and Napoleon Bonaparte, Emperor of France.

Of the numerous books that have been written through the years on the subject of Wellington's defeat of Napoleon at Waterloo, none, I feel, have done justice to the gallant stand made by the 27th

Inniskillings on that wet day in June 1815. Nor have the exploits of the 6th Inniskilling Dragoons, as part of Ponsonby's Union Brigade, received true recognition for their outstanding valour.

The purpose of this book is to correct an oversight which, in my opinion, has been perpetuated for nigh on two hundred years. By recounting the valiant conduct of both regiments I hope in some small way to set the record straight and will have produced a work, which acknowledges the vital role played by the only two Irish Regiments to take part in the Battle of Waterloo.

The 27th Regiment of Foot, the Royal Inniskilling Fusiliers, is a Regiment with a long and valiant history. It can trace its history from the seventeenth century to its amalgamation in 1968 with the Royal Irish Fusiliers and the Royal Ulster Rifles to form the Royal Irish Rangers. Throughout its long history, there have been certain actions which have won it special recognition. It can indeed chart its history through battles and engagements which have shaped history and rewritten the maps of nations, but none more so than at the Battle of Waterloo.

However, though they, virtually single-handed, held Wellington's centre and thus robbed Napoleon of what would have undoubtedly been certain victory, their efforts on 18 June 1815 have been greatly overshadowed by what may be termed more glamorous regiments. The Guards Regiments and the cavalry may indeed have performed sterling work on that day, but it was the infantry, in particular the 27th Regiment of Foot, who bore the brunt of the battle and won the day for Wellington.

All those under Wellington's command demonstrated the utmost determination and gallantry. Every regiment deserves credit for its tenacity and steadfastness and in emphasizing the role of the Inniskilling Fusiliers as part of the 10th (British) Infantry Brigade and the Inniskilling Dragoons as part of Ponsonby's Union Brigade, I do not wish to detract from the bravery or sacrifice of others. I merely wish to acknowledge the vital roll played by these two fine Irish regiments, which I feel has been lessened by the presence of more 'fashionable' regiments who have stolen the limelight simply by nature of their name or country of origin.

To fully appreciate the significance of what took place at Waterloo it is first necessary to look at the Peninsular War in some detail. I shall do so from the perspective the 27th Inniskilling Fusiliers and I make no apology for this. I also make frequent reference to the diary/memoirs of Lieutenant Charles Crowe, 2nd Battalion the 27th Foot. Although not always in the thick of the fighting, his very human account of life during the campaign gives us a brief insight into the likes, dislikes, routines and sacrifices of campaign life.

His account is highly informative and makes fascinating reading. Unfortunately I cannot do justice to it here in its entirety. But I hope that those passages which I have chosen to illustrate the campaign will allow us an insight into, not only the period, but also the man.

In truth, there is little real glory to be found in war. There is only an overwhelming momentary feeling of terror superseded by an enormous feeling of relief and melancholy among those who survive. War is a dirty, squalid affair which degenerates and dehumanizes the participants. There is nothing glorious in the sight of a battlefield strewn with the dead and dying in the aftermath of a battle or the drunken excesses of troops let loose upon a defenceless town or city in the aftermath of a siege, such as Ciudad Rodrigo or Badajoz.

Glory, if glory it be, in the form of flag-waving, medals and battle honours are attributed after the event, oftener than not by individuals who took little or no part in the affair. This book is not intended as a glorification of war; rather it is a factual account, which hopes to recognize the sacrifice of all.

A Chronology of Dates and Events Through the Peninsula until the Battle of Waterloo

1808

May 1808: Marched from Enniskillen to the Curragh.
18 July: Marched from the Curragh to
Middleton Barracks, Co. Cork.
9 September: Sailed from Cork to Falmouth, England.
9 October: Sailed from Falmouth bound for Spain.
14 October: Arrived off Corunna.
25 October: Embarked for Lisbon.
3 November: Arrived off Lisbon.

1809

January 1809: Savacen, near Lisbon, until embarked for Cadiz.
11 February: Returned to Lisbon.
14 March: Occupied Bellen Barracks.
22 April: Arrived Leria.
2 May: Abrantes.
June: Returned to Lisbon on account of ill health.
28 September: Left Lisbon.
8 October: Arrived Badajoz.

1810

17 January 1810: At Celerica, to Guarda until September.
27 September: Battle of Busaco.
Autumn: Village of Patemeira.
Winter: The vicinity of Azambija and Virtudas.

1811

11 March 1811: Engaged in skirmish at Redinha;
marched via Thomar, Barquinta,
Anonchis, Campo Mayor, Elvas, Olivenze to Badajoz.
May: First siege of Badajoz.
16 June: Battle of Albuera; then to Elvas.
End of July: Aldee da Bisbo.
Winter: Almedia.

1812

9–19 January: Siege of Ciudad Rodrigo; then to Villa de Corvo.
3 March: Marched via Penemaçon, Castellobranco
and Portalegre to Badajoz.
March to 6 April: Third siege of Badajoz.
Early May: St Joas de Perquèire.
18 July: Skirmish at Castrajon.
22 July: Battle of Salamanca.
12 August: Madrid; were in quarters at Escurial until
3 October until they marched towards Portugal.
12 November: Passed through Alma de Tormes.
14 November: 1st Battalion left Sicily and embarked for Alicante.
Winter: Wintered in Villa de Corvo, near Almedia.
10 December: 2nd Battalion left Sicily and embarked for Alicante.

1813

Early months 1813: Stationed at Meda,
Escalhao and Estramousa (3rd Battalion).
7 March: Skirmish at Alcoy (1st & 2nd Battalions).
12 & 13 April: Battle of Castalla (1st & 2nd Battalions).
2–12 June: Siege of Tarragona (1st & 2nd Battalions).
21 June: Battle of Vitoria (3rd Battalion).
13 September: Action at Ordal (2nd Battalion).
10 November: Battle of the Nivelle (3rd Battalion).
9–13 December: Passage of the Nive (3rd Battalion).
Winter: Wintered in the vicinity of Tarragona (1st & 2nd
Battalions).

1814

27 February 1814: Battle of Orthez (3rd Battalion).
February to April: Blockade of Barcelona (1st & 2nd Battalion).
10 April: Battle of Toulouse (3rd Battalion).
14 April: March to Bordeaux via Lerida, Saragossa, Pamplona and Irun, arriving May 24th (1st & 2nd Battalion).
May: Bordeaux (3rd Battalion).
June: Sailed from Bordeaux for N. America (1st & 3rd Battalion).
June: Sailed Ireland and then Gosport (2nd Battalion).

1815

9 May 1815: Returned from America arriving Portsmouth (1st Battalion).
24 May: Arrived Ostend, proceeded to Ghent (1st Battalion).
18 June: Battle of Waterloo (1st Battalion).
7 July – 28 October: Quartered at Neuilly outside Paris (1st Battalion).
15 June: Returned to England (3rd Battalion).
Until 25 July: Quartered at Gosport before embarking for Ireland (2nd Battalion).
3 August: Sailed for Ostend and from there to Neuilly with the 1st Battalion (3rd Battalion).
13 August: Arrived Cork (2nd Battalion).
25 December: Abbeville (3rd Battalion).

Chapter One

3rd Battalion The 27th Inniskilling Fusiliers 1807–1811

As is the case with all military institutions when peace is declared, the Inniskillings were scaled down to a single battalion following the Peace of Amiens.[1]* This marked a stalemate between Britain and France. Under the terms of the peace Britain was to return Malta to the Knights of St John and all her colonial conquests, with the exception of Trinidad and Ceylon, to their former rulers. In return Britain agreed to recognize the French Republic. Similarly France was to return Egypt to Turkey whilst evacuating Southern Italy and Rome. However, the peace was short-lived, following moves by France to build up her fleet, with the result that in March 1803 King George III informed the British Parliament that it would be foolish to allow itself to be lulled into a state of complacency and prudent to act now by preparing for a war which, on all accounts, appeared inevitable.

As a result, the 2nd Battalion 27th Regiment was reformed at Glasgow in November 1803, having previously been disbanded on 25 March of the preceding year. As the French threat increased a further battalion, the 3rd Inniskillings, was formed at Edinburgh on 25 September 1805 before it moved to Dunbar in October of the same year.

*   See Notes p. 201

1

1807

By mid-1807 Napoleon was at the height of his power, following his decisive victories at Austerlitz, Jena and Friedland. With Europe in his grip, a treaty was signed with Russia at Tilsit[2] virtually dividing a huge part of Europe between the two empires of France and Russia. However, though country after country systematically submitted to Napoleon's authority, there remained one who held out, refusing to bend the knee – Britain.

In an effort to exert pressure on Britain, Napoleon instigated a Continental Blockade[3] designed to isolate Britain from mainland Europe and thus force her to fall into line. Napoleon determined to force Britain into submission by starvation, having ruined her economic foundations by barring her access to her outside markets. However, Britain was not so easily intimidated. Instead she took up the gauntlet and set about blockading and harassing French interests whenever and wherever the Royal Navy could.

As an ally of Britain, Portugal came under increased pressure from Napoleon to close her ports to all British trade. However, the Portuguese delayed taking any action and infuriated the French by their apparent failure to submit to their demands. So Napoleon sent a force of 2,500 French troops under the command of Marshal Andoche Junot to Portugal in October, 1807. This marked the beginning of a long and bitter conflict which would drain the coffers of the French government. Not only would Napoleon's army be pitted against the combined might of the British, Portuguese and Spanish armies, it would also have to contend with ferocious opposition from local guerrilla forces operating within both Spain and Portugal. The Peninsular War had begun.

1808

Such are the battle honours of the 3rd Battalion the 27th Foot that they resemble a *Who's Who* of the Peninsular War. In May of 1808 the battalion was ordered from Enniskillen to the Curragh in preparation for its impending departure for Portugal and Spain. After an initial period of training it moved to Middleton Barracks, Cork, prior to embarking for Falmouth, England, on 9 September. A month to the day following their departure from Ireland the Regiment sailed

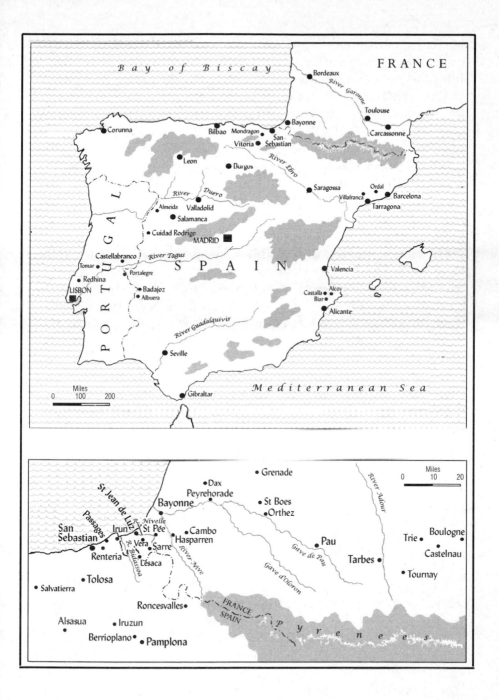

from Falmouth as part of an expeditionary force of five thousand men under the command of Sir David Baird[4], destined for Spain to join Sir John Moore's[5] force in the campaign against the French.

The 3rd Battalion actually landed in spain at Corunna on 14 October 1808, four years before her sister battalions. They were sent south on 25 October to join a force under the command of Lieutenant-General Cradock[6] with the specific intent of defending Lisbon against possible French attack, arriving there on 3 November. By early January 1809 the battalion had moved to Sacarem, a town on the River Tagus a few miles north of Lisbon. At this time the regimental records state the battalion's effective strength to be seven hundred and eighty-one.

On receiving news of the Battle of Corunna,[7] 16 January 1809, Cradock ordered a force of brigade strength, under the command of Major-General Mackenzie,[8] south by sea to Cadiz, fearing that the city was in imminent danger of French invasion. On its arrival, however, the brigade, which consisted of the 27th, 9th, 31st and 40th Regiments, rather than being received with open arms, was actually refused permission to land by the local authorities and forced to return to Lisbon on 11 February after a month of inactivity lying off the port.

Plagued by ill luck, disease and fatigue, the Battalion remained in Portugal and so missed the Talavera campaign of 27–28 July 1809. Again, although present at the battle of Busaco, 27 September 1810, as part of the Fourth Division under the command of Sir Galbraith Lowry Cole,[9] they played no significant role.

During the autumn of 1810 the Inniskillings, as part of the Fourth Division, were billeted in the small village of Patemeira. The Regimental History says that so close were the enemy that the troops often met up with their French counterparts in the surrounding fields and orchards.

However, with the onset of winter the Division had moved on to winter quarters in Asambija and Virtudas, where they remained until March of 1811. The Spanish winter was harsh and unrelenting. Wellington's troops, however, were not alone in feeling the strain of fighting a campaign in an alien environment. Such were the hardships endured by the French that by the early months of 1811 Marshal André Masséna[10] took the step of withdrawing his force back into Spain. Food and munitions all but exhausted, the French abandoned Torres Novos on 5/6 March. As a result, the 27th was ordered to

4

pursue and harass the retreating French at every opportunity. What followed was a series of minor skirmishes, most notable of which was the encounter at Redinha during which the Inniskillings lost several men, being commended for their bravery by General Spenser.

However, the pursuit of the French had hardly lasted more than a few days when the Duke of Wellington sent orders to Lowry Cole to break off and instead make haste to reinforce General William Carr Beresford[11] who had been ordered to lay siege to the town of Badajoz, which had recently fallen to the French. The importance of Badajoz rested in its strategic position on the left bank of the Guardiana commanding a main road from Portugal to Spain. A town of approximately 20,000 inhabitants, it was the principal town of Estremadura. In making their way to Badajoz the Inniskillings marched via Thomar, Barquinta, Anonchis, Campo Mayor, Elvas and Olivenza.

Whilst passing through the town of Campo Mayor, which had recently undergone the rigors of a siege itself, an officer of the 27th is recorded as commenting:

Half the house I am quartered in has been destroyed by shells, and there is in the room in which I am writing a hole in the roof from one of these of about six feet long and three broad; most of the other houses are in the same condition.[12]

It is from this point that the 3rd Battalion can trace its true baptism of fire in the Peninsular War. Up until then it had only been on the fringe of the conflict, though its troops had tasted the usual discomfiture of campaign service, long marches, extremes of temperature, bad food and an assortment of fevers and diseases.

The first siege of Badajoz was a catalogue of misfortune and ineptness. The investment of the town began on 8 May 1811 with a proposed course of action by the engineers turned down by Beresford who decided against all advice that siege works against the position of San Cristobal alone would suffice. According to Sir John Burgoyne:

Marshal Beresford, saying he would take that first, the consequence was that this small attack, comprising only six or eight guns and three regiments – Twenty-Seventh, Fortieth, and Ninety-Seventh – had to support for three days the whole fire and efforts of the place and fort, being commenced a thousand yards from the former, and four hundred and fifty yards from the latter. In a short time the batteries, traverses, etc. were knocked about the attackers' ears, and every effort to keep up the works was only attended by the useless sacrifice of lives, from the very superior fire from the place. This unfortunate attack, abandoned to itself, was for the whole time a horrid scene of carnage of desolation.[13]

During the first abortive siege of Badajoz the Inniskillings, while manning a British battery under construction just a few hundred yards from the city, were surprised by a force of twelve hundred French who burst without warning from Badajoz. After a lengthy skirmish the French were driven back into the city at a heavy cost to the 27th. In this incident the Inniskillings lost 117 men killed or wounded.

The siege, however, was abruptly abandoned on 12 May when news reached Beresford that Marshal Soult[14] was fast approaching with a relief force. As a result of this futile venture the 27th Inniskillings lost 188 men killed or wounded.

The regiment's next engagement came just a few days later at the Battle of Albuera. However, there seems to be a discrepancy as to what actually occurred on 16 May 1811. According to Ian Fletcher's book *Wellington's Regiments*,[15] the 3rd Battalion of the 27th Inniskillings suffered 77 casualties, while the Regimental records state that, far from having a major role in the battle, the participation of the 3rd Battalion consisted of little more than a working party attached to that part of the 4th Division, which actually saw action at Albuera. As a result it suffered only minor casualties, three rank and file killed and a further five wounded. The main force of the 3rd Battalion, being temporarily attached to Kemmis' Brigade, found themselves on the wrong side of the River Guardiana and did not arrive in position until the day following the battle.

By the end of July the battalion was quartered at Aldee da Bisbo during which time the effective strength was reduced from one thousand and forty-six to six hundred and eighty men due to fatigue and disease. Below strength and ravaged by the rigours of the campaign, the Battalion took little or no part in any significant operations for the remainder of 1811 and wintered at Almeida.

Chapter Two

1812
The 3rd Battalion

The Siege of Badajoz

The beginning of the New Year found the 3rd Battalion in the vicinity of Ciudad Rodrigo, which was under investment at the time. The fact that there are no official returns of dead and wounded sustained by the Inniskillings is generally taken as proof that they arrived late on the scene and therefore took no active part in the trenches or the actual assault. The Official History is vague and undecided on this point.

However, there is little doubt about their participation in the third and final siege of Badajoz, which was to prove a baptism of fire for the Inniskillings. The engagements in which they had taken part to date paled into insignificance in the face of what was to come. Although they had suffered casualties as a result of the first siege they were not present at the second. On 3 March 1812 the battalion marched from Villa de Corvo to take up its position for the investment of Badajoz via Penemaçon, Castellobranco and Portalegre.

Having previously failed on two occasions, Wellington now adopted a new strategy on his third attempt to take the city. Concentrating his artillery on a section not previously put under any great pressure, he succeeded after a time in breaching the wall in several places. As a diversionary force assaulted other areas of the city, it was left to Lowry Cole's 4th Division under the command of Major-General Colville, together with the Light Division, to storm the breach at La Trinidad. The castle itself was to be stormed by the 3rd Division under Picton[1] whilst Leith's[2] 5th Division was to take the bastion of San Vincente.

Although the walls of the city had been breached at several points, the garrison commander, Governor Philippon,[3] an able and highly experienced soldier, was prepared for any such eventuality. The task facing the Inniskillings was far from straightforward. Each column was to be led by a contingent of the "Forlorn Hope" (see Note 3, Chapter 4), followed closely by a storming party of five hundred men. Behind these the main body was to divide into two sections, one to advance on the breaches whilst the other would engage the French from the ramparts. As a back-up, a party of one thousand men was held in reserve behind each division to lend support as the battle unfolded.

The carnage and loss of life that occurred as a result of the breaking of the siege was immeasurable.

A little before 10 o'clock the advance troops of the Fourth Division crossed the glacis[4] and swarmed into the ditch without much loss; but, when the moat was full of men, the French suddenly exploded the fuses, shells and powder-barrels with which they had lined the foot of the breach and the bottom of the ditch. The effect was terrible; many men were blown to pieces, and the survivors, losing their direction and mistaking the rough face of an unfinished ravelin[5] for the breach which they had been ordered to attack, scaled it, only to find that a deep chasm separated them from the enemy, whose riflemen, securely posted behind the ramparts, shot them down by scores. The soldiers, seeing a difficult descent before they could even reach the foot of the real breach, hesitated, and had begun to return the French musketry, when the troops of the Third Division, who also had lost their bearings and mistaken the ravelin for their objective [the breach of Santa Maria], joined those of the Fourth Division on the summit. The divisions thus became mixed, and, though the officers did their best to restore order, to reform the ranks and lead their men to their proper points of attack, the uproar and confusion made their task most difficult.[6]

The panic and confusion that ensued in the darkness allowed the French riflemen to pick Wellington's men off at will. Those who did find their way to the breaches were confronted by booby-traps and seasoned troops ready for all eventualities. Attempt after attempt was made by Wellington's troops to overcome stubborn French opposition and gain entry to the city, but time and again they failed, with increased loss of life.

By midnight Picton's Division had successfully taken the castle, but the town itself still remained in the hands of the French. At this point, realizing the futility of the attacks on La Trinidad and Santa Maria, an order to retire and form up for a second assault was issued. Such was the loss of life in these abortive attacks that the troops fared little better retreating from the ditch.

> This retreat from the ditch was not effected without further carnage and confusion. The French never slackened; a cry arose that the enemy was making a sally from the distant flanks, and there was a rush towards the ladders. Then the groans and lamentations of the wounded who could not move, and expected to be slain, increased; and many officers, who had not heard the order, endeavoured to stop the soldiers from going back; some would even have removed the ladders, but were unable to break the crowd.[7]

Throughout the ensuing confusion British and Portuguese troops elsewhere in the battle had more success at various points along the walled city, with the result that, having broken their way through the breaches, they were able to make their way round the ramparts, thus outflanking those defenders holding the 4th and Light Divisions at bay.

The following is the strength of the 27th before the battle on 1 April 1812, when, even at that stage, they had already lost fifty-one NCOs and ORs killed and wounded.

- Present in camp before Badajoz   560
- Sick in camp   14
- Sick out of camp (i.e. in hospital)   331
- On command   73
  Total   978

For those two hours between 10 o'clock and midnight on 6 April 1812 the casualties of the 27th amounted to:

- Officers killed   4
- NCOs and ORs killed   37

9

- Officers mortally wounded   1
- Officers wounded   11
- NCOs wounded   9
- ORs wounded   123

    Total   185

The Inniskillings lost over one-third of their effective strength in a period of two hours. According to the regular returns of the Regiment dated 25 April 1812 the effective strength is shown as nine officers, including the quartermaster, and eleven officers 'sick'. Furthermore, out of nine hundred and twenty-one men on the roll, five hundred and six appeared as 'sick'.

In the aftermath of such carnage and devastation it is no wonder that those who did survive sacked and pillaged the city. The anger felt at the slaughter of their comrades and the steadfastness of the French resistance, combined with the sheer exhilaration of simply being alive, was vented on the townsfolk. Wellington's troops rampaged through the city for several days and nights, entirely out of control, until Wellington brought them to heel by the use of fresh troops drafted in for that purpose, plus the unenviable and sobering threat of the 'rope'.

With the costly experience of Badajoz behind him Wellington would have much preferred to follow up his success with a march against Marmont,[6] who was ensconced at Salamanca, but the sheer logistics of such a move put it out of the question. The severe mauling inflicted upon his troops at Badajoz dictated that time was needed for the sick and wounded to return to their regiments.

It is difficult for us to visualize the deprivations and the agony the troops were forced to endure in those early years of the nineteenth century. Hospitals were no more than temporary makeshift establishments often located in fortresses, convents or anywhere else it was possible to house a large contingent of men. Totally unsuited to the purpose, even the most rudimentary hygiene was absent. Doctors were in short supply and trained medical orderlies simply didn't exist. Where there were doctors available, their level of skill was basic to say the least. These hospitals, and I use the term with reservation, were places of such a squalid nature that men were left to die of horrific wounds as septicaemia and gangrene could turn a wound into a protracted and agonizing death. According to the graphic account of a sergeant belonging to the same brigade as the 27th:

The patients lay on heaps of straw in the long stone-paved corridors, where the small, high windows afforded so little ventilation that to purify the air it was found necessary to burn huge logs of pine in the corner of the wards, although the smoke greatly distressed the sick. The food was infamous; men still weak from typhoid were fed on biscuits and salt pork. No wonder that the soldiers who survived such treatment were so hardy that nothing short of a well-placed French bullet could kill them.[8]

Following Wellington's success at Badajoz the 3rd Battalion found itself at St Joas de Perquèire in early May. The fact that the action at Badajoz was not directly followed up was, in itself, not a bad thing, as it allowed the army valuable time to regroup and strengthen its numbers, so depleted by the siege.

For a number of weeks immediately after the siege, due to the enormous number of casualties sustained, Captain Archibald Mair, commanded the Battalion. Its official strength at 15 May 1812 records that out of a total complement of nine hundred and ten men only a mere three hundred and fifty-eight were classified as "present". It also denoted that no less than five hundred and three were "not present", i.e. in hospital. As a result, and in recognition of their outstanding valour and sacrifice, the Regiment was permitted on 7 December 1812 to add the title Badajoz to its already impressive list of Battle Honours.

The Battle of Salamanca

The days prior to the battle on 22 July 1812 were spent in minor engagements and skirmishes to secure outlying forts, which had to be taken before the real action at Salamanca could begin. The 3rd Battalion suffered a number of casualties during this period, including the loss of Lieutenant Radcliffe and Lieutenant and Adjutant James Davidson, eleven other ranks killed and Captain Archibald Mair and fifty-eight NCOs and ORs wounded.

Although the action at Salamanca was a masterly piece of manoeuvring on Wellington's part, the outcome at first sight was anything but assured. Outwitted and outflanked by Marmont,[9] Wellington was only too keenly aware that fresh French reinforcements could arrive at any time.

From the determination with which Marmont seized the French hermanito,[10] Wellington divined his antagonist's intention to turn his right flank. He therefore executed an enormous change of front and, while leaving the First and Light Divisions on the original line of battle, concealed the remainder of his army behind the broken ridges which faced southwards, with their left resting on the hermanito, guarded by the Twenty-Seventh, and their right near the village of Aldea Tejada. He also recalled the Third Division and D'Urban's Horse from the right bank of the Tormes and, undetected by the French, posted them behind a hill commanding the path which he saw Marmont's turning columns must follow. Thus the rear became the front, and the army in its new position stood at right angles to its old alignment. . . . From the summit of the hermanito, Wellington, surrounded by the Inniskillings, stood for some time, watching the gradual dissemination of Marmont's forces with stern contentment.[11]

On this occasion, although the Inniskillings were actively engaged in the battle, their casualties were light, suffering one officer, Lieutenant Philip Gordon, and seven rank and file wounded.[12]

Chapter Three

1813

In all the 27th had three battalions which saw service in Spain and Portugal during the Peninsular War. All, in the course of the campaign, would cover themselves in glory but only the 1st Battalion would take part in the final battle at Waterloo, which would seal the fate of Napoleon for ever.

Lord William Bentinck, Commander-in-Chief of the crown forces in Sicily, selected both the 1st and 2nd battalions to embark for Spain as part of a joint Anglo-Sicilian expedition with the aim of counteracting a strong force of French under the command of Marshal Suchet.[1] It was feared that such a force already ensconced on the shores of eastern Spain would threaten Wellington's anticipated advance north from Portugal.

As a result, having arrived at Alicante, on the south-eastern coast of Spain in the winter of 1812, both battalions remained in quarters until March of 1813. During that year they were engaged in a number of actions, the most notable of which were Alcoy, Alfafara, just south of the city of Valencia, Biar and Castalla.

The first of these actions was a skirmish with the French on 7 March 1813 when the 2nd Battalion came upon the French near the town of Alcoy. This was the first encounter the 2nd Battalion had with the French. Under the command of Major-General Donkin, the Quartermaster General, the Inniskillings harassed the rear of the French Division. The attack was so fiercely contested that the French General halted his Division, wheeled around and formed a line of battle. Greatly outnumbered, the 27th were lucky the 58th came to their assistance, otherwise things could have been much worse. As it was, they escaped with the loss of four killed and thirteen wounded.

The first occasion on which the 1st and 2nd Battalions had to engage in a joint action was at the Battle of Castalla. A force under the command of Lieutenant-General Sir John Murray had recently occupied the town, but was now in danger of losing ground to Marshal Suchet. On 12 April Murray decided to draw Suchet into a trap and used the 2nd Battalion of the 27th as bait. While Murray positioned his force on the heights above a ravine leading to the village of Biar, the 27th, as part of a detachment under the command of Colonel F. Adam, was ordered to fight a delaying action to entice the French. Besides the Inniskillings, the detachment comprised a section of German light infantry and riflemen, the 1st Italian Legion, the Calabrese Free Corps, a small section of Allied cavalry and several mountain guns. The one weak spot in the defence of Castalla was to the rear of the town, which, it was rightly assumed, the French would not overlook.

As soon as it was seen that they were gaining ground on the flanks of the village, the signal was sounded to those in the town to retire behind the line formed in rear of the place. This was smartly executed. After some hesitation, the enemy debouched from the village, covered by numbers of tirailleurs. These were met and well punished by German riflemen and the light company of the 27th and driven back on their columns, while the Calabrese and the Italians kept up a heavy fire. Notwithstanding, they deployed and moved forward in line, supported by several heavy columns. Colonel Adam's orders were to fall back gradually, but to dispute the ground where practicable. They therefore withdrew to a new position. The 27th executed this movement by wings, the riflemen and light infantry thumping the enemy's tirailleurs handsomely. At this point in the action, Colonel Adam was wounded, but continued in charge of his division. The action became rather warm, when a body of cuirassiers were observed gaining the road in front of the left of the 27th. Lieutenant-Colonel Reeves,[2] recognizing their intentions, detached Captain Hare,[3] with three companies, to take post behind some rocks where the road made an angle, and there wait until the cuirassiers had committed themselves, which they soon did, galloping down the road and calling to the 27th, 'Bas vos armes!' At this juncture they received a volley from the ambuscade that made them reel, and those that could galloped back, leaving the best part of them kicking in the road. It was remarked that the musket balls passed through cuirass and man; in fact, the muskets almost touched some of them. This had

14

good effect, as the line formed in front of the 27th fell back, throwing out sharpshooters. Here was an opportunity for a charge; but the 27th had orders to fall back, and did so, in ordinary time.

The last check made the French much less pressing, and they brought up several guns. Under this fire the column of attack again moved forward, as usual covered by sharpshooters, and, as usual, were met by our light troops. Lieutenants B.T. Duhigg, C. Manley and J.K. Jameson of the 27th were by this time wounded, all severely, and several of our men; but the enemy fell very quickly. Colonel Adam having had his wound dressed, came up and gave orders to fall back gently, which was done. The enemy seemed glad to get rid of us, and, after five hours' fighting, we marched into our position on the left of the army at Castalla.[4]

The following day, 13 April, Marshal Suchet's Division emerged from the defile into which they had been driven, only to find that Murray had occupied the surrounding high ground. The Inniskillings and Mackenzie's Division held the crest of the hills and thus the centre of Murray's Allied army. To their left was positioned a section of Spanish troops, whilst to their right the ground dipped so dramatically that it was deemed suicide for the French even to attempt to take it.

Marshal Suchet tried to break the Allied line by bombarding the centre with his artillery whilst simultaneously attacking the Spanish contingent on the right with his cavalry. Although the French had some initial success with their cavalry, the Allied line held, as they met with sterner opposition ascending the hill to face the 27th.

Their skirmishers, spreading over the mountain, and here and there attaining the summit, were partially driven down again, but where the main body met the 2nd battalion of the 27th there was a terrible crash. The ground had an abrupt declination, which enabled the French to form line under cover, close to the British, who were lying down to wait for the moment of charging. A grenadier officer seized the opportunity to advance and challenge Waldron, also a captain of grenadiers, to a duel. That agile, vigorous Irishman instantly leaped forward, the hostile lines looked on, the swords of the champions glittered in the sun, the Frenchman's head was cleft in twain, and the 27th, rising up with

15

a deafening shout, fired a deadly volley, and charged with such a shock that, maugre[5] their bravery and numbers, Suchet's men were overthrown, and the side of the Sierra was covered with killed and wounded.[6]

With the French in full flight, Sir John Murray made the mistake of failing to capitalize on his victory. Rather than pursuing the fleeing French army he allowed Suchet's troops to make their retreat from the plain of Castalla with relatively little loss.

Casualties for the 27th for the two-day period in the vicinity of Castalla and Biar were:

1st Battalion.
- Killed   2
- Wounded   7

2nd Battalion.
- Officers wounded   2
  (Lieutenant B.T. Duhigg and Lieutenant J.K. Jameson)
- Killed   18
  (One sergeant, one drummer, sixteen rank and file)
- Wounded   85
  (Three sergeants and eighty-two privates)[7]

Following the abortive siege of the city of Tarragona, not far short of Barcelona, both battalions were summoned back to Alicante.

The attempted siege itself was nothing short of farce. Under orders from Wellington, Sir John Murray embarked on board ship and set sail for Tarragona with fourteen thousand men and an assortment of siege equipment, which included the guns which had worked so effectively at Badajoz. A combination of inter-service rivalry between the Army and Navy, combined with an inability to see eye to eye with his officers, doomed Murray's operation to failure from the outset. No sooner had the army disembarked and laid siege to Tarragona than, as the Regimental History records:

Hardly, however, had the bombardment begun, when, in a groundless panic, Murray ordered the siege to be discontinued and the troops to be re-embarked. The men were sent on board their transports on the night of June 12th, and many of the stores were

16

shipped on the 13th, without the slightest interruption from the enemy; but eighteen or nineteen battering-pieces, the guns of Badajoz, were abandoned to the French garrison, who, though only one thousand six hundred strong, in full view of the British fleet and the British army, triumphantly dragged the guns into the fortress. Weighing anchor, the General sailed down the coast as far as the port of Belaguer, where he again disembarked with his whole force; but on the 17th he had for a second time ordered his army to regain their ships, when the arrival of Lord Bentinck from Sicily put an end to Sir John Murray's command.[8]

With this change in command the troops were ordered back to Alicante for a period of reorganization. This was partly because fourteen of the fleet's transports had run aground at the mouth of the Ebro.

Tarragona would eventually fall to Bentinck, though not through any great effort on the part of the allied troops. Owing to the course of the war elsewhere in the peninsula, the French partially demolished its Roman walls before Suchet abandoned the city altogether. The city now in Allied hands, Bentinck pushed on towards Villafranca, a town midway between Tarragona and Barcelona.

By June 1813 the French were on the run before Wellington's advancing army as he pushed further and further north towards the Pyrenees and France. Successive defeats had for the moment demoralized the French as they retreated north toward the town of Vitoria.

Taking up a position in front of the town at the junction of the roads from Bilbao and Madrid and covering their lines of communication between Bayonne and St Jean Pied-de-Port, the French were attacked by Wellington's troops and routed. The 3rd Battalion of the 27th formed a section of Anson's Brigade, in conjunction with the 40th, 1st Battalion the 48th, and a detachment of the Queen's and 53rd.

The following extract is recorded in the Regimental History and is taken from the *Historical Records of the 40th Regiment*, pp. 140–1, by Captain Raymond Smythies:

Major Hill, an officer of the Fortieth Regiment, thus described the action: 'The duty assigned Anson's brigade was the attack of the position above the bridge of Nanclares, which was defended from

17

the heights by various artillery, and it was carried. Every arrangement for the attack was made by nine o'clock. At ten o'clock we advanced to attack the enemy's left. The moment we showed ourselves we were saluted by a burst of artillery, which was answered by a shout from our brigade. We were not exposed longer than about ten minutes to this cannonade, for, having got under cover of some rising ground, we continued advancing along a hollow, which obliged their guns to fall back until we came to about four hundred yards of their lines, which were formed up on a hill about as high as Primrose Hill, Chalk Farm, extending about half a mile in length. We then deployed in two lines, one about fifty yards in front of the other, under fire of their line. When done, the front line, consisting of the 27th and 53rd gave the enemy a volley, uncased their colours and advanced to charge the hill. The 40th and 48th Regiments formed the second line, and (situated on the right rear of the first line) were appointed to force the left of the hill in this form. We then moved on the enemy, but under heavy fire of shells. Few of them, however, fell upon our lines. The French thought proper to retire without a charge, or evincing any desire to court from our side a closer contact. By the time that both lines had ascended and crowned the position, we again found them drawn up on another hill in rear of it, from which they kept up a continuous fire of musketry, but with little execution. We again advanced precisely as before, and they in their turn also retired and again formed on every rising ground they came to . . . this sort of movement and fighting continued without any variation for about eight miles, when night favoured their flight.'[9]

Casualties suffered by the 3rd Battalion on this occasion were slight:

- Officers Killed   1
  (Lieutenant Philip Gordon)
- Other Ranks killed or died of wounds   7
- Officers wounded   3
  (Lieutenant William Weir, Lieutenant J. Hill,
  Volunteer Murray)
- Other ranks wounded   32
  (Two sergeants, thirty rank and file)[10]

Chapter Four

Lieutenant Charles Crowe

At this point reference must be made to the memoirs of Lieutenant Charles Crowe, 2nd Battalion, the 27th Foot. His graphic account of nineteenth century Portugal and Spain, together with aspects of life in the Regiment from the perspective of a junior officer, is both intriguing and entertaining. His account of life during the Peninsular campaign is informative, as it brings to life aspects of the everyday campaign which tend to be glossed over in favour of more momentous happenings.

So from now on we will concentrate on the campaign as dictated by the movements of Lieutenant Crowe, for who better to portray the hardships, triumphs and dangers of this period than an actual participant?

Historians may regurgitate facts and figures in an effort to convey atmosphere, but there can be no substitute for first-hand evidence. Military history must go hand in hand with social history. Put simply, the military aspect of war is more than just battles, it is the accumulated sacrifice of men and women alike. Therefore, to get to the heart of a conflict it is essential to view the whole campaign, not simply to gloss over what seems mundane in favour of those incidents which stand in the forefront of events.

August 15th 1813
Sunday. This morning at 5 o'clock I started, with bag and baggage, script and scrippage.

As I rode along, I was amused by observing the effect of the sun on the mist in the valleys between the mountains. I could but remark how absolute was His power, wherever His rays penetrated. I could almost have found arguments for the Hindoos in their worship of the grand luminary. But reflection hinted that were His power, however potent, it was not absolute, since he himself is subject to laws! Then, "Plato thou reasonest well! For there is a Power above", and that "all nature cries aloud through all her works"!!

Then how thankful ought the Christian to be, for having been trained in that religion, which offers him an unerring path to the protection of "That Divine Power"!!

"Lord what is man that Thou art mindful of him" or "the son of man that Thou so regardest him?" As these reflections were not inappropriate to the day, I encouraged them, and my meditations were greatly assisted by the numerous dead bodies along the road.

"When Nature's beauties spread beneath the eye,
And all above the worlds blue canopy,
When reason's self doth elevate the mind
How good, how virtuous, feels the heart inclined!"

A serjeant of the 66th Regiment joined us and seemed well pleased with company as we were. I invited him to keep company, as far as our routes would allow. We passed the village from whence we drove the French on the 1st inst. and parted at the bridge of San Estivan.

The roads had been bad and certainly I was hungry, thus I felt confident that the distance in my route, of 3 leagues was not correct. My servant agreed with me that it was 5 leagues or 15 miles. I obtained a good billet and I liked my room for being up two flights. As my servant placed the breakfast things on the table, I was astonished at the multitude of flies, which congregated on every fresh article as soon as placed on the table. The hot tea pot only was free. My sugar canister was coated with a black horde. It was equal to one of the plagues of Egypt. In spite of all, I made a good breakfast and walked forth to examine the town.

The natives were then going to church, the curiosity of a traveller induced me likewise. The edifice was lofty and handsome, decorated as most Roman Catholic churches, with separate shrines and tawdry draped figures. I did not think to ascertain the particular day celebrated but every person had a small basket before them, spread with a clean napkin, on which were a number of cakes and small loaves or rolls, and three or four wax tapers burning before each basket. Four priests were hard at work in different ceremonies at the same time, making such a hubbub that it was totally impossible for any of the congregation to understand what either of them was about. I could not participate in the apparent devotion which I noticed in those around me, who were chiefly females. Disgust was my predominant feeling, and I retired as quickly as possible, returned to my billet, opened my portmanteau for my prayer book and fervently read the morning service of my own church, which dissipated all my polemical reflections.

On making my second sally I certainly felt more amiable, and meeting the congregation on their return, I was not in the least inclined to quarrel with anything, and certainly not with any person, for I beheld many fine countenances and many lovely girls, whose beautiful faces seemed brightened by the conviction of having fulfilled the bounden duty of keeping the Sabbath day holy.

I did not trouble myself to define whether it was the sparkling of so many black eyes, or whether it was the delight of once more beholding social society, but confess that I enjoyed the scene to the very utmost.

It is quite apparent from the frequent reference in Lieutenant Crowe's diary that he was a devout man, deeply entrenched in his own brand of Protestantism and staunchly intolerant of Roman Catholicism. Whilst he can appreciate the beauty of his surroundings, especially the obvious attraction of the flower of Spanish womanhood, he can never for a moment relax his religious bias and staunch reformist upbringing. He seems almost apologetic for having enjoyed the Sabbath, as if to show any inquisitiveness in another religion, no matter how innocent, should in some ways endanger his own steadfast beliefs. He obviously found it extremely difficult to reconcile his more puritanical view of religion with the more demonstrative, gregarious nature of Portuguese and Spanish Catholicism.

I found the town surrounded by a wall of loose construction about 14 feet high pierced with loopholes for musketry against guerrillas, for the French never dreamed of our reaching that secluded spot. And every house near the walls was looped most effectively. A large detached house south-east of the walls was made a fortress of no small consequence, every one of its lofty stories had a separate range, nor could any force but field pieces, have silenced its fire. The yards around were protected by a wall ten feet high, and also looped. The two gateways were protected by *chevaux de frise*,[1] forming, together as a great a defence against the valley as the house, for a longer range. I imagine that after the thrashing the French received from our 7th Division on the 30ult. at Larvy, they were convinced it would be futile to stay here.

A serjeant of our German Hussars stationed here assured me it is only three leagues to Lizasso, my next stage, and that by starting at 2 p.m. I should have plenty of time. On leaving San Estivan I re-crossed the bridge which I reconnoitred on the 1st inst. and retraced that day's march along the southern bank of the Bidasoa, hidden, for the most part from our view by blocks of rock, which reflecting the heat of the meridian sun, rendered the course most intolerably hot. There was not a breath of air to fan our scorched faces.

A deeply complex character, his observance of the Sabbath was fundamental to his Christian belief. A further aspect of his character was his preoccupation with all matters medical, confirming that he was somewhat of a hypochondriac. His entries relate over and over again to the state of his health and the infallibility of his own self-diagnosis. He feels genuinely aggrieved that the Surgeons, in particular one Doctor Burmester, should take his condition so lightly when in his own opinion he was so gravely ill. Yet even he is aware of his fixation when he records:

I had not a dry thread about me, but the extreme heat of the road soon dried everything, and left a painful burning heat, pervading every part of me, as if I were within the focus of an immense burning glass or lens! It is impossible to describe my agonising sufferings at this juncture! Had my pony felt the increase of weight as I did myself, he must have fallen under it. The oppression on my head and shoulders made me think of the representation of Atlas bearing the whole heavens! Subsequently I learnt that all this was decidedly a *coup de soleil*! which is generally fatal, especially in India. These combined events caused me much future suffering and misery, and I must carry their mark to my grave. In the interim I cannot be too thankful for the preservation not only of my life but of my eyesight!!! The remainder of my diary abounds, I find, with memoranda of my daily suffering, which I must endeavour to curtail.

August 17th

Started in good time this morning and found the roads much improved in the neighbourhood of Pamplona by what the troops had done to them. I met numerous stores going to the Spanish Army, on their rudely constructed cars. I halted for breakfast at an isolated house at Berrioplano by the roadside and had no objection to ascend two flights of stairs to my room, to gain a fresh current of air. The house stood above the road, not a tree within sight; no bank or rock behind; no house within a quarter of a mile; I was on the third storey with a draught through, yet the flies were innumerable. I thought them bad enough at St Estivan but here they were ten times more numerous. I was obliged to draw my small cloth off to cover over the table, but it was difficult to eat or drink without swallowing flies.

The garrison made much noise with their large guns, while I stayed here. The natives were become accustomed to them, and only when the breeze brought a stronger sound that they exclaimed. 'Ah! Diable!!'

As I proceeded on the Grand Camino Real I met a Dragoon officer and his baggage. He asked me many questions about the road, and the halting places. I questioned him also, and learned that Harry Franklin, our assistant surgeon was at the next depot. This was most welcome news, and I was impatient till I could take my good friend by the hand.

Irurzun is a good town protected by walls of some importance. On arriving I reported myself to the commandant, Captain Gun of the 91st. Regiment and obtained my ration return. This was a "good shot" and I quickly made for Franklin's quarters. He was surprised to see me. But I found him quite in low spirits for want of society, and impatient to rejoin his regiment. However, a conversation about old friends soon roused him! I felt convinced that we rendered much good to each other.

August 18th

My good friend would not allow me to depart until I had partaken of his hospitable breakfast. I left the Grand Camino and, the road I took proving very tolerable, I arrived at Lacanza in good time, and Alsasua about 6. p.m. where, by the assistance of a private of the 5th Dragoon Guards, I obtained a very comfortable billet at an old surgeon's. The Dragoon was tipsy and became so very officious

23

that I was obliged to give him to understand I stood in no further need of his kind services.

August 19th

Reached Salvatierra about 10 a.m.; from its external appearance, as we passed on the 22nd June, I expected to have found a place of some importance, but to my surprise, only three parallel streets surrounded by an old and defensive wall. It is absurd to note it in the maps as a fortified town for guerrillas would laugh at it. Two hours from hence brought me in sight of Vitoria, but the road was so circuitous that I did not arrive till dark. When searching for the commandant's I fortunately met with my old friend Lieutenant Duke of the 48th, who took me to his own quarters and procured me a bed on the floor of his room, it being too late to procure a billet.

August 20th

The greater part of this day was occupied in getting rid of my charge, and thereby contributing to the comforts of the afflicted. The performance of this duty introduced me to so many brave fellows suffering severely from "the fate of war"! that my military ardour was very far from "fever heat!" In the truth my spirits were much below par!! that I was glad to divert my mind by asking for my billet, which by assistance of my two brother officers, Pollock and Radcliffe, I made at N. 16 Coireria Street, up two flights of stairs, a large and airy room facing south-west with a glass door into a balcony.

Not expecting me so soon, my servant was absent, with the key of my apartment, so I patiently seated myself on the stairs till he should return. Major Fitzgerald of the 82nd Regiment occupying the opposite apartment, on seeing me, insisted on my going into his room. The Major was wounded in a similar manner as Captain Butler of ours. A ball had perforated both cheeks knocked out all his teeth and cut his tongue so severely that it was difficult to understand what he was saying. He seemed to be quite the polished Irish gentleman and soon gave me to understand, in a most courteous way, his anxiety to have the house to himself, in as much that in the balcony beyond my room, was a certain con-venience, highly required for an invalid, to which he was obliged to resort.

August 21st

Desirous of contributing to the comforts of the other people, when I can, I obtained another billet and left the Major full enjoyment of the balcony. My new quarters were in the Street Herreria, near my two chums. The accommodation was but indifferent and the inhabitants very reluctant to admit me, although my billet was regularly issued from the Alcalda's office. I did not wonder at this for since June 21st they had never been free from sick or wounded officers. Certes![2] We are fighting for their freedom, and therefore have a claim for accommodation but I am equally certain that John Bull would not relish foreigners at free quarters.

August 22nd

I find the Sabbath here is kept in a Catholic i.e. Roman Catholic manner. It is considered more a day of rest and recreation than for Divine worship! All customs in extreme are bad and so is this! Many a frusty old Saint, on his or her day has more strict observance and prayer that is ever thought of on that day, which Holy Writ hath ordered to be kept holy! I noticed that two young girls in the opposite house, were dressed in five different garbs, during the day. In the crowded afternoon mall we met many bare and bald headed fat priests, monks or friars, with lovely girls of gentlemanly appearance, holding reluctantly on their arms.

August 23rd to 26th

I had fully resolved to have returned to my Regiment but the excessive pain in my head and eyes which I have endured all the week obliged me to conform to the advice of my friend Harry Franklin and to apply for medical advice.

August 28th

Our poor brother officer Lieutenant Phillip Gordon died this morning; after most severe suffering from his wound received 21st June, by a musket ball which broke the thigh so high up that amputation at the hip joint, was the only expedient. This arduous operation required greater skill than could be found in a new, and hastily formed, Hospital Station, and his case was too far gone e'er such skill did arrive.

Gordon, the Senior Lieutenant of our three battalions, had entered the Peninsula with the 3rd Battalion in 1808 and consequently had seen much service. He was a large raw-boned Scotchman and his national reserve never suffered him to drop a hint as to what had been his career. He must have been full fifty years of age and consequently either risen from the ranks or entered the army late in life. He was on good terms with everyone; but there was no glimpse of the gentleman in his appearance or conversation. He lived the hard life of a soldier, had his own tent and never indulged in anything beyond his bare rations. So that poor Phil Gordon always had spare dollars to cash a bill on England for any officer who wanted to raise "the wind"! And this parsimony was "The ruling passion e'en in death!!", for the Staff Surgeon who attended him thrice urged us to request Gordon to live more generously.

August 29th
We buried poor Gordon this day in a most respectable manner. We three, with cape on our arms and swords, followed as chief mourner; accompanied by all officers of the Division who were able to attend. The coffin was covered with black cloth, studded with brass nails. The ceremony attracted a vast concourse of inhabitants who behaved with utmost decorum, and evidently were much impressed by the solemnity of the 'funeral ceremony' although they did not comprehend a single word.

August 31st
We had heard of an assault on St Sebastian, its failure, and that many Portuguese, of whom the storming party mainly consisted, were taken prisoner.

This day Pollock received a letter from Weir, stating that Jack Harding, a serjeant, and twelve men had marched to the second attack of St Sebastian, being our quota of the number *required* from our Division by a letter from the Adjutant General to General Cole in which he states "by Lord Wellington's order, that 100 British, and 50 Portuguese are wanted to set an example to a column of attack, in a point of great moment: but which only required to insure success!" This remarkable order spoke his Lordship's chagrin at the failure of the first assault and put every one concerned on their mettle.

Harding was acting as Adjutant, and therefore decidedly off the roster: but finding that the turn for duty came to his name, he was resolved to take it, regardless of our colonel's remonstrations, and even solicitations – had I been with the regiment, and Harding not taken the perilous duty, it would have fallen on me – General Sir Lowry Cole was excessively pleased that "a Forlorn Hope"[3] should be called from his Division in such a manner. He inspected the marching off of the party and, shaking every officer by the hand, desired them to remember the 4th Division!! – The Light, and 1st Divisions furnished the same complement.

September 2nd
Late this evening intelligence arrived of the taking of San Sebastian, in the afternoon of the 31st ult. The bells began to jangle immediately in the most absurd and discordant manner, resembling the alarm of fire in an English village. But yet, perchance the Spanish would say with the Portuguese, that, "the English have fine bells, but know not how to ring them!" Lights were exhibited at every house and bonfires in every street, with men, women, and children dancing to the monotonous beating of lozenge shaped tambourines covered on both sides and singing their loyal airs which want cadence, as much as their music and variety as much as their dance!

I had recently listened to the sound of the guitar when passing the streets and from what I heard concluded all performers as novitiates. A wounded English officer, a very handsome and gentlemanly fellow although a decided coxcomb,[4] had a good quarter in the lower part of the plaza near the mall. Frequently in the evening, he would stand in either balcony to his windows, a monkey on one side and a parrot on the other, touching his guitar in a scientific style to the Spanish, Scotch and Irish airs, which he sang admirably, while the assembled crowd below, priests and peasants, listened with wonder and delight.

I could not have imagined that a nation like the Spanish, which, not long ago, asserted its due preponderance in the affairs of Europe, and was famed for her Moorish wars, her riches, her colonies, her armada should be so devoid of the general refinements of society.

It requires, apparently, some great excitement like the present, to rouse their innate indolence to action.

September 3rd
The Governor has received intelligence of the gallant conduct of the Spaniards near the mouth of the Bidassoa on the 31st ult, and has

ordered bull-baiting and illuminations for four nights. Immense placards at the corner of every street blazon forth the bravery of the Spanish soldiery. All this, we imagined, was instigated by the Spanish General Alava,[5] who is Lord of all the lands around. He loses no opportunity of rousing the lethargy of his countrymen.

We, likewise, received particulars of the taking of St Sebastian; and had to mourn the loss of our highly esteemed friend Harding, of Vunjon the volunteer, the adopted pet of my chum and self. Ten days after his death his commission as ensign was received! Had this arrived sooner he would have been saved!! Pollock felt as a brother the loss of his messmate Harding!!! – another volunteer, who had been very recently attached to our regiment, was also killed. He had been one of the senior Lieutenants in the Marines. He had been cashiered by an order from the Admiralty for having been a second in a fatal duel at Portsmouth.

Of our little devoted band, that is, poor Jack Harding, one serjeant, 12 men, and two volunteers, only four survived! Half way to the breach Jack was struck on the thigh by a grape shot. When he fell, his whole party halted, but Jack raised himself on his hands, and called out, "Serjeant Achison, what are you about? Go forward and do your duty! Look to the castle on your buttons, and prove yourself an Enniskillener!" This was like an electric shock, the serjeant put his cap on his halbert,[6] waving it and shouting, gained the breach and with three men survived to tell the sad history. The Colonel made him a colour serjeant for his brave conduct; but being of a volatile disposition he soon afterwards lost his colours.

September 4th
I felt better this day; and in the evening rode out with my friend Pollock and Vandermeulan of 48th. We traversed part of the battle field of June 21st [Battle of Vitoria] "fought our battle o'er again!" and confirmed in our former opinions, that we were not assisted by our cavalry as we ought to have been.

September 5th
Dined with my worthy friend Duke. And afterwards walked with him to examine the cannons taken June 21st collected beyond the city; beside the road to Tolosa: and a most gratifying sight it was, such a park of artillery was never before taken from the enemy!

123 Guns of various calibre.

33 Howitzers large, and new.

3 mortars of small size.

159 I counted but we were informed that very many had been sent away. Some of the largest were made in 1703 by Charles 3rd. Many of the field pieces were of French manufacture during the Republic, with Liberté et Egalité on their muzzles. A few were marked Ferdinando 7th. And some few Λ.N. The remainder were Carlos 4th excepting one of great length and octagon shaped, with an escutcheon of five stars. We could not decipher the motto. Unquestionably it was a great curiosity. The calibre not more than six pounds although its length is equal to the Egyptian gun in St James Park. There was a due proportion of ammunition wagons to the above, with a great number of various descriptions, and the remains of 17 coaches, the whole occupying an immense space of ground.

The impression one gets is of a soldier not too impressed by his surroundings, his superiors or the Spanish people, their traditions and religion. Whilst his comments are highly informative, he cannot help but reveal his inherent cynicism and bias. Nevertheless, his diary account is a wonderful insight into the haughty life of a commissioned soldier around the turn of the nineteenth century. Facts and figures, dates and statistics can never properly afford the reader a proper insight into the everyday movements, dangers and even humdrum of campaign life.

The Battle of Ordal

It was Lord Bentinck's intention to locate the main body of his force at Ordal; therefore a detachment of some 3,500 men comprising the 2nd Battalion the Inniskillings under the command of Colonel Adam was sent ahead to occupy the heights of Ordal.

Approximately ten miles to the front of Villafranca rose the heights of Ordal, an area which would cost the 2nd Battalion dearly. In the ensuing battle eight officers and three hundred other ranks were either killed or wounded. Again, as in the case of Tarragona, this action wasn't so much a farce as criminal neglect on the part of those in command. A position which, given ample consideration, should have been relatively simple to defend was, through a catalogue of errors, left exposed and vulnerable.

The 2nd Battalion, the only British contingent in an Allied Army, under the command of Colonel Adam, was ordered to hold the steep heights of a ravine accessible only by a road bridge. Confronted with a numerically superior French force and warned of the likelihood of an impending attack Adam ignored the possibility and failed to take even the most rudimentary precautions. As a result, the bridge was left unmanned and unprotected, allowing advanced French patrols to cross and reconnoitre the Allied position.

When the attack did come, it was swift and decisive. As darkness fell Colonel Adam further compounded the situation by placing his troops on the heights to the rear of the ravine. In such a position they were effectively removed from lending assistance if the bridge was compromised. At nightfall those sentries in the vicinity of the bridge were taken unawares by French infantry columns as they stormed across the bridge at midnight.

Had it not been for the forward pickets putting up such stiff opposition, the main body of Adam's force would never have had time to stand to arms before being overrun. As the French came across the bridge one of the first to fall wounded was Adams himself, as a result of which the command fell to Lieutenant-Colonel Reeves of the 27th. Now it became obvious that the Allied position was untenable. The following account by Captain Waldron of the 27th Inniskillings reported to Colonel Carey of the Calabrese, who had assumed command of the force when Reeves fell wounded, gives a graphic account of the action as it unfolded:

On the night of the 12th instant, about 12 o'clock, the enemy, in great force, attacked the position of the 2nd battalion 27th Regiment at Ordal; and, shortly after, Lieutenant-Colonel Reeves and Captain Mills being wounded, the command of the battalion devolved to me. At this time the fire from the enemy's sharpshooters was extremely heavy, as well as that of his artillery, under cover of which heavy columns of infantry were advancing upon my front and upon my right flank. Notwithstanding the inferiority of my force, and the loss already sustained, I was determined to keep my ground as long as possible, more especially when I witnessed the gallant, brave and determined conduct of the Spanish troops on my left, who charged with the bayonet three times, and forced the enemy to retire with great loss.

I continued to maintain the position for an hour and three-quarters, exposed to an incessant fire along my front, the enemy's light troops on my right flank, and even in rear of it. I did not think of falling back until I saw the gallant Spanish overpowered by numbers and almost destroyed. My left thus being uncovered, I conceived it my duty to save as many as I could of the battalion, and, accordingly, I retired with five officers, eight sergeants and sixty-six rank and file, under a heavy fire, and followed by the enemy's cavalry.

I beg leave to state that nothing could exceed the brave, determined conduct of the officers and men of the 2nd battalion 27th Regiment; and I feel it justice to mention the good conduct of Lieutenant Felix, of the Royal Marines, attached to the battalion.

I have the satisfaction to add that many of the brave men who were unavoidably dispersed during the action have since joined; and I trust our loss altogether will not exceed two hundred men.[7]

The outcome of the Battle of Ordal was that a retreat soon became a rout. So heavily outnumbered were the Allied troops that little else was possible. Although a detachment of Spanish cavalry and an officer and twelve men of the 27th covered the retreat of the artillery, four pieces fell into the hands of the French. As a result of this action, the numbers of those killed, wounded and missing are inconsistent. A vast number of men were displaced due to the nature of the retreat and only succeeded in rejoining their units in the days and weeks that followed the battle. However, 25 September seems to have been accepted as a cut-off point, as few stragglers returned after that date. Therefore the figure estimated in the manuscript Record of Service Book is generally taken as more or less correct. This document concludes that the 27th Inniskillings lost at Ordal a total of three hundred killed, wounded and missing. The total losses among the Allies as a whole in this engagement amounted to approximately one thousand.

September 26th
Agreeable to the doctor's orders I last night swallowed his copious dose of calomel, and consequently did not leave my own quarters until dinner time. During this interval I was surprised by an Orderly Corporal showing me Garrison Orders, stating that having been reported fit, I was ordered on depot duty. This

annoyed me excessively!! I was as unfit as I had been from the start! Moreover, it was a very plain intimation that my surgeon thought I was skulking. In the evening Pollock and Radcliffe went to the theatre, and I returned home.

September 29th

Our baggage started soon after nine o'clock and we followed at eleven. The day was fine, although the clouds were threatening. The road wound round the mountains in a pleasing manner. We all enjoyed our ride, and reached Salinis about three. Like old soldiers we pursued our first day's march leisurely, and I found myself much fatigued. Our baggage arrived half an hour after, and was just housed when one of our servants apprehended the man who had stolen Radcliffe's horses from Vitoria. Of course the villain stoutly denied the charge. But fortunately Lieutenant Colonel Rudd of the 77th Regiment with a serjeant and party were in the own, on their way to Vitoria to attend a court martial, of which the Colonel was to be President. He ordered his party to take charge of the culprit. The town of Salinis is barricaded as usual. And at the gate a toll is collected for the repairs of the Camino Real which passes it. The town is situated half way down a mountain looking delightfully into a fertile valley. In the Grand Plaza, or Market Place, a fountain affords an abundant supply of excellent water.

The Adjutant of the Brunswick Oels,[8] an acquaintance of Radcliffe's, had overtaken us on the road, and conversed with us some long time. Like my companions, his wounds were not healed but he was likewise impatient to rejoin his Regiment.

We found on our arrival that he was engaged to dine with Lieutenant Colonel Rudd. And they joined us afterwards. We found the adjutant a most entertaining companion: One of those brave heroes, who preferring "death or victory!" – the motto and war cry of the corps – to French thraldom, followed their prince through hosts of enemies and innumerable dangers to England. He was wounded and taken prisoner in the last encounter with the enemy, and did not reach Heligoland till two months after the prince arrived in England. Norman was a small active fellow strongly imbued with "esprit de corps"! His animated conversation was a strong contrast to, and compensated for, the bestiality of the Lieutenant Colonel; who was drunk when he came, and yet

32

was thirsty – at all events he drank to and with the last. Converse he could not; all his thoughts and ideas were fixed on wine. It was quite grievous to see a well-known brave soldier and good-hearted fellow thus lose himself. Before he became too much inebriated he amused us much, by relating that at the Battle of Albuera a cannon ball carried away his valise[9] from behind him, with the skirts of his jacket.

September 30th

Radcliffe was obliged to return to prosecute the stealer of his horses. Pollock and I proceeded along a most delightful valley, favoured with a lovely day. The peasants' houses ranged on each side at the distance of two, three and four hundred yards from each other: that at every turning of the road, they had the appearance of a long-continued street and the well-cultivated fields looked like one extensive garden. In peaceable times this must be a nucleus of content, industry, and earthly happiness! We passed through Mondragon, a large and good town. On approaching Bergara the road was diversified and interesting, capable of forming, with the river, a very formidable military position. The large gateway, a handsome stone arch over the road, had the direction of different routes inscribed thereon. Under the arch to Vere, to the left Bilbao and the right to France. The latter reminds us that we were on the great road to Bayonne and gave rise to many reflections and remarks which were arrested by our passing a most admirably planned blockhouse commanding the road we had so attentively noticed. On enquiring, we learned that ten thousand French, who retired from Bilbao, resolved to make a stand here and fortified the spot accordingly.

I will not say that our troops would not have assailed this spot, but I can say that many brave fellows would have fallen in the attack. Bergara is a fine well-built town and has not suffered from the calamities of war, which have dilapidated half the Peninsula. At the entrance we noticed a nunnery in an unfinished state and made enquiries of the number of nuns, and Order for which it was intended. But it was very evident that our interrogations gave displeasure. No horses are allowed to pass through the plaza, where stands the town hall, where the gateway was formerly. A low, but handsome and ornamented building. The following motto is cut on its front.

Oque Mucho to de Alla
Oque poco to de Ava.

Signifying, where there is much sin, or transgression, there is little grace, or pardon.

We found our billets better than usual.

October 1st

We had a short and pleasant ride to Villa Real, but as we must draw our rations here, we could not advance further. The road passes through the town and, during the six years the French occupied it, they fortified themselves to the utmost of its locality, against the mountaineers. We were informed that no troops were allowed to be stationed here, they were always hurrying to and fro.

October 2nd

The weather was unfavourable and prevented our starting at our usual early hour. It cleared up however before we had travelled a league along the continued delightful valley, where nature was refreshed by the showers, during the night and morning. At Villa Franca, we had to put up with the worst billets we had hitherto experienced.

The gateway led us to expect a good town, but we found ourselves woefully mistaken! I sat down without the walls, to watch the approach of our baggage, and Pollock soon joined me. An old weather-beaten and lame sailor, who had asked us in vain for charity, as we rode in, was passing us in silence, not deigning even a look at those who had disregarded his entreaties. I felt the reproof and gave him somewhat. We asked the particulars of his wounded leg. He said he was wounded when fighting against the English nine years ago, in the West Indies; he could not stand to work and charity was his sole dependence. "And a pitiful dependence that is," thought I, for most of those who pass are soldiers, and though their hearts do not want the inclination, their pockets lack means!!

October 3rd Sunday

Knowing Tolosa to be the residence of the Paymaster General with the grand military chest, we fully expected to find it a town of some importance, and were mightily chagrined to find only three parallel dirty streets. We obtained salted mackerel and sardines, alias sprats, for dinner.

October 4th

It was fortunate that we reached Ornania at an early hour, for it was crowded with artillery and cavalry as we were sent to a farm-house across the river as our billet. We were well pleased with our quarters; the description of which may prove interesting. The house was about 20 yards square, the entrance in the centre. On the right hand was a kitchen some nine feet square; all the rest of the ground floor was used as a stable. In the middle a broad ladder led through the floor above, and the apartment was open to the very roof, excepting small bedrooms, right and left of the western side, nine feet long and four broad, the intermediate space occupied by two large wooden chests, and a small door to a balcony. The eastern side was, for the most part, open to the weather, hot or cold. The furniture consisted of a low table and two broken chairs.

The floor was well stored with ears of maize, or Indian corn, which were thrown there in a heap for our occupation. For this occupation the tenant pays so many Reals, in proportion to the number of castanos, or chestnut trees. An extensive orchard joins the farmyard, but apple trees form no part of the covenants. His rent is registered, and for every hundred Reals he pays eight as a government duty or land tax. He was hard at work, delighted with the conviction that now he should have to pay only 8 instead of 20 and aftimes 50 Reals, levied by the French. He admitted that 8 Reals was trifling. Moreover he added, "I pay that on my own lawful government." When the little table was prepared for our dinners, with our silver spoons and forks and Pollock's plated goblets, the contrast to the other parts of the house was very great.

This day on route, we passed through a village occupied by Horse Artillery. I saw an officer sitting on the bridge and was about to pass him unheedingly; his earnest look at me induced me to look at him, when we had again exchanged looks, he sprang forward, exclaiming, "Good Lord, is not your name Crowe?" "Yes! And is not your name Day?" It was James Day from Norwich. And had we been more nearly related we could not have been more mutu-ally pleased with the encounter.

October 5th

We ordered the baggage to take the direct route to Renteirea, and leaving our rural abode about 8 o'clock made the best of our time to visit the ruins of the famed fortress of San Sebastian. The morning was most lovely and the blue sea bursting suddenly to our view, after a brief observation, wafted our thoughts, our fond thoughts, to England for some time.

We reached the spot our engineers first broke ground, which rising, did not, at first, require much labour to render the approaches safe. A large convent on the right had been transmuted into a fortress of considerable importance, as an advanced position. It was taken by Portuguese, and very much was said about their gallant conduct on the occasion. Within a few days the French recaptured it, and deserved infinite praise for the boldness of the attempt and the bravery with which they retained it.

This convent, converted, riveted our attention for some time, and we were surprised to see it still standing. We could not conjecture, why one brick was left on another, as our lines so entirely commanded its situation. In our progress we could, by the gabions[10] still standing, mark the admirable position of our various batteries, all of which had a good command or range, until our lines reached the sea shore. When our engineers advanced their approaches in rear of the convent they exhumed many coffins of French officers and placed them in their ramparts, which being now levelled, these coffins were exposed, to the weather, more or less. Our regrets and indignation were much excited, that these coffins had not been placed in the trenches, and again buried. When we came in full view of the fortress we noticed that the sea wall on the east had been carefully repaired; to effect which, the workmen had cleared away and made use of chief of the material battered down from the awful breaches, on which our own immediate comrades had died, and by which our brave soldiers had reached the heights. This circumstance was a great disappointment to us! For we had fully resolved to have secured our steeds, and with a melancholy satisfaction passed up over the footsteps of our lost comrades, and searched out the spots where our much lamented friend Jack Harding, poor Kenyon, and other brave fellows had died! The town showed all the horrors of a bombardment, excepting the houses on the rock, on which the citadel is built which our guns could not reach, not one remained entire. They had been uniform and handsome, with stone basements, and had extensive and handsome balconies to the upper windows. The streets are parallel, and at right angles. We could not discover a lane or alley anywhere.

The ascent from the town to the citadel on the south side of the rock was *en barbette*,[11] but the French built a parapet with flat loose stones, sufficiently high to screen passers up and down. When ascending this road we arrived at the fatal south-east angle commanding the main breach, from whence the besieged incessantly poured forth death and destruction on their assailants. This parapet originally had but one large gun; in consequence of our attack, however, it became a most important place, and the French, by cutting into the face of the rock, and other expedients, established three twenty-four-pounders on traversing carriages. These kept up such an unceasing fire, that their touch-holes, the size of this quill with which I am writing, were fused, like holes in a honeycomb, which admitted my four fingers! The centre gun was dismounted and burst, by one of our shots sticking in the muzzle. From this spot we had a full view of the breach, and well contented that our turn of duty had not forced us into it, I reflected upon it with acute feelings for had I been with the Regiment and Harding availed himself of his office as acting adjutant I must have risked my life there. Approaching the castle we had a view of the north side of the rock furrowed by the shot and shells from our guns which had passed over the citadel, to which the garrison retired, after our troops had taken possession of the town, but next day surrendered. And well they might! Their ammunition was exhausted. We found the flour magazine no longer proof against the weather, and the few remaining bags were so mouldy that they could not be lifted.

On passing through the different apartments of the castle we were surprised to observe how remarkably thin the walls of the upper rooms were. We could distinctly perceive that our balls from our batteries, and also from our ships in the bay, had passed directly through both walls although so elevated. Every room had, from two to six perforations of this kind, excepting the Donjon, which being in the rock, had escaped.

Crowe graphically depicts the scene in an around San Sebastian in the aftermath of the siege. He can appreciate the sacrifice of the troops involved, especially his friend Jack Harding, who, on all accounts, detailed himself as one of the Forlorn Hope in Crowe's stead.

The 400 Portuguese taken prisoner by the French when they recaptured the convent were confined in the upper part of the castle, sixty of whom were killed by our shots. Having attentively surveyed the fortifications collectively, we were strongly inclined to the opinion that the engineer who constructed these works, relied too much on the apparent strength of the conical-shaped rock. For had it not been the additions which the French made in various parts the capture would not have cost us so dearly.

It will be many years ere the town and fortress can be restored to their original grandeur and importance.

On leaving San Sebastian we passed by the route along poor Jack Harding and his gallant party must have also advanced to their death bed.

On arriving at Renteiria we found our servants waiting, having received our billet for another country quarter, full half a league back the road we had come. There was no redress, though it proved worse than our last night's abode. From the field in front of the house we had a very picturesque view of Passages, or Pas-sa-haes, from whence the packets sailed for England. It is probably the most extraordinary port in the whole world. I cannot suppose there is such another. Without any appearance of the proximity of the sea, we found a basin, of less than a hundred acres in extent, with an unruffled surface, and vessels from six to eight hundred tons safely moored to the banks. The egress is a chasm between two perpendicular rocks, twice the height of the mast head of a large brig. On the eastern rock is a neglected fort, destitute of guns. A casual observer would imagine this to be a secure post, and such it is, but ingress and egress are dangerous, for in case of any swell in the bay, towards the opening, vessels are in danger of being driven on the rocks on either side. No ship ventures out but with an ebbing tide, for in such a confined place sails are useless. The passage is no more than 150 feet wide.

October 6th
We could obtain nothing but salt meat, or regular junk, for our rations, at Renteiria and moved off little satisfied with our cargo.

We passed through Carazun, and between one and two after noon took possession for the night of a forsaken house by the roadside. The valley was very picturesque, the day fine and the clear river most inviting, that we took a cold bath before dinner.

I must admit our quarters were most capacious, but by no means accommodating, or comfortable, for as the night advanced the wind and rain drove in most bitterly, and the shutters to the windows in front having been destroyed we were compelled to force the doors off the back apartments to fence out the weather. Moreover our situation was so lonesome that we considered it requisite to keep watch throughout the night.

Fortunately the ground floor was a wine store and had no opening but the main entrance to the house. Over which was a wooden balcony, under whose partial shelter our servants kept a good fire with the abundance of fuel, which we had providentially secured. And we ordered them to stand sentry by turns and give the alarm should any person approach. Pollock and I did not undress, but, with drawn swords in hand, crept under our blankets. This precaution was soon tested. For about 11 o'clock my servant, being on duty, fired a shot and called out, "Stand to your arms!" My friend and I had not long made our appearance below, when a very suspicious and desperate looking fellow, wearing a pisan,[12] came towards us, pretending to be looking for his lost mule. We told him very plainly that we knew he was a flam,[13] for the sentry heard him conversing with his comrades before the shot was fired. And that if he, or any man, or any number of men dared to come near the house during the night we would show them no mercy. During this parlance we frequently stirred up the fire with our drawn swords. Our vigilance and alertness had a good effect. For although we kept a dog watch, we rested ourselves unmolested for the remainder of the night.

October 7th

We moved off in good time, but the road was so very steep and bad we could precede but slowly, and were obliged to dismount and walk chief of the way. On approaching to Lesaca we were informed that the whole front of the army was engaged. We left our baggage and hurried forward through Lesaca, reaching Bara between two and three o'clock.

Here we ascertained that our own Division had only moved up

in support of the Light Division and the Spaniards, in driving the enemy from their numerous breastworks, which, as I have before stated intersected our lines, and on which they had been actively working during their long sojourn in the locality. We ascended that heights, following the track of the contending parties, and were grieved to see so many sad proofs of the undaunted manner in which our gallant riflemen had advanced. We did not, I think, pass any one of these fieldworks without seeing two or three of these brave fellows dead, evidently shot in surmounting the embankment, and fallen back into the ditch. A large work near the centre of the position had been contested most bravely, as evinced by the many dead on both sides. But our attention was riveted for some time to two who had bayoneted each other, and though opposed in life, were united in death, for it would have required considerable force to have unclenched their grasp of their muskets!! We could not but compare the two countenances; the contrast forced itself on our notice. The Frenchman was evidently an old soldier and had perhaps witnessed many a hard-fought battle, his cap, low on his brow, was well secured under his chin, and his lurid countenance still wore the satanic and malicious grin of desperation! The young Rifleman's cap had rolled back into the ditch, leaving his full and curling hair floating in the breeze. A good-tempered smile rested on his ruddy face, which seemed to say, "I bear no malice to any one, I have only done my duty!!" His sword bayonet was thrust with all the vigour of youth far through his antagonist.

We overtook our Regiment about four o'clock and accompanied them to their ground above Lesaca, under the mountain that was still contested by the Spaniards and French.

Our baggage came up in good time for us to pitch our tents for the night, allowing me time, before it was quite dark, to run and shake hands with my old friends Captains Reid and Wauch of the 48th who had joined during my absence.

I received a letter from my father, dated July 24th.

October 9th
We advanced at daybreak in support of the Spaniards, who were sharply attacked at an early hour. After halting for many hours we took up our ground in a young oak wood. Our baggage was late in reaching up. I was excessively ill, but fortunately fell in with

Captain Smith of the 20th Regiment, nephew of Sir Sidney Smith, who gave me two cups of tea, which revived me much.

We are decidedly in France near Sarre.

October 12th

Dined with the Colonel. I am removed to the 8th Company under Captain Chitty, who lately came from the 2nd Battn in Valencia. An Englishman, very gentlemanly and agreeable, we chum very pleasantly. Our tent was near the road, with a good view of the Crown mountain. In the evening Harry Franklin and Pollock sat chatting with us, when the 20th Regiment retired to their camp. As he passed we asked Captain Smith how he was. He replied in his ever cheerful and jocular way. ' Oh my dear fellows we are all alive, although fagged out with two nights bivouac in support of those rascally Spaniards, but lying on the ground they had occupied, we are most animated, for we have lice in all our quarters!!" Soon afterwards we saw Downie, the Spanish General, approaching a fine rattling Irishman, formerly a Commissar of our Army attached to the Spanish service in the Alentejo, when Portugal was the seat of war and an old acquaintance of Franklin's. As soon as he saw Harry's cheerful face, with three bounds in was in the midst of us! Pulling off his gorgeous sash and sword, he threw himself down in our tent, exclaiming, "I am going on very important business, and have not a minute to spare, but it is impossible to pass Harry Franklin. Come lads give me some wine, for I am as dry as a lime-burner's wig. Oh! How delightful to be once more in the company of good fellows!!! My curse on those lousy dastardly Spaniards! What a laborious task have I had with them in those mountains!! If you redcoats had not remained so close at our heels, I never could have urged the villains on. Oh! How I wish myself back in my old post!"

Franklin reminded him of his rank and pay as General Officer. "Psha! Nonsense," he replied. "I tell you that I should be a far richer, and much happier man with my old corps."

"But recollect your honours, and your legion with Downie cut of tin in front of their caps."

"My dear fellow I cannot stop to talk of such trumpery. I must be going!" With sword and sash in hand, he sprang up on his feet and went off with the elastic step of a native mountaineer. When Franklin exclaimed, "How extraordinary has been that man's

41

career! Soon after the commencement of the Peninsular War he came out in the Commissariat Department. In the South of Spain he was Commissary of a Spanish force stationed in the Alentejo near the French lines, which were strong, and kept our advanced guard in check. A party of the enemy, one night, assaulted the station and behaved with all their wanted cruelty and wanton desperation. Downie roused the Spaniards to action, mustered all capable of bearing arms, pursued and routed the assailants and, following up his Army, retired (with the full persuasion that it was a general attack by our Army) and maintained his ground until relieved by the advanced guard.

"This gallant event opened the field for others most important; and having been effected by Spaniards, their government became wild with enthusiasm, instantly appointed Downie as full General in their service. And the Cortes gave him the sword of Pizarro!!! A legion, or Brigade, was quickly formed, of which every man had a tin plate round the bottom of his cap, with Downie cut in front."

October 13th

This day began at a very early hour, for soon after midnight we were awakened by very sharp firing, and arose in full expectation of a sudden order to advance. No order arriving we laid down on our blankets till about 5 o'clock when we advanced to support the Spaniards. We found that they had decidedly lost the advanced redoubt, nor did we marvel for it was quite within the French lines that we were surprised that they had been suffered to retain it a whole week. Availing themselves of the huts formed from branches, which they had erected, the French endeavoured to regain the second redoubt, but the Spaniards set fire to the huts and secured their own position. Regardless of all this, the French strove hard for this second redoubt and the two guns they had left there, which they were anxious to redeem. Ere noon they gave it up as a bad job. And in the afternoon we levelled the works, rolling the guns down to the ravine beneath.

Agreeable to the Brigade orders of yesterday for an officer to be sent to the advanced posts to report to General Sir Lowry Cole what occurred in front, I was ordered to remain, when the Brigade retired to their camp. I remained till dark and returned with the working party.

October 14th

A rainy morning. I have sent my pony with the foraging party to Passages for corn. Wrote a letter to Ratcliffe.

October 19th

So ill I could not raise myself the whole day, my head was in agony. Applied to Franklin, who made for me some calomel pills, and surgeon would not allow but next day ordered me to the rear.

October 21st

Our paymaster having received orders for the short and long bat[14] and forage, advanced me ten guineas on account. I have so arranged the accounts of the 5th Company that my friend Boyle can settle them for me. And I started this morning with my servant, Barney Bradley, and baggage. I had not travelled a league, ere I was attacked by a fit of fever. It was fortunate the day was so fine, for thrice was I obliged to dismount and lay down, that I preceded but slowly on my route. I arrived at Irun about sunset, but it was so crowded with Spanish soldiers that a billet was refused, and I was ordered to proceed to Fontarabia, which was out of my way. I arrived before it was dark, and was sent a mile further to a house by the sea beach.

Fontarabia, situated on the south bank of the Bidasoa just above its confluence with the sea, is a very striking object and would from many points make a good picture. Its lofty walls, formed on rock, but now collapsed, prove that once it was of some importance. The entrance has double gates, with drawbridges to it.

October 22nd

I started in a pelting rain for Passages, the hospital station to which I was ordered. Reported myself to staff surgeon Doctor Baxter, late surgeon in the 48th Regiment. And to whom my good friends, Paymaster Hughes, and Captain Parry, had given me letters of introduction. But the town was so full that I was ordered to return to this mudhole, Renteiria. And only obtained a billet in a very ordinary house, already occupied by a conductor of stores, a sub-ordinate of the commissariat. I asserted my priority of rank, and obtained the only bed, such as it is, for my friends in England would be astonished at its component parts, the fourteen inches high of a stump, bedstead being filled with branches pruned from

43

the vine, and which, although very elastic, were not at all soft or agreeable, despite the thin bed of I know not what placed above. I must endeavour to obtain better quarters. I wish I could obtain the opposite house, where my brother officer Lieutenant Shaw waits for a passage to England.

Lieutenant Harnet, with a party for arms,[15] left the regiment the same day as myself, has accomplished his mission and will return on the morrow.

October 23rd
Shaw is ordered to Passages to take his passage. The commandant will not grant me his quarters, but has ordered my companion the Conductor off. Having the house to myself, and the stable beneath being more than usually secure, I will be content with my lot, in spite of my uncomfortable bed with swarms of fleas. My servant and baggage shall occupy the small room out of mine, now vacant.

The people are as dirty as the house, but very civil as soon as they comprehend our signs of what we want, but as true Biscayans they understood the Spanish language as little as English or French. During the afternoon when we were endeavouring to make our quarters as clean and comfortable as we could, my servant went to ask our hostess the loan of a broom, an article unknown! He returned in a great wrath, exclaiming, "Troth, but these are the queerest folk I ever came near!" "How so Barney?" "Why, sure now, they don't understand their own language, when I spake Spanish to them, and when I spake Portuguese they knew as little of that!!" "Truly Barney, I know not what you are going to do, unless you talk Irish to them!" "Is it now Irish that you are talking about?" he indignantly replied. "Sure they have not wit enough to understand that!"

October 24th Sunday
I was too ill to do more than read the service for the morning. But, as Sterne's Corporal Trim states, "a soldier, when he has time, prays as fervently as a parson!"

October 27th
A detachment of the 4th Division arrived from Vitoria. Ensign Clunis, of our Regiment, was with it. He breakfasted with me. And as the day was fine I escorted him to Passages and we returned to a

late dinner. I was rejoiced to find he had recovered from the very singular wound received at Pamplona. A bullet entered about six inches above the left knee; a slight inflammation showed its upward course. The surgeons fearing that it had entered the lower part of the body, kept their patient in bed. But finding, after long observation, no further trace, ordered him to take exercise. Some time after the ball was cut out of the corresponding spot above the right knee!

October 28th
Torrents of rain all day.

October 29th
Clunis and the detachment returned this morning. I am greatly surprised by the receipt of a letter from the sister of my friend Lieut. Joe Hill, dated Sept. 24th in reply to my letter of the 6th of that month to inform his mother of the loss of his leg high above the left knee. I wrote a second letter this day. Considering that the letter was directed to me at Vitoria was sent from thence to the regiment, and followed me hither, it is an unusually quick transit, and would not have tired my patience had a young lady been interested for me instead of her brother.

November 2nd
A fine morning. I accompanied Byrnes and Lieutenant Boyle of the 82nd Regiment to Passages. We found the harbour quite full, many transports having entered yesterday. Some from St Andero with convalescents, and some from England with reinforcements, of which a detachment for our regiment Ensign Phibbs, Ensigns Weir and Slattery, with 105 fine young men. They were quickly landed, and marched off to Oarazun, near to Irun, where I suppose they will halt a day or two. Byrnes and I introduced ourselves to Ensign Kater, who is sick here. A good-tempered, thoughtless, rattling little fellow, who will not be able to stand much hard service. On our return we met Ensign Weir with Doctor Felton, who had recognised him, in the evening Lieutenant Fairfield arrived from the Regiment.

November 4th
I omitted the other day to mention a letter I received from our Colonel, requesting me to ascertain if any regimental clothing or stores had arrived by these numerous transports. Having written

my official report that there was nothing arrived here, I gladly availed myself of this fine, lovely morning to go to Passages and put my reply into the letter box in the office of the commandant, who I found in a rather warm altercation with a captain of the Royal Navy, whose back was towards me, but his voice interested me much more than the topic of conversation, some what about the duty of transport, and their mode of entering the harbour. I did not heed what it was all about, for I felt confident that I knew the voice, although more excited than I ever heard before. The captain closed the debate rather with warmth, saying, "I cannot wait any longer, I am under sailing orders, and my frigate is standing off and on, waiting my return. But as I have charge of this coast I tell you major, these orders must be obeyed."

I marked the limp as he turned around, which confirmed my surmises, and instantly I was face to face with Frederick Langford, with whom I parted a few years since in my father's house at Swaffham. He fixed his eyes on mine, in an enquiring state of surprise for a few seconds, then seized my hand exclaiming, "Why Charles, is it possible, that we meet again on foreign service! I am heartily glad to see you, but you look cursedly ill!" I told him I was suffering from *coup de soleil*. "Oh! That is a bad case," he replied. "I wish I was not under sail. I would have taken you on board my ship and soon made you well! Now I cannot stop, for this trouble-some business has already detained me too long. Goodbye, my dear fellow! I hope you will soon get well, and give the French a good d. . .d good licking in the spring!" And off he went.

Two more transports have arrived, with reinforcements, and many very, very, young officers. I have not, for a long time, seen so many smart new jackets, for, young-soldier-like, they all came ashore rigged out in their very best. One young chap of the Fusiliers sported his tall bearskin Grenadier cap and looked tremendously fine and grand! Poor lad! He will very soon be glad to leave it in some ravine, never to see daylight again. During my absence Phibbs and Weir came over for their baggage. In the evening I went over and sat with Boyle of the 82nd [The Prince of Wales's Volunteer Foot].

November 5th
I ought to have stated that "the limp as Captain Langford turned round" was caused by the severe wound he received in the hip,

from a grape shot, when cutting out some French gunboat from Boulogne harbour. And that Lady Hamilton of notoriety (see Life of Nelson) attended his sick bed daily, till he recovered.

Pamplona having surrendered, the garrison was this evening marched into this town to wait transport to England. They are a remarkably fine body of men; their looks and hilarity do not denote the great hardships and privations which they must have suffered. Provisions were so scarce that it is supposed they have not left even a rat or mouse alive in the fortification. A strong guard at each gateway keep them within the walls of this town.

November 6th

These Frenchmen have kept up an incessant jabbering throughout the night. Most heartily do I wish them safely in Foctin or Yaxley Depots. The church is appropriated to them as their barrack and is already in a most filthy state, for in addition to the natural want of cleanliness in these people, they are all, more or less, suffering from diarrhoea in consequence of their late privations, and some of them to such an extreme that they cannot get out to relieve themselves.

We were told that 1500 were too ill to leave the fortress. My brother officer, Byrne, who lodges with me, has charge of 664 of these prisoners. There are 1915 in the town and at Leso the same number, making a garrison of 5330 men, a much larger number than was estimated when we invested Pamplona. The prisoners have abundance of money and eagerly purchase bread at any price. Disgusted with Byrne's duty Tom Radcliffe has marched with the detachment and sent a man with a note to me to order his baggage to overtake him this night. The Commandant has enough to engage his attention, and may therefore overlook this bold attempt by my friend. But Tom is confident our Colonel will not censure him! He has forfeited, by this disobedience of orders, three days' rations for himself, servant and animals! But Tom is an excellent forager. I am confident that his servant will look out for something for the poor "bastes" as well as his own mouth.

I passed the medical board this morning, where I fell in with Lieut. Moore of the 45th Regiment [1st Nottinghamshire Foot] who informed me that when the Army advanced after the Battle of Pamplona, his Division, the 3rd, returned to Roncesvalles, and that on his progress, his attention was drawn to a naked corpse in the

47

garden, with the bowels protruding from a desperate wound across the abdomen, and that on close attention he recognised the face of his schoolfellow Charles Crawford! I felt quite a disgust to this man, when I found that he was not the old schoolfellow who did bury poor Crawford's remains!

November 8th

At Passages I was informed that the rumour on Friday of the Army attacking was false. Most of the Army remains in status quo as when I left it. I saw a packet come in with a mail from England and profusion of stores of every description landing from transports.

I met Lieutenant Wilbraham, R.N. who walked with Hambley and myself from Barricalia to Pumhete on our route from Lisbon, where he was agent for transports. I should have been glad, could he have assured me his long and arduous services had been rewarded by promotion.

A sutler[16] asked 50 Dollars, just fifteen pounds for canteens, which I could have purchased at Portsmouth for three guineas and a half!

November 9th

A large blister was last night applied to my neck, that now, if not minded, I am stiff-necked! This troublesome companion instead of relieving made my poor head more miserable! Then I wandered along the mud wall of the harbour until I was opposite the convent on the other side, which is close to Passages. The tide was excessively high, and the busy boats of various shapes, kinds and nations, scudding about, aided by the fine weather, presented an interesting scene, had I been well enough to have enjoyed it.

A detachment of the 77th Regiment is come round from Lisbon to escort these French prisoners to England. I found that Taylor is of this party. He was with the regimental depot at Danbury barracks, when I was there with the 2nd Battalion 48th Regiment. The air and duty of Lisbon has agreed with him.

After I was returned to my quarters I heard much talking with heavy footsteps on the stairs and went to ascertain the cause, when I met three Spanish officers attended by the Alcalda, or Mayor, coming up to enforce three billets in this house. I told them there were two English officers and their servants here, besides the two families, that there was no room for more. One of the officers was extremely indignant and endeavoured to pull me downstairs, but received in kind what he so officiously intended for me. I knocked him down upon the Alcalda. As soon as he could recover his feet he drew his sword and cut furiously at me. I put my fist to his nose and calmly assured him that, although I was without a sword, if he did not instantly sheath his I would break it over his head! The Alcalda interposed and desired the Ruffian to descend; consequently I allowed the rest of the party to descend. At this juncture Byrnes and my servant came to my support, they coolly opened the window shutters, determined to bundle both the officers and the Alcalda out into the street, their indignation was so furious that I had great difficulty to establish a cessation of hostilities. If I had not succeeded in this, as senior in rank, I should have been in a very awkward predicament. For however custom justified me in resisting encroachment of my own billet, I had no right to resist the Alcalda in locating one of the Spaniards on the poor family in the attics.

November 10th

The French prisoners were marched off this morning, by an officer of Quarter Master General's Staff. The church is open for ventilation, and unfortunately the wind is in the south, and blows the stench up to my quarters, rendering my room insufferable. I was compelled to walk out for fresh air. Curiosity induced me to go up to the church door, in spite of my olfactory nerves; the floor was really ankle-deep with filth! I never witnessed such a sight. And the street on the south side of the church was like an open sewer!! I never saw such an accumulation of filth! I was obliged to wander beyond the bridge to relieve my miserable head.

November 11th

Today I was in even greater pain and vainly expected my doctors, for they did not come. Received a letter from Close.

November 12th

Endured great agony. About four in the afternoon the assistant staff surgeon, attended by an hospital mate, or assistant, and ordered my head shaved. Which operation Byrnes kindly performed for me, and put on the capacious blister, which the hospital mate sent.

November 15th

I am informed Lord Wellington had appointed a certain number of the prisoners from Pamplona to be exchanged, including the governor, who has petitioned to be allowed to proceed to England, rather than return to France. Six hundred prisoners from the front marched to Passages for transport, escorted by a party of the 16th Light Dragoons.

November 17th

I was compelled to sit up in my bed this morning to make out my return for drawing rations. I found myself better for the exertion, and wrote to my friend Close of the 48th and Boyle of our own regiment. Before I finished, my fellow lodger Byrnes came to take leave of me, he having an unexpected order to escort some prisoners to Headquarters at St Pée, who were to be exchanged. My blistered head is healed, but, contrary to the surgeon's expectations, I am in great pain, that in spite of my reluctance I much fear I shall be obliged to return to England when I am in orders to do so. For the present according to general orders promulgated this day, I have a month's sick leave to Bilbao. How truly absurd and annoying this! How is it possible for me to move and for what!

When Doctor Fenton came to see me in compliance with my request sent I stated how much I was molested by the order, he promised me a certificate, if necessary, that I was incapable of removing. I learn that I must remain in durance vile, until 5th December when my leave will expire, and I appear before another board of strange medical officers, who will know only the official statement of my case, and the black marks put against my name, for I have a strong impression that some of the medicos imagine that I am skulking, despite the severe treatment received from them, and my frequent repeated disinclination to return to England!

The assistant staff surgeon in his attendance this day did deviate from his usually sententious remarks, by relating an attempt by two men of the 83rd Regiment to rob his house last night and that they are to be tried tomorrow. He also told me that two men, the other night, entered the room where two officers of the 16th Dragoons were in bed in two recesses. The villains had a light and deliberately ransacked the clothes on the chair beside the first bed, unlocked the baggage, and took whatever they pleased. Then proceeded to the other recess, and when satisfied quickly retired with their booty. The two officers confessed that they were awakened and saw all that passed, but did not dare to resist, for fear of having their throats cut! Oh! What valiant Heroes! Their swords stood within their reach, but they were afraid to use them! What are we to expect from troops led by such doughty commanders!

Ever aggrieved at the perceived callous treatment he received at the hands of the medical profession, Lieutenant Crowe appears less than impressed with their diagnosis and apparent total disregard of his obvious plight. Apparently, according to his expert self-diagnosis, too ill to return to normal duty, he was reluctant to be returned to England. To do so, as any young officer of the day knew, was disastrous. Promotion and advancement in the Army very much depended upon being in the thick of things. Returning invalided to England would most certainly have put paid to any chance of promotion in the interim whilst others in the field would advance at his cost.

November 21st Sunday
McNicoll informs me that there was much sharp fighting with the enemy on the 10th, [Battle of Nivelle] and that our regiment came in for its share of hard knocks. Major Johnson was killed, and his little son, who came out with him, and joined us in June as a volunteer must now return to England, to solicit for a commission. He will doubtless succeed under such circumstances. Lieutenant Crawley of the Light Coy. was taken prisoner. Ensigns Phibbs, Galbraith, and Ireland (late Sergeant Major) were wounded, and fourteen men: and nineteen of our men were killed.

November 22nd
By the frostiness of this lovely day I fervently hope the weather will become more settled. In my walk to day I met Colonel Erskine of the 48th on his way back to England. Two months ago when at Vitoria, on his route to join the old corps, I passed without saluting him. Now he was glad to find any one to speak to him, he condescended to recognise me. We had a long conversation, but I was very cavalier with him, for I always disliked the man. My antipathy began with our first acquaintance. When I introduced myself on

joining the 2nd Battalion of the 48th Regiment at Northampton, Colonel Erskine said, "You come from the West Suffolk Militia, they have excellent bugles, drummers and fifers. On the next volunteering from the militia, I shall send you to your old Corps to obtain as many as possible." I instantly replied, "I hope and request, Colonel, you will not send me on such an errand, for I could not be able to fulfil your wishes! Sir William Parker, my late Colonel, is justly proud of his bugles and fifers, having perfected them at his own expense instead of taxing his officers for the support of a band of music. I have received much personal kindness, and strong marks of friendship from Sir William, and I could not undertake so ungracious a duty!"

This of course placed me on the Colonel's black list, that is, I was no favourite. It is very curious that some such coincidence always attended me, on joining a new corps.

When I joined the West Suffolk Militia at Sunderland Sir William Parker reproved me for making my appearance on the 25th of the month, instead of on or before the 24th. Whereas the voyage from Lym in Norfolk oft times accomplished in sixteen hours, had, by the perverseness of the wind and waves, detained me sixteen nights and days! I have before stated the malignant prejudices I had to contend against on joining the 27th Regiment.

I am reluctant to forego the history of this Colonel Erskine, because it will elucidate the evils of a military life, which rarely meet the eye and cognisance of civilians.

When Major, and in command of the regiment, at Oporto, he dismounted and headed the Grenadiers in their valiant charge. He was wounded and sent to England, but his object was attained: he was promoted to Lieutenant Colonel; in this rank an officer must wait to gradation of promotion, and Erskine's military ardour evaporated. After a full absence for a slight wound he returned to the Peninsula. And as field officer of the working party, before Badajoz he skulked and was hustled and jostled in the entrenchment by his own men, when a sortie was made by the garrison. After which he somehow obtained leave to return to England and, under the interest of his wife's family, who were engaged about Court, managed to stay at home a very long time, during which I joined the 48th.

He remained at Northampton with us, but a short time. And I saw him no more until I passed him in Vitoria. When I rejoined the

Army in October I heard much of his ill fame from my old comrades. In the camp, of which we took possession October 9th the ground studded with stumps of the young oak trees which had been cut down, Colonel Erskine had the rashness and folly to order the whole regiment to practice the go, or goss-step, the initiation of recruits on a level barrack square! This, and many other ill judged petty acts of want of judgement, and of abused authority, roused the Corps of Veterans, who had done their duty manfully in many a hard fought battle, almost to open rebellion!! I never learnt the particulars of the result, except that Colonel Erskine was attacked by ague (i.e. a shaking fit!) and the doctors recommended him to return to England. I encountered him under these circumstances, and must add I never saw any man in full enjoyment of health!!! In 1816 my communication with my old corps, then stationed at Naas, near Dublin, informed me, that Erskine, in command, had pursued his wonted tyrannical conduct, to such an extent that Lieutenant General Sir Lowry Cole, KCB, was sent by the Commander of the Forces in Ireland, to enquire into the case. Having done so, Cole told Erskine that if he did not alter his conduct, he should be demised from the service!!! This quieted Erskine in a great measure, but when the Regiment received orders to prepare for foreign service, brevet Major Thwaites, the senior captain, with some others, resolved to forego their long and arduous services, and chances of promotion, rather than be under such a man, and retired on half pay. The regiment was sent to New South Wales where Erskine's tyranny again effervesced and very many of my brother officers (my crony Close and Val Blomfield inclusive) exchanged their commissions for grants of land, and became settlers. The regiment next moved to Bombay, where Colonel Erskine died, if not "unshrived," certainly unwept, "unhonoured and unsung!"

There is no doubt Lieutenant Charles Crowe's diary is a treasure trove of information, demonstrating a very human feature of the Peninsular War which we seldom get a chance to experience in more statistical less human accounts. His day-by-day description of the period, which I cannot transcribe here in its entirety, makes the period come alive in a way no outside commentary could. His are the thoughts, recollections, gripes and observation which can only come from someone who experienced those eventful years at first hand. It appears from his narrative that, although a deeply religious man, this religious fervour did not extend to turning the other cheek. Thus we witness more than a passing elation at the disgrace of his former commanding officer Colonel Erskine.

His account of the events of 22 November 1813 differs somewhat from his usual entries, in that he obviously added the details concerning Colonel Erskine at a later date. So strong did he feel on the subject of this particular individual that he could not let his account stand without returning at a later date to elucidate further.

It may be said that many of Lieutenant Crowe's entries have little to do with the actual conduct of the war and therefore irrelevant. I disagree. While it is my intention to catalogue the exploits of the 27th Inniskilling Fusiliers during the Peninsular campaign from embarkation until the epic Battle of Waterloo, I wish to portray those years in their entirety. I want to produce both an informative yet entertaining narrative. The individuals we encounter along the way are not fictional, as in the case of Bernard Cornwell's Major Richard Sharpe. They were genuine individuals caught up in actual events. As previously stated, history should be more than a mere regurgitation of facts and figures; it should be a living representation of the past in all its many facets.

As such, it is interesting to note the medical procedures carried out during this period. According to Lieutenant Crowe's diary he seems to have gone from one ailment to the next. Never one to spare us the sordid details of his illnesses and suffering, he records with increasing clarity each detail almost with perverse delight. He had apparently been ill for quite some time and regularly attended by the surgeon who applied various remedies, some quite barbaric by today's standards of medical practice.

November 24th
A party is come from the regiment to escort the clothing and stores, of which I can gain no intelligence. Sent one of the Grenadiers, with a pass, to make enquiries at Tolosa. Took a short walk at flood time in the harbour, and returned quite exhausted.

November 25th
Ensign Kater came from Passages to see me. When he had lunched, I accompanied him back to the ferry opposite the convent. On my way I missed the Brigade of battering guns, and was informed they

moved off this morning for Bayonne. This looks as if something was about to take place in good earnest.

November 26th
The Grenadier returned from Tolosa, but no intelligence of the clothing etc. He brought the information that the Paymaster General has moved his quarters on the 21st to Irun.

November 29th
I learn that the next medical board will be composed of entirely new medicos. Be that as it may, I cannot imagine it will alter my destination. I borrowed from Kater a fine edition of Campbell's Pleasures of Hope! I wished I had not for some parts of it excited very painful reflections!

December 1st
This day a party arrived from my own Regiment, under the command of Ensign Owens who dined with me. He was heartily grieved at finding me so ill, and expressed his sympathy in the kindest manner. Yet this very little but queer chap was particularly active in exciting the enmity which he encountered from the junior officers on joining the 27th Regiment.

December 7th
Lieutenant Norton of the 34th Regiment came to the billet above. Although a stranger I invited him down for a chat after dinner, and found him very intelligent and gentlemanly. He had once been in my state, was restored by leeches, and gave me great hopes of my recovering. Speaking Spanish freely, Norton had been conversing with a priest about the dialect of this province, Biscay, which is called Vascuence,[17] scarcely comprehensible to any one, not borne with it on their tongue; like the Irish and North Scotch, most difficult to be taught, written or construed. Yet, this prejudiced fanatic, this drone on the earth, most perniciously insisted that it was the most genuine and natural language, so much so that, could a child, on first coming into the world, before it had heard any person speak, as for what it needed it would talk Vascuence! Nay, he even asserted that it was the language of Adam and Eve!

What vast utility has this man's twenty years of study in the university been to him! And how greatly it will benefit society!

December 9th
My new doctor, Staff Surgeon Donoghue, a hearty good fellow, visited me, and has recommended the application of leeches if they can be obtained, but of that he has many doubts.

December 12th Sunday
Too ill to leave my bed, until summoned by young sculapias to rise, and undergo the operation of bleeding at the temporal arteries. I made all the haste I could, assisted by my doughty squire, Barney Bradley. But the weather was very frosty and the sudden transition from a warm bed to a room with open windows chilled and retarded the circulation and probably benumbed my feeling the doctor's knife. The sensation, however, was quite bad enough, being so close to the ear, I heard, as well as felt, the incision. The medico found that my temporal arteries were deeply seated, and made a second cut, and expressed his surprise; he made a third but poor Barney Bradley at that was quite overcome, he lustily pushed the doctor aside, and offered him battle, exclaiming, "By Jasus you want to kill my poor Master!"

Even with the blood trickling down to, and dropping from, my chin, I could not but smile at the event. The medico laughed heartily! At my injunction poor Barney promised to command his feelings, and the artery was opened, but with so slight an effect, that the left side was operated upon, but proved equally unsatisfactory. The medico formed two pledgets[18] by wrapping lint over two copper vintems, coins as broad as a half-crown; these he applied on either side, by means of a tight bandage, ordering me not to disturb them until he should take them off some weeks hence.

This woeful operation occupied a full hour and half. Quite exhausted, I threw myself on the bed and remained almost motionless till night, when I undressed. And the next day was not inclined to move.

December 14th
I was rejoiced to find my health much relieved from pain. And was able to rise and amuse myself by writing to my good friend Close. Also to fill up and return the receipt for my travelling expenses to Portsmouth this time twelve months, which Colonel Hutchinson so kindly assisted me in obtaining. I was likewise glad to look out

and notice some fine German soldiers as they passed along the street, belonging to a regiment which came bodily over to us from the French, with their arms, and accoutrements. They are come here to wait for transport to England, on their way back to Germany.

December 16th
Here is great rumour of there having been much fighting in the front. And as no corn party has arrived, though four days past the time I am inclined to think something has occurred.

What Crowe is referring to here is the engagement, which took place in and around the Nive. Marshal Soult had occupied Bayonne whilst Wellington had placed his troops two miles to Soult's front in lines, which extended from the coast to Nivelle. It wasn't the most ideal position, but it did allow Wellington's troops to rest and recuperate somewhat after the hardships they had endured under canvas in the mountains. Wellington at this point was more intent on recouping his strengths and fortifying his lines of supply than actually taking on the enemy. Once up to strength, however, he viewed the area between the Nive and the Adour essential if he were to restrict the movement of Soult and keep him more or less confined to the area of his own cantonment.

By 9 December the Allies had moved. Wellington's left wing advanced by the road to St Jean de Luz, affording them a commanding position over the enemy's entrenchment. Whilst this was in progress, the right wing of his force crossed the Nive north of Cambo, whilst a makeshift pontoon constructed of boats allowed Lieutenant-General Sir Henry Clinton to move his troops across the river by Nostariz. Taking up such a position, it was clear the French were now compelled to fall back on Bayonne or be cut off.

Even at this stage the advantage still remained with Soult. Whereas he had the luxury of falling back upon the fortifications of Bayonne, the Allies were stretched across two rivers, the Nive and the Adour, confounded by a poor road system as the weather conditions deteriorated. Hay's 5th Division on the left occupied the heights of Barouillet with a Portuguese division commanded by Campbell to their front, whilst the Light Division was a full two miles away at Arrangues. Extended in such a formation, it was nigh on impossible for either to lend assistance to the other or even hold out individually should the French attack. Predictably Soult did not overlook Wellington's predicament.

The French attack came on 10 December as Marshal Soult launched a fierce assault on both the 5th Division on the left and the Light Division simultaneously. Driven back, the French held the intervening ground but failed to occupy the heights due to stiff Allied opposition. During the day Soult made several attempts to gain further ground but a bold move by the British and Portuguese to turn the French rear forced the enemy to retreat and as Wellington reached the field the position at nightfall was back to square one.

Such was the carnage on both sides that the 1st Division took over the position held by the 5th, while the 4th and 7th were held in reserve should Soult make a further attempt to take the Barouillet.

The morning of 11 December brought a resumption of hostilities. An attack against the Allied force at Arrangues masked Soult's real goal, Barouillet. As the French tirailleurs pressed forward they met with the same stiff opposition from the 1st Division which they had encountered from the 5th the previous day. Once again the French were driven back with heavy casualties.

The following day, 12 December, brought more of the same. As in the case of the previous two days, Marshal Soult threatened the heights of Barouillet, which covered the route to his intended goal, St Jean de Luz, but with similar effect. The Allies held their ground as casualties on both sides mounted.

New tactics being called for, Marshal Soult, on 13 December, launched a full-scale, all-out attack on the right wing of the Allied force held by troops commanded by Sir Rowland Hill. Unfortunately for Soult, Wellington had anticipated his move and placed the 6th Division in support of Hill whilst the 3rd and 4th remained in readiness should they be called upon to lend support. As the battle unfolded Hill's approximate force of 14,000 was more than a match for Soult's force of 30,000 given the advantage of the terrain and their displacement.

Fierce fighting continued throughout the long day as wave after wave of attack was repelled by wave after wave of counter-attack. Positions changed hourly as divisions and brigades battled for superiority throughout the day. Casualties on both sides mounted horrifically as men fell to the scything effects of grape shot and withering fusillade after fusillade of musket fire. Not only did Hill succeed in holding off Soult's force, he initiated a counter-attack and pursued the French, assisted by both Byng's Brigade and that of the Portuguese. The consequence was that his counter-attack resulted in a retreat by the French with the loss of a huge number of men and ancillary equipment.

In these continued actions the losses on both sides were immense. In the casualties of the 9th, 10th, 11th, 12th and 13th of December, the total, including four generals, amounted to five thousand and sixty-one *hors de combat*.[19]

December 20th

The corn parties begin to make their appearance. Ensign Armit is arrived from our regiment and is gone to Kater for accommodation. This is fortunate for me; the pair are well suited. I learnt from Armit that our Division has had many marches to support other troops, but is now in front and performing outpost duty, no other material change has occurred. Armit has much Irish volatility in his manner, and amused me very much by describing the arrival at our advanced picquet of a French brigadier with a flag of truce, to enquire if Lord Wellington was likely to recover from his wound in the head. And if General Clinton's wounds were dangerous? When assured that neither had been injured, he expressed his chagrin in very plain terms.

December 21st

I went last evening to the kitchen fire (the only one) to warm my feet, as usual, before going to bed. The whole family party were seated around. On the further side sat the anxious mother, ministering to the comfort of her only son, a guerrilla, come home to be nursed and restored from hard living, and hard service. His legs were bound in cabbage leaves as blisters. He is rather undersize but had seen much service. He and my man Barney were great cronies. Next sat the good man of the family and his daughter. His niece Catline, or Catherine, sat on my right. A very good-looking young woman of about six and twenty but not of the Spanish cast of beauty. Her hair was black but her eyes were brown, and very animated, her face fair, round and plump. Finding me low in spirits Catline with the utmost good nature tried to rouse me, but talking her Vascuence to me, but our conversation was more by eye than tongue. During which I had received great warmth from the fire, my blood circulated more freely, which caused an irritation on my right temple, and induced me to put my finger and rub around the pledget. The sensation was so pleasing that I went too far, a small scale fell off the wound, and blood burst out with such a vehemence that poor Catline's fair face and neck were covered. Horrified at the circumstance she could not rise from her stool, but vehemently crossed herself, fumbled her scanty rosary and with extended hands muttered her Ave Marias. I clapped my finger on the wound to stop the blood and sent Barney to fetch the hospital mate. Who on arriving, availed himself of the event to bleed me to his heart's content, for he took full a pint of blood. He altered the pledgets and bandage, most painfully incommoding my ears and half-healed blisters that I passed a most comfortless night.

Received another kind letter from my friend Close. A strong detachment from our Division has arrived for a supply of muskets, under command of Captain Bignall, with Ensign O'Shea of our regiment, and my old friend Lieutenant Duke of the 48th.

December 22nd & 23rd

My worthy friend Duke has made many kind visits, and we have had much interesting conversation about mutual friends, and the old and bold 48th. Captain Bignell called. And Frank was as anxiously kind as his frank and rough manner would enable him to express. In the evening I was surprised by a visit from Lieutenant Rawlings of the 4th Regiment [The King's Own Regiment] in the 5th Division, to whom I relinquished my turn of volunteering from the West Suffolk Militia, by which he joined the 4th Regiment. I must admit he is much polished, since we parted at Liverpool, but is still a rough warm-hearted fellow! This man's history might fill a volume! He was a natural son of a wealthy farmer in the Fens in Norfolk, who was Captain in the Downham Volunteers, when the different corps were enrolled as local militia, in which he obtained an ensigncy for his hopeful scion. During the fortnight's permanent duty we performed at Norwich, this shrewd intelligent chap attached himself to me. Subsequently finding that I had joined the W. S. Militia, he made interest and followed me and was well known by the cognomen of "the Fenman". He amused me with his history since we parted. On the death of his father, he obtained

60

leave to return to England, and received his legacy of five hundred pounds, with which he joined the depot of his regiment at Colchester. He started a tandem,[20] and a livery servant; spent his legacy, ran into debt and was rejoiced on being ordered to return to the Peninsula.

Waiting at Portsmouth for the sailing of the fleet of transports he was accosted by a stranger who was desirous to enquire for Lieut. Rawlings. He replied with the greatest self-command and assured the stranger that poor Rawlings was safe on board his transport, as his only protection from arrest! The discomforted sheriff's officer or bumbailiff[21] thanked him for his information, and walked away greatly disappointed. Rawlings took the hint, returned to his hotel and paid his bill, then purchased from the chambermaid some female garments in which he dressed himself, and quickly went on board, thereby escaping the fangs of the law and his creditors. He assured me that he had remitted money sufficient to clear off all his debts, and had plenty to spare. I expressed my astonishment, which he soon dispelled by informing me he had formed a connection with Marsden who has a contract to supply the Army with horses and mules, and with cattle, who had supplied him with money at first starting, also a good English horse, on which, when he was clear of the routine of regimental duty he scoured the country round, and bought animals of every description and made a great profit. I can easily imagine him well qualified for such an undertaking; his Fenman's judgement will serve him well.

December 26th

The swelling on my temple was much reduced by morning, by a considerable discharge of pus from the incision, but my head has been excessively painful. In the evening the artery again burst out. My servant, however, managed to stop it.

December 27th

I took the precaution of burning a lamp all night, for fear of the artery proving troublesome. I slept well, but awoke so ill and full of pain that I wrote a note to and requested a visit from Staff Surgeon Donoghue himself. He kindly obeyed my summons and evinced the utmost sympathy for my sufferings, expressed his astonishment at finding me so very ill, contrary to the reports he had received of my case, and promised for the future my head should be better treated. He likewise gave me a requisition on the purveyor for a bottle of porter and for two bottles of port wine. Soon afterwards he sent the rattle-headed hospital mate to dress my sadly featured head. The young medico is evidently much chagrined at having been reported. I trust it will do him good!

December 29th

An order from Headquarters disallows forage to all subalterns not commanding Companies. I am truly rejoiced that I sold my mule! The corn parties are again reappearing. And I hope to see my old friend Close.

I am informed a Rocket Brigade has arrived and marched to the front. They will greatly surprise the rich inhabitants of Bayonne! All accounts agree that there is immense treasure in that city. I am also told that the Spanish officers taken in the French service have pledged themselves to show a practicable plan for taking Bayonne. They may be right and honest, but I doubt much Lord Wellington's faith in rascals who have fought against their own country.

December 30th

The batmen of my own regiment under Ensign McLeod caused me, through my servant, much trouble, in their attempts to occupy my stable, beneath. But Barney at length drove them away. I should have had no peace by day or by night. The person who bought my mule paid me four doubloons and promised to bring the balance about the 8th of next month.

December 31st

Again no corn. A large fleet arrived from England, but the artillery by precedence has taken all the corn, leaving the reinforcements of the Rocket Brigade, and a large supply of arms, to follow as they can. I wrote to the Paymaster. Also to my friend Pollock, requesting him to report to the Colonel, confidentially, the shameful conduct of our batmen. The artery again broke, but bled only a small quantity. And thus painfully I finished this eventful year.

With the onset of winter, military operations all but ceased while the troops attempted to regain their strength and new arrivals joined their regiments. The effect of the constant persistently heavy rain having made the road systems impassable, combined with the severe bitter cold, forced the troops to remain in winter quarters, though the possibility of attack was never far from their minds.

Chapter Five

1814

New Year 1814 found Wellington's army held up in quarters due to the severity of the weather conditions. Both the Allies and French were equally aware it was nigh impossible to move either men or ancillary equipment under such circumstances. Wellington's troops therefore settled into their encampments to the south and east of Bayonne, to await a change in the worsening weather. Marshal Soult, for his part, could only bide his time and rue the failure of his numerically superior force to overwhelm Wellington's army some weeks previous. Twice he had tried and twice he failed. Having fallen back on Bayonne, Soult attempted to strengthen his existing lines of defence, whilst Wellington similarly bided his time and planned his next move, which out of necessity involved finding a way to cross the Adour.

As January passed into February the snows receded and the weather slowly improved sufficiently to allow Wellington to move supplies and reinforcements up to the front. However, in an attempt to deceive Marshal Soult from his true objective, the Adour, Wellington threatened the French left on the Bidassoa. Taking the initiative, he ordered a Spanish Corps under the command of Morillo[1] and the 2nd Division under Stewart to march on, and take St Palais and the surrounding heights. The French, commanded by General Jean Isidore Harispe,[2] were dislodged and forced to fall back upon Gave de Mauleon. In their retreat they destroyed the Navarette Bridge in a desperate attempt to halt the allied advance. However, the Allies were successful in fording the river and dislodged Harispe's troops from their positions.

Realizing the severity of his situation, Soult attempted to slow the allied advance by destroying the bridges over the Adour before leaving Bayonne in the hands of a strong garrison with orders to protect this vital city.

The landing of reinforcements and ancillary equipment at Passages witnessed by Lieutenant Crowe indicated that something was in the wind. Such a build-up despite the severity of the weather was a clear indication to Crowe that, come a break in the weather, the Army would soon be on the move once more.

January 1st 1814

I was awoke this New Year's morning by the congratulations and kind wishes of my esteemed friend Close, in his blankets on the floor of my room. This is a holy day with the native here, and I gave my host a piece of junk or salt beef, which I had received as part of my rations, and I was glad it proved a great treat to all the family, they scarcely ever eat meat, it being too expensive. From the statement of my servant of the uncomfortable state of the officer in the billet above me, Lieutenant Robinson of the 57th Regiment [The West Middlesex Regiment] or the Old Die Hards, as they were called after their dauntless intrepidity at Albuera, where they fell in ranks, I sent him an invitation to dine with me. Poor fellow, the fortune of war has been most severe on him, for, in addition to a shot through his thigh and another through his body, a third ploughed its way up from the middle of his forehead, carried away the frontal bone, and laid the brains bare but unscathed. His head is bound round with many folds of black ribbon, for contact with the air produces insensibility. This poor young fellow embarked for England, with Major Johnson's son in November. They were driven about in adverse winds, once nearly into Bayonne, another close under St Andaro. I am induced by his statement to conclude that the excitement was too much for him; for the Master of the transport put back and re-landed him. He confessed that his wound had caused derangement and his present resolve to rejoin his regiment proves he is not free.

I well remember that in November, when passing along one of these streets, my attention was drawn to the opposite side by the audible and fervent prayers in my own language of some poor sufferer. I now recognize my guest as the supplicant.

January 3rd

Close left me early to breakfast with his brother officer Lieutenant McDougall. I had a painful and restless night, consequently feel very indifferent. My medico warned me for the board on the 5th and seemed surprised when I declared I could not walk to attend it. I do not understand, nor am I at all satisfied with his report of my head. He says it is quite superficial, yet I find the discharge increases considerably.

January 4th
I sent my servant to Passages with a very peremptory note to Kater, for the volume of Shakespeare, foolishly lent to him, and which he had lent to another person. A vague answer was all I received, and my book is, I fear irrevocably lost. In the afternoon a surgeon called to assure me the board would on the morrow come to my room. My head and eyes were excessively painful all day and after dinner I had much fever. Impelled, however, by an irresistible impulse I exerted myself, and turned out my writing case, reperused old letters, and tore them to pieces. The kindness expressed in many overcame my weak feelings.

January 5th
The medical board has been too fully occupied to visit the out-patients, thus I must endure another night of suspense and uncertainty. Buckeley called and chatted some time. I congratulated him on the improvement of his looks, and he kindly expressed a fervent wish he could have returned my courtesy but it was too evident that I suffered much pain.

January 6th
My servant awoke me this morning by his abrupt entrance announcing the arrival of the medical board. The outcome so surprised me, that I shook in my bed. The president, Doctor Bermester, asked many questions, but did not wait for a reply to any one and I began to feel a rising indignation when he exclaimed, 'I think Sir, you would be much better with your regiment!" This gave me utterance, and I replied, "And a d. . . fine effective soldier I should make on picquet, don't you think?' The paper was filled up by Doctor Christie and I sullenly signed it, in compliance with Christie's request. I could perceive that the good fellow's feelings were nearly as deeply wounded as my own! Doctor Burmester then examined my head, abused my servant for not washing the wound clean and myself for lying in bed. Again my indignation was roused, and I calmly, but very significantly replied, "It is evident doctor,

66

that both of us are victims of misrepresentation. For that scape-grace[3] of an hospital mate who has attended me would not allow the wound to be washed. And, contrary to my remonstrance, insisted on my remaining in bed!!" But I might as well have whistled jigs to a milestone, or a tune to a horse, for this military Abernethy[4] took himself off, as his monotype[5] would have done, leaving me to digest as I could the ill-judged calumny that I was skulking.

As the artery was pronounced to be healed, I resolved to become my own doctor and joyfully left my bed at noon, walked across to Slattery and in the evening wrote to Pollock and to Close.

January 8th
Lieutenant Campbell of the 71st Regiment [Glasgow Highland Light Infantry] from the opposite house came in last evening with a friend, a Rifle officer. They gave me a good hash of European politics, with which I was much amused and highly gratified by the favourable tenor. Our conversation lasted so long that it was eleven o'clock before I could fulfil my intention and get to bed. Campbell has sent five newspapers for my amusement, and they have proved a great treat.

January 9th Sunday
Awoke so ill, and full of pain I could not rise till noon, and with exertion read the service for the morning. The day, also, rainy and cold, is as cheerless as myself. Moreover, I feel I did not retire to rest at peace with all mankind. Doctor Burmester's unfeeling conduct and slur he cast on my character rankle deeply in my mind!! Had I the strength I would wring the rascal's nose and he then might test my want of pluck.

January 10th
Arose about noon, somewhat better, and as the weather had cleared up, by great exertion rode to opposite the convent, but returned much fatigued. I found a regular formed depot of ammunition for our ensuing campaign. The British Artillery flag is duly hoisted. A brigade of 18 pounders, with numerous wagons of ammunition are waiting an order to advance. Numerous reports are afloat. One asserts that our Division is gone to General Hill, to allow his Light Brigade, the 50th, 71st & 92nd, to come here tomorrow for their new clothing. True, the stores are here, but it

is not probable that three regiments can be spared at one time. Another report states, that Soult has sent a flag of truce to inform Lord Wellington that an armistice had been formed in the north. But his Lordship begs leave to await the announcement from his own government. My neighbour Campbell assured me that Colonel Napier of the 50th landed from England yesterday, and started immediately for Headquarters.

January 11th

Finding myself better this morning I rode towards Oarazun, but the wind from the snow-clad Pyrenees made me sneeze. On my return met Campbell, who informed me he had been to Passages, and read the general orders, wherein my sick leave was stated to be for three days! I kept the utmost restraint on my indignation, hastened home, and wrote to Doctor Burmester to know if this was correct. He very officially referred me to the general orders recently promulgated. My indignation and wrath now rose considerably above fever heat, and my resentment strongly prompted me to evince somehow my sense of the affront!

January 12th

Rose this morning in a most determined disposition. Called on Slattery and Kater. Returned home, swallowed some meagre soup. Rode to the ferry, it was low water, that the boat was obliged to keep the tortuous course of the river. On landing I went direct to the quarters of my old friend Quartermaster Stubbs of the 48th. He was not at home, but Mrs Stubbs gave me some wine; this short rest gave me fresh energy, and I proceeded into town, where I met my friend Bulkley who informed me, that he was *modestly ordered* by the general orders to join his regiment "for change of air!" Likewise Lieutenant Steele of the 48th.

As Bulkley and I pursued our walk, we met staff surgeons Baxter and O'Connor. I mentioned my leave, and my feelings; both of them laughed heartily, but declared they never before knew of such unfeeling treatment. When I showed them my poor head, they shook theirs! Bulkley declared he never saw so ugly a wound!! I went to the commandant's office, and read the general orders, in compliance with Doctor Burmester's *"kindly feeling"* reference, and saw my fate. Slattery is ordered to return to England. I fear he will experience a hard fate should a peace be established.

January 14th

While dressing this morning I heard the well-known voice of my friend Lieutenant Vandermeulen of the 48th, who, after billeting his corn party, returned to breakfast. After which we went to Passages. I found two letters for me at the office. One from my good friend Paymaster Hughes of the 48th containing my account, with a balance of £20 against me, but he had given me credit for some 8 or 9 pounds for the accounts of the men of the detachment which accompanied me from England. I must rectify this when I join the Regiment. The other from Close giving me the *shaves*! or *on bits*[6] of the day. Also an account of General Cole's particular (and I could say more!!!) request, for a certificate from each officer of the number of animals he has! No Division, nay, only our Brigade is thus persecuted, by "the insolence of office!" "And thereby hangs a tale"!

These are strong words indeed from a junior officer safe in the knowledge that his writings will remain private. However, a note of caution still permeates his comments. General Sir Lowry Cole was the Commanding Officer of the 4th Division of which the 27th Inniskillings formed an integral part.

January 15th

I am grieved to learn that my friend Pollock is very ill, I wish I was near him. The weather was too fickle to induce me to venture over the harbour. Vander [Vandermeulen] went, and was fully occupied all day by endeavouring to obtain corn. I looked at two mules of the 48th, which are for sale. Finding them not what I wanted, started off in a resolute fit, to examine one, priced at a hundred dollars belonging to Colonel Gough of the 87th Regiment [the Prince of Wales's Irish]. On my way met Lieutenant Drummond of the 82nd [the Prince of Wales's Volunteers] who introduced me to one of his brother officers from whom I purchased an active cob horse and pack saddle for forty dollars. Returned home, and laid down till my friend Vander came to dinner. He had not been able to obtain the complement of corn, or allowances which he claimed, and gave me the checks for the residue. I scrumpled[7] to receive them, as encroaching on government supplies. Vander, however, overruled my fastidious honesty by the assurance that, after the hubbub he had made, if I did not avail myself of the supply, the commissariat clerk would.

January 17th
Rose this morning the worse for the searching wind from over the water yesterday, the succeeding hurricane all night, and the cold rain all this day. I will have hot water for my feet, and go early to bed at night. My intended trip to Passages to lay in a stock of articles in readiness for my march to the regiment has been thus prevented.

January 18th
Having drawn my rations, I went to Passages. Purchased an old horse with a good bridle and saddle for ten dollars from the same officer. Also bought many other things, which cost me much money. I will equip the old horse with my old bridle and saddle, and sell them together. Met Bulkley and Ensign Fox of the 48th with whom I parted at Chelmsford. At the post office, that is at the Commandant's Office, I was informed that a packet, without the mails fortunately, was lost near San Sebastian, two days ago, and only two of the crew saved. A fleet sailed this afternoon, with a very strong wind, from West North West, which caused great roughness within the harbour. With my ration return I sent my friend Vander's checks, for straw, wood and corn. Of the first two articles, nothing was forthcoming. But my servant received 420 lbs. of barley. And, ere I returned, he sold a bag full of it, for five dollars. I took a late dinner with Kater, agreeable to promise, that I might make the utmost of a long day.

January 19th
When rising this morning my nose began to bleed, which I encouraged. My head was greatly relieved thereby. Received a kind letter from my chum Radcliffe, offering to send his pony to convey my baggage to the regiment. But from the orders I saw yesterday recently issued by the commandant, I much fear I shall not be able to get off with a detachment, and by no means so soon as I have planned for! I will test the point tomorrow, although my pony "is absent without leave", having made his way out of the stable, and I have sold horse and gear to Kater, for the price I gave for him.

January 22nd

Yesterday was, throughout, rainy and comfortless, and I as equally cheerless. But rose this morning better. And as the weather invited, I went to Passages. The roughness of the harbour proved there had been foul weather abroad. Signals from the Admiral and Commodore foretold a fleet was beating into harbour, and away went all the boats. With a crowd I went up to the fort on the rock and looked down on an English cutter as she was towed in and moved alongside the Admiral. A large fleet made their way in, main part of which, were ships which sailed three days ago, forced back by stress of weather, but some of them are lost! A packet arrived, too late to venture an entrance, so sent the mail on shore.

In the crowd was a person whom I imagined was the master of a vessel, accompanied by his wife. An extremely nice little English woman, dressed very neatly. I was so much pleased with her appearance that my lips almost itched to kiss my country woman's pretty mouth. And I lost no opportunity of gazing at her, when I could do so, without impertinence.

In my progress I overtook the master and his little wife. The skipper was making all sail ahead, leaving his rib[8] to follow in his wake, as she could, down the steep and slippery pathway. On my discerning them the active volition of thought offered me a chuckling laugh by bringing to my recollection a caricature print, oft seen in cottages at home, of, "six weeks after marriage"! The husband stalks away, leaving his wife, with an umbrella under her arm, to get over the stile and pass a narrow foot-bridge by herself!

For a brief moment we see another side of Lieutenant Charles Crowe. For once, not preoccupied with the plight of his own ill health and obvious intolerance of all things Spanish and Catholic, he actually demonstrated a degree of humour and a liking for the opposite sex previously undisclosed.

January 24th

The ground is covered with a thick coat of snow, which precludes riding or walking. I must again have the caldera,[9] although it did yesterday burn through the dirt and char the floor.

I noticed that my last ration return was signed by a new official. A. Barton, Captain 39th Regiment [Dorsetshire Regiment] that induced me, personally to present my return this day, to ascertain

71

how far my surmises were correct. As soon as I entered the room I recognized Alfred Barton from Norwich, his small neat features not a jot altered, since he left my father's house twelve years ago! I placed my return on the table. Barton looked at it, then at me, and again he looked at both. "Pray," he said, "did we ever meet before?" I replied quaintly, "not since you left me at Swaffham!" He was much pleased with the recognition and promised to call on me as soon as he could to talk about "days o' auld lang syne".

Snow continued all day. I wrote to Captain Chitty, which was as much as I was able to do, for my poor head is not on good terms with this inclement weather.

January 25th

I had not finished breakfast when my brother officer Lieutenant Gough arrived. He had billeted his corn party, so I brewed him some fresh tea, which he much enjoyed. Afterwards he went to visit his cousin Colonel Gough, before mentioned, who lies here badly wounded, I find.

Regardless of the snow and dirt, I accompanied Gough to Passages. The fleet has not been able to get out. I met Hanley and requested him to take charge of my letter to my sister. I will not send the one to Chitty, now Gough has arrived. We found a General Court Martial sitting at Passages. Colonel Barnes, of the Royals is president.

January 26th

The morning milder; but the afternoon rainy. No corn to be obtained till night. Gough is to dine with his cousin and I with McAdam of the 9th [East Norfolk Regiment] to meet Bulkley. Two men of the 50th Regiment [West Kent Regiment] were too drunk last night to find their homes and slept in the snow. One is dead and the other despaired of. I learned that the commissary received rum, direct from Jamaica. It matters not from whence it came; it is much more like *aqua fortis* than a liquor! The clark gave me a taste of brandy, equally vile.

January 28th

I think I never knew such a terrible night as we have experienced! The tremendous hurricanes of wind were succeeded by torrents of rain, accompanied by most vivid lightning and terrific peals of thunder!! Even more loud than we experienced on the heights of Pamplona. One clap exceeded all power of description! The whole house shook, and my bed rocked. Every person that I have met this day expressed the horror they felt and declared that an earthquake could scarcely cause more consternation! The heavy rain had effectively washed away all traces left by the French prisoners. I joined a party of officers in the market place, where we walked for two or three hours. Lieutenant Allcock of the 58th [Rutlandshire Regiment] was attended by a poodle dog, which was delighted by such an assemblage of good companions, and exhibited his various and entertaining postures and tricks for the amusement of the party. And not less so to that of some Spaniards who, wrapped in the dark capotes, or cloaks, with their low, and broad-verged hats pulled over their brows, had watched the whole proceedings. Both master and dog were exhilarated by the fun they had made.

One of the Spaniards was crossing the square. On a signal from his master, the dog seized and nearly pulled the Don's capote off. I can never forget the fellow's indignant look, and this hand was instantly in his breast, grasping his poniard![10]

Allcock laughed heartily at the event, but we thought more seriously of it, gathered round and forced him to return to his quarters with his dog.

January 30th Sunday
My night was painful and restless, yet I am better than yesterday. Filled up my rations return and visited Kater; found him much better. The morning cleared, and induced me to take a walk in the plaza. I learned that every sick man capable of being removed is to be sent to England. Also, that a ship is arrived laden with arms and accoutrements. If this be true, detachments will soon be sent to the Army. This intelligence awakens many reflections in my mind, whether to take myself off, running all risks or to wait for a detachment. I had not been long in my room when the depot Serjeant Major entered with the order book, warning me to sit on a court martial. This, to my great annoyance, proved that my name is duly registered. And now I must have patience. But the sooner I can get away the better, for I am truly ashamed, if not of my profession, certes, of my abidance! In consequence of the tales I hear of the conduct of officers and men relative to the peculations on commissariat stores etc. etc. etc.

January 31st

The court martial was comprised of Captain Davy, 7th Fusiliers, president; Lieutenant Martin of the 43rd; Balls 58th; McDougall 48th and myself. I hope never again to meet two such oafs as the second and fourth! I well knew that the latter was a dolt and Martin was equally a nonentity! Both declared they never had written the Proceedings of a Court and I could readily believe them, for truly I could not imagine either equal to the arduous task. Although the youngest of the party, I was too much of an old soldier to proffer my services in recording the heavy charges produced. Drunkenness! Insolence! Forgery! And theft! But promptly availed myself of the privilege as Junior to speak first, and strongly second the president's proposition that Lieut. Ball should be the amanuensis.

The charges so heavy that we could decide on only two prisoners and adjourned till the morrow.

I dined with Captain Barton. We had a long chat about Norwich, Norfolk friends, and events of bygone times. His chum, Lieutenant Fairfield of the 88th, [Connaught Rangers] long a subaltern, is brother to Fairfield of our regiment, and, excepting, his natural power of singing, as his brother has, is an equally negative character. And the two brothers would match well with the two members I met this morning. I admit I was rather prejudiced against the identical Fairfield having heard him one day protest, "that the only way to take an advantage in the service, was, never to look at an order book." This cockscombed bluster disgusts me.

As January passed into February the weather took a turn for the better. The climatic conditions of Portugal and Spain are varied, dependent upon the particular region in question. Portugal, lying on the western seaboard adjacent to the Atlantic, can experience cool wet winters and quite humid conditions along the coast during summer. Temperatures range from approximately eleven degrees centigrade in winter to the mid-twenties during summer. Spain likewise has a varied climate, the central zone of the country experiencing very cold winters and intolerably warm summers, temperatures ranging from as little as nine degrees centigrade in places like Santander in January to the upper twenties and even early thirties in Seville during summer. Therefore it is understandable how difficult Allied troops found the whole process of acclimatizing to such extremes. Likewise, from a purely militaristic point of view, the movement of large numbers of troops in conjunction with vast amounts of heavy ancillary equipment, such as siege guns and heavily laden supply wagons, was inefficient and impracticable, especially during the winter months.

February 2nd

The weather promises more favourably. Some ships, five weeks from England, have brought a great import of new officers. Lord Wellington, attended by only one Aide de Camp and an Orderly Serjeant of Dragoons, passed through to the ferry, on his way to Passages. He returned in a few hours. It is surmised he went to adjust a difference between the Quartermaster General and the Alcalda respecting billeting. A detachment is ordered to march on the 4th for our Division. This tedious court martial will prevent my joining them.

February 3rd

The court could not reassemble today, the president being obliged to attend at Passages, with Detachments, for arms and accoutrements. And from what I hear, our detachment cannot march for some days. The weather is rainy, but from the shifting pains in my head, I am inclined to think I will soon become more settled. The great Major-General of cavalry, Terence O'Loughlin, and suite, returned from headquarters and was at a loss for a billet, his old one being assigned to Lord Dalhousie.[11] Thus even a Life guardsman must take second rate fare.

February 6th Sunday

A fine frosty morning induced. I did not breakfast till late, thinking someone might arrive with a corn party. After the duty of the day I took a good walk. Campbell brought me a letter from my brother, dated October 19th. It is much worn and dirtied. On rejoining my regiment, I will call the Drum Major to account for not forwarding it. My brother suggests the policy of my entering the Spanish service. Could he know the discipline, and organisation of the Spanish army, and our Commander-in-Chief's want of confidence, Phillip, as an old soldier, would not urge the measure! I should hesitate accepting even an appointment as a field officer, that is a Lieutenant Colonelcy, especially being confident in my standing in the estimation of my own Colonel!!

I must be a Lieutenant two years before I could obtain my Captaincy in the Portuguese Service. The same regulations may pertain to Spanish. In either, I must put on the semblance of being a Roman Catholic, or be considered a heretic, and have no authority! The Spanish Major-General Doyle[12] is related to Sir John Doyle, was Lieutenant in the 88th Regiment and on the staff of our Army. In the south he rallied a Spanish regiment and led them forward. He distinguished himself so much that the Spanish government offered him promotion. Having good friends, he was soon appointed Colonel, and resigned our service. Now he has a Brigade, bearing his name on their caps.

I likewise mentioned the career of Major-General Downie, as I had detailed under date October 29th, to which I added Captain Donavon, who lately exchanged into our Regiment is a Lieutenant Colonel of Spanish cavalry, but writes that he is disgusted with the service and heartily wishes himself back amongst us. These are the only British officers I have met, or know, in the Spanish service, although I have seen the greater part of that Army. Also of Don Carlos' and Don Julian's which are considered much more effective. When Lord Wellington was made Field Marshal of Spain, that Army was 12 to 18 months in arrears of pay and clothing. To rectify which His Lordship travelled to Madrid and would not leave until the Junta promised to place their Army on the same footing as that of Portugal, which is always in advance of the British, especially in pay.

During the long cantonments near Lesaca, in the autumn, the Spaniards, from the want of a well regulated commissariat, were compelled to live on bread and apples, with what few animals they could find in the mountains. This produced much dysentery, which killed many. And in their present cantonments the Spaniards suffer severely from hunger. A quarter of a pound of bread, one pound of potatoes (i.e. when they can be procured), two tablespoons full of oil is the ration for a Spanish soldier per diem. Poor John Bull would look very blue with such allowances in winter!!

The Spanish Army has, in no wise, improved by its intercourse with the British. Their characteristic haughtiness, jealousy and thirst for revenge for the slightest offence, which cannot be satisfied but by the blood of the imagined offender, have deterred British officers from joining them.

A Field Officer of the 27th
Regiment (Inniskillings) 1805.

Troops of the 27th Inniskillings
Light Division, (Light Bobs).

An officer of the 27th
Inniskillings circa 1810.

A fusilier of the 27th
Inniskillings circa 1810

Major John Hare, 27th Regiment.

General George MacDonald. Served in the 27th Regiment 1805-16.

Major General George James Reeves, CB, KH. Served in the 27th Regiment 1805-15.

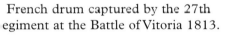

French drum captured by the 27th Regiment at the Battle of Vitoria 1813.

Battle of Castalla, 3 April 1813. The 27th Regiment, led by Colonel Reeves, charge the French on the crest of the hill and drive them off their position.

WATERLOO

W OF THE GROUND IN FRONT OF THE POSITION OCCUPIED BY THE REGIMEN

EXECUTED IN 1816.

An Officer of the 27th Regiment
(Light Company) circa 1815.

General the Hon. Sir Galbraith Lowry
Cole, GCB, Colonel of the 27th
Regiment 1826-42.

Major General Sir John Maclean,
KCB, Colonel of the 27th Regiment
1842-48.

LIEUT. GENERAL. SIR THOS PICTON.

FIELD MARSHAL VON BLÜCHER, PRINCE OF WAGSTADT.

NAPOLEON BONAPARTE, EMPEROR OF FRANCE.

London, Published May 2 1815 by Rich.d Evans, White's Row, Spital Fields.

The detachment of our Division, strange to say, marched yesterday, under officers belonging to the 2nd Division! This want of system in our commandant will induce me to alter all my plans.

February 8th

The alternations of the weather for some days past have not suited me. I have written to Pollock to solicit the Colonel to appoint me to the charge of the clothing, that I may make escape from the control of our twaddling Commandant – a wary, sententious Scotsman, who tries to make 'every word weigh a pound!" to impress on every one the importance of himself and his office, by way of cloak to his incapacity to that office. A detachment has this day been selected here, to proceed to the Army, but I have not received notice to be in readiness.

I heard of a great battle[13] in the north of Europe between the Allies and French on the 27th, 28th & 29th January.

February 9th

The Detachment was duly mustered this morning. I left them in the plaza, waiting the arrival of the noble commandant. To get out of his way, I accompanied Lieutenant Allcock of 58th to Passages. We beguiled our walk by talking about two brother officers, my early schoolfellows in Norfolk, William and Anthony Bale. Allcock declared he never knew two such handsome and stupid fellows. Anthony had left the service, and William was continued on the recruiting service, for which he was well adapted, as he procured more recruits than any other officer. I replied I could readily imagine such, having seen him draw his sword in a most portentous manner and, with his large cocked-hat square to the front, surmounted by a prodigious plume, precede his recruiting party through a village fair.

Allcock was greatly amused by my anecdote. We agreed that Bale was a very fine young man, but his handsome face was so devoid of intelligence that physiognomists[14] would be puzzled. At Passages we met Mr Sousher. His frank and gentlemanly manners do credit to his maternal English blood! His father is an eminent merchant at Lisbon. We went with him on board the lately arrived packet. She left England 31st ultimo and reached this port on the sixth day, February 5th. I found only a few pickles, and some ordinary boots and shoes, for sale. I was gratified by looking over this packet. All was quite in Man o' War's trim. A passage to England is 82 dollars, and six for a bed. At the present exchange of six shillings and three pence the dollar this is equal to seven and twenty pounds!

February 10th

I was roused from my slumber by the welcome voice of my friend Lieutenant Boyle. After breakfast we proceeded to Passages, where he gladly purchased 100 lbs of potatoes for two dollars. The same was worth 10 dollars near the army. The fleet, which on the 6th made an attempt to sail, had been driven back. Boyle and I reached the fort in time to see them again venture out. The wind was favourable and they at once made an offing. We noticed Kirkland and Hanley on the deck of their vessel. And although much above the mast's head, we held a converse with them while they were towed out. Boyle tells me it is supposed our whole Army will advance as soon as the weather will permit. I hope and pray that I may join the regiment before this occurs.

February 12th

I could not find at Passages letters, or any news. The wind was direct and I watched four brigs come straight into the harbour. Our regimental clothing and stores are on board the transport No 199, that I only wait the Colonel's orders, and be very busy, and likewise free from control of the commandant. The weather continues fine and appears to bed decidedly settled.

February 14th

The Adjutant General has been here today and kicked up a fine dust on finding so many men, arms, and accoutrements uselessly detained. And has left peremptory orders that every effective man be furnished and marched off for the Army the day after tomorrow.

I received an answer from my friend Pollock, assuring me that the Colonel in compliance with my requests had written to the commandant an injunction to allow me to proceed forthwith to rejoin my regiment. Thus I may expect soon to leave this place and on the morrow will prepare accordingly.

February 15th

In full confidence of receiving a marching order, I expended a doubloon at Passages and secured an excellent stock of requisites for camp or field. On my return an Orderly Serjeant produced the Order Book, warning me to march all the men of our Division, in the morning at daybreak, round to Passages, to be furnished with arms and necessaries. I was well pleased to notice in both depots that the functionaries were roused by the Adjutant General into action, and every one of them, instead of listlessly drawing their heels after them, was on the full trot. I heard much of a sortie of the garrison of Bayonne, on General Hill's Division investing, and that the 1st Division marched long before daylight to his support.

February 17th

Our men mustered this morning in good order. We impatiently waited the arrival of the commandant, who gave the order for marching at 8 o'clock. Detachments followed us for 3rd, 6th and 7th Divisions, in all 690 men. And as the detachment for the 2nd Division marched yesterday 300 strong, there is no marvel why the Adjutant General stormed and swore so furiously.

The first of our march was mild and pleasant, but, having passed Oarazun and ascended the Pyrenees, we encountered a sharp biting wind from the north sea which gave me great pain the whole day. Our first day's march was too long for convalescents, long unaccustomed to marching, that we were obliged to make many long halts. Our engineers have repaired the wooden bridge over the Bidasoa at Irun, which the French burnt on their retreat; we were able to march along the capital road, the Camino Real. As we crossed the bridge and entered France our road was still better, except where it had been broken up by the enemy to impede our artillery.

Every part of our route now became most interesting, by the numerous field-works constructed by the French to defend the right of their position. True it is, nature formed the country, but certainly the engineers proved their judgement in their selection of the inequalities of the ground, for erecting their redoubts and breast works. Even in this short distance, the contrast of the two kingdoms was most striking. Small enclosures well cultivated; numerous country houses, with neighbouring cottages, all bespoke more industry, comfort and cleanliness!!!

February 18th

On my way to the barracks I learned that we were not to march today, and that a Lieutenant Daniels of the 7th Fusiliers was to take the command of our detachment. Such being the case, I was obliged to again seek a quarter. After four attempts I house myself tolerably well at No 6 Rue St Jacques. In my search for a billet I was excessively annoyed at finding in numerous places the name of some officer of the Guards chalked on the door, with his brevet rank! I made a trial at a Captain's house, knowing that in the regiment, he was like myself only a Lieutenant. A servant of livery, a private servant, that is a civilian, assured me the Captain always came to his billet whenever duty would allow him to leave Lord Hill's Division before Bayonne. Thus I discovered that these Guardsmen retain, permanently, their marine quarters to the great inconvenience of all other troops! Most fervently did I wish these cockscombs were under the control of the stringent order of our Division!

As can be observed from his comments here and elsewhere, Lieutenant Crowe was less than enamoured of Guardsmen. He considered them lazy overbearing oafs who held their position as officers in the Guards much superior than merely holding a commission in the infantry. Throughout his narrative he comes to the conclusion that they were further from being gentlemen than they were from being actual soldiers. Officers with little appetite for the job inevitably placed a greater burden upon senior non-commissioned officers who were forced to bear the brunt of their incompetence.

> Here are no marks of the devastation of war! But everything in this large town bespoke a flourishing, commercial depot, built in almost a quagmire, in a most daring manner not much above the water of the Bay of Biscay, in defiance of its loud roar and drenching surf.
>
> When the wind is dead-on-shore, the swell is so great with a flowing tide that boats have great difficulty and danger in getting to sea through the vast surf, for the entrance or channel of the harbour is narrow and shallow, that only small craft can enter. Soon after gaining possession of this town, Lord Wellington ordered a hut of faggots to be constructed on the neck of the sand between the basin and the sea. Some heavy guns were hauled up

to the strand and fired some large rockets. The first was too strong, for the range, but the second set the hut in a blaze to the great consternation of the spectators. And the fame of our rockets spread like wildfire through the country. The Provost, or Mayor, of this town is an elderly man, speaks very good English. He is very polite and attentive to the British, but I am inclined to think he is actuated by policy, for he received his office from Bonaparte.

February 19th

No order for our marching. The wind is bitterly cold and makes my poor head very painful. Regardless of which I went to witness a Brigade of the battering train of 24 pounder guns, crossing the lofty pile bridges from the south, or Spanish, side of the Nivelle River. But it is scarcely worth the name of river! It begins from the summit of the Pyrenees, west of the pass of Maya; is rapid in its narrow channel at this season of the year, through a bed of ooze, more than a quarter of a mile broad, to the south-west of the town, over which the pile bridges are erected. But they had been built many years and tottered most fearfully at every gun drawn over, although twelve of the fourteen horses were taken off, and the artillery men at the drag ropes were extended on the platform. I was much interested by the sight. And each gun made it more attractive. For the hauling of the last was truly awful. The great, and oft repeated, vibration, on the lofty piles had rendered them so unstable in the ooze below that every bridge reeled like a ship at sea!!!

When attending our parades, I saw evidently that our new commander, Lieutenant Daniels, felt very much out of his sphere, in this land of the "Philistines", and in commiseration gave him the courtesy of the morning. He is a broad set fellow, about 5 feet 6 or 7 and full forty years of age. Whatever "swell" he might have made when young, he has now totally lost the debonair appearance of a gallant Fusilier!

In our afternoon's conversation Daniels confessed he felt quite out of his element and truly miserable. He had been in the regiment chief of his life, for very many years had been on the recruiting service in various parts of England and sent many hundreds of recruits to Headquarters. But did not perceive that his success in this way would not forward him in the promotion in the army. He had for some time been the senior Lieutenant of the regiment and finding that many of his juniors obtained their rank as captains, over his head, he sent a remonstrance to the War Office, to which he received the laconic reply, "Sir, I am ordered by the Commander in Chief to inform you that unless you join your Regiment in service you can not expect any promotion!" Under such circumstances poor Daniels had torn himself from his wife and family, at a late period of life to act the young cavalier!

I fully sympathized with the poor fellow, but at the same time saw the force of Sir John Moore's remark that "matrimony spoils the soldier"!

After tea I accompanied Daniels, by request, to a coffee house in the market place, to meet a friend of his. On entering, I looked around and did not feel quite satisfied but that it was below the dignity of a commissioned British officer to enter such a rendezvous, until I saw many other officers come in, when I thought of Sterne's reflection, "they manage these things better in France!" This was an easy method of conforming to circumstances, nevertheless I did not sit on velvet! The assemblage of company was most incongruous. At one table was a commissariat clerk, 'hail fellow well met,' with a capatazt[15] of muleteers. At another serjeants of Dragoons and Guards. In other places officers, with merchants of their own and other nations. Clerks of the Ordnance and sutlers, servants of livery, and women in men's clothing. I did not heed the purport of the meeting of Daniel and his friend, for I was watching the mixed medley.

February 21st
When a full league past Herrerity we left our road and proceeded on Bonaparte's military road, both of which we found better than we expected, after the many severe frosts. We distinctly saw the French picquets on the opposite hills. On passing we noticed how well Garrett's house had been prepared by the French for defence, by numerous field works. After a long day's march we reached our night's quarters in good time, but I can not say in good order! In course of the evening I made Daniels read my copy of the Standing Orders of our Division, and pointed out the necessity of his exerting himself, or he would stand a chance of being reported at Headquarters, which would still further impede his promotion. The poor fellow was so desperately frightened at the onerous responsibility which had been forced upon him that he entreated

me to take command of the Detachment. I assured him that plan was futile, for many crafty old soldiers, of whom we had charge, knew, as well we did, who was the junior officer! I called to his recollection the three officers of our Division who had on this day given us the go-by. although they confessed that they had been ordered to join us. The only expedient I could suggest was that when the party was mustered for march on the morrow, Daniels should announce to the men that he had appointed me to act as Adjutant. This would enable me to take the lead, without the appearance of superseding Daniels, or McDougall, who gave himself no trouble about, but preceded the party every day.

February 22nd

Some of the sunburnt veterans looked very significantly at me, when Daniels made the announcement! I fully met the look and said, "Men, you know the order of march as well as I do. We are now so near the Army that if we do not observe the order we shall all be found fault with. Give me no trouble, and I will not trouble you!! Left face! Quick march! Left countermarch!" and away we went, Left in front, very compact and very contented. We were all marching merrily forward, enjoying the goodness of the road and the fine morning, Daniels and myself in the rear, in close conversation, when we heard a horseman in our rear. I looked back and had only time to say, "Here is Lord Wellington! Salute as he passes!"

"How do you do, how do you do!!" he said. "What Division?" I replied, "The Fourth, my Lord!"

"Thank you! Thank you! I'll tell Cole of you!!" and he galloped on. Soon after we were overtaken by Lieutenant Hare of the 2nd or Queen's Regiment. He said he had been ordered to join, and take command of our detachment. He requested to look at our route. After minutely inspecting it, he said, "Thank you! My name is not inserted in your route, so I will say good-day and wish you well with your regiments." I felt excessively annoyed that I was clenched into the collar of detachment duty by my name being on the Route! Fortunately for me our road was excellent, for I endured much pain in my knee, from wringing my foot at San Jean de Luz, where I slipped on the pavement. Moreover, I experienced a very great deal of fever, and began to feel serious apprehension that I should knock up on the road. By very great exertion I persevered and was grieved, on reaching Hasharn, to learn there was not room for us in the town, but must proceed to the adjacent neighbourhood. We could only see that it was a very neat and extensive town. We soon housed our men. And our unsociable compeer McDougall took possession of the next cottage, rather than move his fat carcass in search of the billet he had received.

February 23rd
We could not learn any intelligence of our Division. We advanced to Bastide about noon, and on our way heard a heavy cannonading at Bayonne. Proceeded to Bardash, where our Division had been all winter, and managed to quarter off our men before it was dark. Our own billet was the very reverse of our last night's quarters. The house was small and dirty, the inhabitants churlish. I could have fancied myself again in Portugal.

By all accounts Lieutenant Crowe appears to have never been afraid to speak his mind, even though that may have been confined to his writing, as the men, his brother officers or the situation in which he found himself often felt the brunt. Having been laid up in quarters for the past number of months, discipline amongst the men appears lax, especially amongst the old stagers who instantly recognized inexperienced, wet-behind-the-ears young officers fresh out from England. Such junior officers were 'food and drink' to many old soldiers. Out of necessity or simply as an act of survival, junior officers had to make their authority felt from the very outset or else experienced troops could make their lives a misery. Rank alone did not warrant respect. Soldiers of this period actually expected and demanded the aloofness, authority and position which rank conferred.

February 24th
We ought to have drawn rations for our men yesterday, but none were to be procured. And here the exhausted commissariat stores afforded only 40 lbs. of bread and 40 lbs. of meat, not a third of the quantity we required. We three officers declined drawing anything for ourselves, or our servants, that what we could obtain was served out to the party. Nevertheless it was but too evident that our men were very dissatisfied. And my word of Attention, preparatory for marching was sullenly disregarded. I approached and remonstrated with them. A surly, malignant fellow of the 7th

Fusiliers [Royal Fusiliers] seized a musket, fixed bayonet and presented it to me! I looked sternly for some time at the scoundrel, but he was not to be cowed in any way! Very deliberately I drew my sword and said, "You old villain, if you advance one step from the ranks, I will run you through the body! Order your arms, and unfix your bayonet!" Finding that I was not to be trifled with, the old rascal obeyed, very sullenly. On which I appealed to the men of the 48th and those of my own regiment (but they were chiefly young soldiers, had been but little time in the regiment and scarcely knew one officer from another) whether they ever found me negligent in securing comfort for the men? The inconvenience we now feel is only the chance of service and could not be guarded against. "On joining our regiments this day we will report that you have been three days without rations! And, as for you, Sir," advancing two steps towards the mutineer, "I know not your character, but strongly suspect that, so often as you have been skulking in the rear, you must have experienced this inconvenience many a time!" By the fellow's involuntary start, I found that I had struck the right chord, therefore added, "Were it not that your gallant comrades are in front of the enemy and have no time to attend to such a worthless chap I would myself march you a prisoner to your Regiment and give in a written charge against you! Now Lads! Attention! Shoulder arms! Right face! Quick march!" And away we silently trudged.

Having quelled the unrest and averted the possibility of a potential mutiny, Lieutenant Daniels' detachment moved forward to link up with the main body of the Army. On their arrival each section of the detachment joined up once more with their respective regiments and prepared for the engagement to come.

February 25th
We marched at noon, forded the Gaison River without much inconvenience, and were dry again ere we reached the larger stream of the Gave d'Oleron. Luckily I succeeded in getting into a ferry boat, for the water reached the waist, and our men had to take their ammunition and bayonets under their arms. We soon took up ground for our camp, but it was night before the baggage could reach us. As the stream was rapid, the animals were not suffered to pass collectively, but by sections.

The night was very cold, and but little wood could be procured for our fires. I dined with Captain Hamilton on eggs, ham and roast lamb! Tom is an excellent forager and had procured some very excellent claret from the adjoining town of Sorde.

In this town is a large building which originally was an English monastery. During the French Revolution the monks were killed and the Mayor has taken the mansion as his official residence.

The eventual crossing of the River Adour was accomplished by means of a flotilla of ships, which formed a pontoon bridge. In order to protect the pontoon from possible destruction by French fire ships a series of booms were stretched across the river. However, prior to the pontoon being set in place a number of attempts were made to ford the river with limited success.

At the same time the Allied troops under the command of Sir John Hope[16] continued their investment of Bayonne, whilst Sir Rowland Hill,[17] by turning the French left, forced Marshal Soult to fall back and take up a defensive position at Orthes. Lieutenant-General Sir Thomas Picton, in command of the 3rd and Light Divisions, followed Hill in his outflanking manoeuvre. Lieutenant-General Sir Henry Clinton crossed the river between Laas and Montford with the 6th Division, whilst Lieutenant-General William Carr Beresford, Marshal of the Portuguese Army used his troops to good advantage by keeping the French firmly in their entrenchment at Peyrehorade.

The French for their part held quite a defensive position. Their left, commanded by General Count Bertrand Clausel, occupied the town of Orthez, whilst Marshal Jean-Baptiste Drouet Count d'Erlon[18] held the centre, which occupied the heights to the rear of the town and the French right extended to the occupied village of St Boes and a little beyond.

The Battle of Orthez, Sunday 27 February 1814

February 27th Sunday
We marched off not suspecting any mischief, but had not managed a league when each of our Brigades marched into three separate fields on the right of the road to allow the Artillery of the 3rd and 6th Division to advance. This took all of us at surprise, and conjecture, but it was evident that a big fight would soon begin. From

the upper part of our field we could look over the intervening high ground and saw the French in position.

When the artillery had passed, our left Brigade was ordered to advance. Captain Smith of the 20th Regiment [East Devonshire] when passing spoke to us, and expressed his opinion that there would not be too much to do today, since we were not in front! But found in the course of the day the fallacy of his conclusion! For the left brigade came in for their share of hard blows. We lost sight of our brave companions when they filed into a hollow road on the left of the road, before reaching a tall farmhouse, which appeared to have an extensive view of the adjacent country. Part of our Portuguese followed them.

Our Brigade advanced soon after, followed by the remaining Portuguese regiment and some filed into another hollow road, a little ravine between two inequalities of ground, this as we found extended more to the left. We were on no pretence to show ourselves on the rising ground, to lie very close and maintain this post until relieved by the 7th Division. The latter part of our orders drew forth many quaint remarks from our old soldiers. "Troth and sure now," said a sturdy Irishman, "and have we not a mighty pretty berth? For should the right of the French line attack us, must not we fight like tigers to maintain this cursed hole?"

Subsequently we learned the brunt of this battle. Marshal Soult had ascertained that only three of our Divisions had passed the rivers, and having 45,000 to our some 18,000 men, resolved on fighting, and giving us a right good licking! And during the last night three regiments of new conscripts had joined him. Our men rested very quietly in the hollow, but curiosity urged some of us officers to the top, to see what was going on, when the French favoured us with shots and shells. And again we were peremptorily ordered not to show ourselves. We afterwards crept up to the summit, and with our swords shoved away the earth until we gained a view of the passing events. Our Light Companies of the Brigade were thrown forward in our front, and experienced much sharp skirmishing, for the enemy well imagined that our left was our weakest point and their skirmishers made many resolute attempts to force their way along the by road which crossed the left opening of our hollow position, but our Light Bobs[19] valiantly kept them back.

Early in the afternoon a dashing young officer of Marshal Soult's

Staff attempted to reconnoitre our position, and galloped along this road in a daring manner. Two men of the 48th Light Company marked him advancing, secreted themselves till he came up, then sprang out and took him prisoner. With two bayonets and loaded muskets close to his body the young cavalier had no alternative and most indignantly threw his sword to the ground. The brave fellows conducted him to our Brigadier, General Anson, who gave him in charge, on parole, to two of his staff. I felt truly grieved for the crestfallen fine handsome fellow, when led past us.

About this time the artillery of our Division came up and opened their fire, in front of the farm house between the roads. Lord Wellington, desirous to obtain a good view of the whole battle, rode up to the house, left his horse with the only Dragoon that accompanied him, and opened the door, but instantly closed it again, sprang into his saddle, and rode off at full speed!! To his utter astonishment he found the room filled with French dragoons, who strange to say, were quietly reposing themselves without a single sentry to guard their post and to inform them of their danger. It is marvellous that the firing of our Brigade of artillery so close to the house had not induced them to look out. Roused by his Lordship's attempt to enter, they hurried to the stable, mounted and then galloped off, helter-skelter between our skirmishers as they could. During all this, the battle was most furious on our right a mile beyond the house, in the village of St Bocs on the Grand Road from Orthez to Dax and Bayonne.

The enemy's cavalry made many determined attempts on our Light, or 2nd and the 3rd Divisions. The additional fire of our Brigade threw consternation into Soult's raw conscripts; they were on the Grand Road from Orthez, opposite our position, and which there passed along a ridge about level of that from which we were watching them. They were wholly terrified, broke from their ranks, but knew not whither to go, then huddled together in an incongruous mass, elevated their muskets and fired a volley at the clouds!

We saw Marshal Soult ride up to them, drop the reins on the neck of his white charger, sword in hand and hat in his left hand, he vehemently exhorted them, for we could plainly see his gestures, although we were too far off to hear his words. He could not prevail; they listened for a short time, but turned tail and bolted off for Peyrehorade on the road to Dax. In the village the case was quite different: the enemy fought in full confidence of their superiority in numbers, were five times driven out, but our Light Division at length succeeded in turning the left flank of the French. Sir John Moore's old regiment, the 52nd [Oxfordshire Light Infantry] made a valorous charge up the rising ground, which decided the battle about 4. p.m. The enemy began his retreat having lost nine guns and many men taken prisoner. We were ordered to emerge from our ravine, and rapidly follow the retiring foe. Which we continued to do until daylight barely allowed us to take our ground for encampment beside the road. Our baggage reached us between 8 and 9 in the evening.

February 28th
We commenced our march at 7 o'clock but were molested by repeated halts, to allow the various Brigades of artillery to pass to our front. Their progress however, and consequently ours, was impeded by destroyed bridges and roads broken up that we did not encamp before it was dark.

The defeat of the French at Orthez went far beyond the loss of men or materials. Many troops abandoned their weapons and deserted their posts in the face of Wellington's troops. The French retreat soon became an all out rout, as Soult's troops, abandoning their equipment, made all haste eastwards towards Toulouse. For the first time Wellington's Allied Army was pushing the French back on their own ground. However, due to the severity of the encounter and the strain on the Allied troops at the Battle of Orthez, coupled with the fact that Wellington himself had suffered a slight wound, his troops failed to follow up their victory. However, the all-important breakthrough had been made both physically and psychologically. The French were now on the run.

March 1st
My birthday, and friends at home, thinking of me, have passed the day much more comfortably than I have! Repeated storms of rain rendered our march and frequent halts most cheerless. The Adour River near San Seirerre is very broad, its long and lofty wooden bridge showed that it was subject to great floods. Today the stream was low and banks of sand were dry between some of the piers. In the centre the current was very rapid.

The enemy burnt a wide chasm in the bridge here and totally destroyed its extremity, availing themselves of the lowliness of the stream. Their stratagem did not much avail them, for while our artificers and engineers constructed a platform over the centre, our Pontoons were towed across, and the passage established. In spite of this delay, many of the timbers were still burning when we crossed. Our camp ground was wet and cold; but being on a stiff clay, we felt some assistance that the tent pegs would not readily draw, even with the boisterous wind which rocked the tent, and frequently obliged us to go out and regulate the weather-cords.

March 2nd

During this day's march we were wet and dry. The heavy squalls of rain frequently drenched our backs and the keen wind dried us. We halted 4 or 5 hours on the military road, near a château, surrounded by vineyards. Our exposed situation was excessively bleak and the wind piercingly cold. Our soldiers tore the vine trees up from their roots and made large fires, around which we stood to dry ourselves from the frequent storms of rain. For some time we could not comprehend what were the movements of this day but at length learnt that we were performing our accustomed duty of supporting some other force.

The 6th Division in our front drove the enemy from the village of Grenade. And there established their own night's quarters. In the evening we were sent to scattered houses beside the road, some more than a mile distant, where our comrades in advance had rested last night. In the small house allotted to our 7th and the 8th Company there was much baggage belonging to the 6th Division, with which remained seven of their soldier's wives, to secure a shelter from the inclement weather. We could not, at such a late hour, compel the batmen to march off with their baggage, but consigned one room to the use of the whole party.

Our house had five rooms below with double that number of doors, but only two windows, certes! There was one upper apartment, of which I will say no more. Fortunately there were small stables, with outbuildings, with plenty of clean straw, by which our men were well off. Better than we five officers in the house. The divisions of the house were merely stakes and clay. And during our dinner a woman with the baggage in the adjoining room was taken in labour! And during the night another woman was delivered.

March 3rd

I searched the bottom of my canteen-basket and found part of a cake of chocolate, which I brought from Lisbon, with which my servant made, not so scientifically as Mrs Glass would have suggested, two good messes for the lying-in women, for which they were very thankful. Some of our soldiers discovered in the garden, behind the house, a hidden well, in which the natives had deposited the chief of their goods and chattels. We placed a sentry over the store, to prevent any articles being taken out, during our sojourn.

March 4th

> Little thinks the Town-man's Wife,
> While at home she tarries,
> What must be the lassie's life,
> Whom a Soldier marries!
>
> Old Song.

The baggage moved off early this morning, and with it the two poor women, with their new-born infants wrapped in soldiers' fatigue-jackets.

At 9 o'clock we marched to the rear for the new clothing. When passing General Sir L. Cole's Headquarters I was verbally ordered to bring the sick of our own regiment, of whom there were not more than half a dozen. Under this impression, I allowed my baggage to proceed, but was amazed, on reporting myself and men, to find that the order pertained to the sick of the whole Division! I represented to the staff surgeon, all the circumstances of my awkward situation. He kindly exonerated me. Our men were well housed in a military hospital and the officers billeted. Ensign Ovens had obtained a good double billet for us two. An excellent and clean bed and the greatest civility, for all which we amply paid.

Captain Chitty joined us at dinner and the worthy hostess charged twelve francs for her culinary science in cooking our ration beef! She never gained so much by her own countrymen! We sent and made diligent enquiries for the famous claret, but could not procure even a bottle. His lordship's staff had engrossed all. We here learned that Lord Wellington had been wounded and was confined to bed for a few days. When reconnoitring, a musket ball passed under and lacerated his thigh.

The Adour is so swollen by the late snow and rain, and the current become so strong that during the night, six of our pontoons were forced from their moorings and carried a long way down-stream.

March 5th
After a fine day, and a long march of four leagues, we were quarter in Sault de Nouvaille.

March 6th
At Orthez we halted for rations during which some of us indulged ourselves by a second breakfast at the Restaurateur à la France. We had an omelette, fresh salmon fried, apples, pears, walnuts, claret, brandy, bread, butter and cheese, for four shillings and sixpence each.

The town is extensive and good. With numerous shops and a capital market, and prices very moderate. At 5. p.m. we halted at Puzo.

March 7th
Passed through Peyrehorade; a good town of one wide street, but far inferior to Orthez. After marching about a league and a half we again crossed the Adour, which here takes an immense curve and appears to flow towards the Pyrenees, but it again turns and flows in to sea at Bayonne. The sudden rise of the river had baffled the exertions of our engineers here. We were ferried over by some natives, who are regularly engaged for that purpose and each man receives forty sous per diem. Two large boats or wherries fastened together by a strong platform, with rails around, to prevent accidents conveyed nearly two companies at once. Having crossed the river we were compelled to march forward in quest of quarters, for the village of Port de Lance was on the opposite bank. And finding the village of San Marie was a full half-mile on the left of the road, we pursued our march, more than a mile, ere the Adjutant, at full gallop, checked our course, with an order to retrace our weary steps. We three, Captain Chitty, myself and Ensign Ovens, were billeted on the Cure or priest.

He was a shrewd fellow, and very civil. It was very evident, from

92

his broad shoulders and sleek sides that he did not "live on bread alone", nor on air!

March 8th

The latter part of this day's march was very bad. When within a league of Bayonne the roads, as well as the adjacent fields were brought to puddles by the constant passing of troops. To avoid which we diverged to our right and, I suspect, went from bad to worse, for more than half a mile a narrow, hollow road was a regular watercourse, mid-leg deep. At sunset we encamped on a firm sandy ground, amongst some scattered oak trees, near the mouth of the Adour and within a mile of the village of Bocos, the Headquarters of General Sir John Hope, commanding the First Division, chiefly composed of Guards and investing Bayonne.

March 9th

When we were quietly enjoying our breakfast, Captain Hamilton looked in. We noticed that Tom was in great wrath, but could not prevail on him to partake with us. And his ablution soon burst forth. "You will scarcely credit what I have witnessed this morning. Desirous of obtaining a good sight of Bayonne during our short sojourn, I mounted my horse very early this morning, and rode to the advanced picquet and asked the serjeant if I could be allowed to go beyond his post. The stupid fellow was astonished by my question, and declared he could not say! What I exclaimed, not say! What the Devil are you placed here for? The fellow did not know!! I demanded where I could find the officer of the picquet. He is in the house was the reply. I entered a nice château, passed long passages, saw many empty apartments, ascended the stairs, and in one of the rooms found Mr Guardsman comfortably reclining on a sofa. I excused my intrusion, explained who I was and why I had come. My gentleman forced himself from his recumbrancy and declared he did not know how far I could advance! Fancying that the fellow was not sufficiently awake to comprehend my enquiries, I repeated them, again he declared he did not know! "Not know, Sir," I exclaimed. "Pray, with what intent are you placed here?" "Oh, I am here on picquet." "On picquet forsooth," I retorted. "Let me tell you, Sir, that when we are with the grand Army on outlying picquet, we know, to an inch, how far any man may advance! Pray, how far off are your advanced sentries?" "On

93

my honour, I cannot say." "Not say, Sir! Why Sir! I am utterly amazed! I am wholly astounded! Good morning to you." Ere I left the room, I again turned towards him, and added, "Before I depart allow me tell you one thing. If you do not better comprehend the duties of an outlying picquet, and be much more on the alert, these French rascals will some day sally from the fortress and give you a cursed licking!" And thus I wasted my morning's exertions, but have fully confirmed the opinion throughout the Army that their Guardsmen are, by their commissions, officers. They are personally brave as chivalrous gentlemen ought to be. But – they are not soldiers!! Were it not for their Adjutant and their superior non-commissioned officers, 'The Guards' would be 'live lumber'! Fully satisfied with his pathos, Tom strutted off to his own breakfast.

Soon after this the Adjutant rode up to our tent and wanted me for a foraging party, to march immediately. I most cordially wished him to have been with Tom Hamilton's advanced sentries, but that availed me not. After a long march of at least four leagues, and by diligent search, we obtained nearly our proper quantity and rejoined the camp before eight in the evening. But I was fairly knocked up. I learnt that Tom Hamilton's prophecy had been verified during my absence.

The garrison made a strong sortie and attacked the Guards with such determination that our regiment had been ordered out to their support and did not return to camp before my party. Sir John Hope was so well pleased with the promptitude with which his unexpected summons was complied that he sent a request of Headquarters that our Regiment might remain as part of his Division. Subsequently events proved that Lord Wellington could not spare such a reduction of the centre division of his main Army, which after all the casualties of eleven months' campaign, was far from the strength requisite. We understood that the Guards had many killed and wounded this day.

March 10th

This morning when we awoke we were much pleased by the brilliant light occasioned by a dense coat of snow covering our tent. Our philosophical reflections had not a very wide scope, for the warmth from our disturbed blankets soon affected the thaw, the dripping water compelled us to start up, and knock the snow off the outside. When we had affected this, we very promptly huddled on our clothes, for the keen March wind penetrating the wet canvas rendered our abode miserably cold. The deep snow dissolved very tardily, keeping us prisoners to our tent chief of the day. I dined with the Colonel in a miserable hovel. But he preferred it to a tent.

March 11th
The new clothing having arrived at the other side of the harbour, we started in light marching order about 11 o'clock to fetch it. We found the harbour constructed with an admirable stone embankment on each side; the great breadth was adapted to the occasional swell of the Adour, not to the depth of the harbour in a general way, for a vessel of 200 tons could not venture an entrance. Twenty-six coasting vessels, of about fifty tons burden, are securely moored, stem and stern with the current; they are cleared between the fore and mizzen masts. Athwart the hawsers, or cables, thick deals[20] were closely placed, affording a free passage for a battering train. We were mightily pleased by noticing the efforts of engineering skill in conquering obstacles! Moreover this admirable bridge is constructed beyond the view of the garrison, and consequently free from any annoyance of its firing.

Three of our gun boats are stationed above the bridge, within sight and range of the forts, between it and a strong boom, or iron chain, supported by logs of wood, which the French had established for defence of the fortress. But they never anticipated the vast service this boom would be to us! Our gun boats and our bridge were secured from any attack. And the velocity of the current was checked, especially when the river was swollen. We did not return to camp till past four o'clock, and had just time sufficient to dry ourselves from the showers of rain before dinner.

March 13th
I had the unpleasant duty of escorting 123 French prisoners, who at various times had made their escape from the garrison, to deliver them over to General Robinson's Brigade of the 5th Division, a few miles beyond the bridge. My friends Pollock and Radcliffe had admonished me not to enter into conversation with the prisoners for they would worry my very life out. I acted on their kind hint and looked very stern and determined on taking the command. With a firm voice I ordered my strong guard to prime and load

before the poltroons and gave them very peremptory orders. We started at 8 o'clock in the morning. On our way to the bridge I found my friends had given me very useful advice.

Most of the prisoners hung back and tried to draw me into conversation, but I sternly ordered them to "march on"! I would not drop a single word of French. One of the party had before been a prisoner; was a long time in Fortin Prison near Gosport. He spoke our language freely and frankly declared his earnest desire to return to his old quarters, where he had good fare and civil treatment, rather than be a prisoner in Bayonne, subject to harassing duties and the stinted allowance of an invested garrison. I noticed that the light-hearted, merry fellow found congenial spirits in my Irishmen, and that a great deal of jocularity was passing freely. He ingratiated himself so adroitly that my men called him Jack.

I halted the party short of the bridge and called for Jack to be my interpreter. I said to him, "Jack! I cannot talk French, but you can understand what I say! You shall hear my orders, and I will then send you to tell them to your comrades. I tell you plainly, that I am a most determined resolute, fellow and I will not be fooled by you French chaps. If any one of you attempt to escape while crossing this bridge he shall be shot and thrown into the river!! I shall stay here with the corporal and four men, and will not cross until my serjeant sends me word that all of you are on the other side."

I then ordered the serjeant to escort the party across and to count his prisoners, and if any were absent, to send back four men to poke with their bayonets into every boat, and if any resistance was offered, for them to shoot the offender. Having allowed time for Jack to impart my orders to his companions, I gave the order to march. My orders were complied with; two prisoners dropped into the centre boats and secreted themselves until forced out at the point of the bayonet.

March 14th
After breakfast I sallied forth, but found the market very scantily supplied. A Muscovy duck for 6/- was the only purchase I could make, with which my companions were well pleased, considering it, in such a locality, as a good catch.

Learning that an order had arrived for us to march immediately, I hastened back, and found that, as our foraging party of yesterday is not returned, we shall not start before the morrow. My attention was attracted by a detachment of "Johnny Newcomers" for the Fusilier Brigade passing our camp, in fierce array, with fixed Bayonets, their officer in front drawn sabre in hand and his large bearskin cap on his head, looking as portentous as possible!

All which afforded us no small amusement, and I was freely enjoying the quiz[21] but discerned that this handsome and fierce-looking bearskin-capped officer was Matthew Higgins, my brother Ensign in 48th Regiment who left us at Chelmsford to join the Fusiliers. He was delighted by my recognition. He readily assented to my proposition to halt his men, and let them stand at ease, while he entered our tent to take wine and receive a regular schooling, for although not Solomon's eldest son, Matthew Higgins was perfectly an Irish gentleman and I ever felt a regard for him.

I well knew my man and gave him some friendly useful hints and said, "Mat, when you left us at Chelmsford, you thought yourself on the high road to promotion! You have been grubbing at home while I and some others of your compeers have given you the 'go by'. Unfix bayonets and march your men with sloped arms; pass what you may, put your sabre into its scabbard; you will find we here rarely draw our swords! And burn that tremendous fur cap this very night."

At this Matthew opened his eyes in astonishment and urged its great cost. "Never heed that," I replied. "Here you will find it useless. I have never seen an officer of either Fusiliers with such an encumbrance. You will be woefully quizzed if you exhibit it to your regiment." Higgins was very thankful for my admonitions, and cheerfully pursued his route. I then packed my trunks and regulated our mess accounts, which occupied me until Captain Chitty's friend came to dine with us, Mr Caldwell, a very gentlemanly, pleasant young man.

March 15th

We started early this morning and found the crossroads much the worse for the constant traffic since we arrived. In our route we passed through the cantonments of a Portuguese brigade. One of their captains my old acquaintance Lieutenant Brown of the 48th and whom I formerly knew at Norwich, where his father was a minor canon, recognised me and insisted on my waiting behind to partake of his breakfast, then on the table. Such a provoke on a march was too good a thing to be refused, for I had been out long enough to have found a second appetite. Brown obtained a Company in the 13th Portuguese Regiment. We crossed the Adour in good time; its current was greatly reduced in breadth and force since we passed on the 7th inst. A Brigade of the battering train is stationed in this town, Port de Lance, but we found plenty of room. Our men were well off. And we could not complain, for our hostess recompensed for the want of room by the ready civility with which she cooked an omelette and fried our sausages.

March 17th

Before daybreak our drums and fifes paraded the town playing "St Patrick's day in the morning" with other Irish airs. And the natives fancied us all run mad, on beholding our caps green with shamrocks! Nor did their terror subside until they saw us march away. We took our former quarters at Sault de Nouvaille, where I felt so ill that I was obliged to sleep, ere I could exert myself to even changing my shoes.

March 18th

Our men, in true Irish spirit, have commemorated St Patrick to excess, and committed many misdemeanours. The natives attended our morning muster with so many complaints that the triangle was pitched and a drumhead court martial[22] summoned. Two or three offenders were tied up and given their deserts on the spot. Scarcely a man was sober until the exercise of marching brought them to their senses. Our route named San Savier was our next halt, but on the way we met some British soldiers who said they had been surprised during the night and narrowly escaped being taken prisoner by some French cavalry.

Our Colonel cross-examined our informants and ordered the Light Company to the front, as an advanced guard. On which we gave the word, "Steady lads!" "Heads up soldiers!" This was like an electric shock and we could have taken our men into any enterprise. On our arrival at the next village we found the natives in the greatest consternation, which our presence pacified. Our Colonel left two Companies here, as a picquet to a brigade of guns, which was advancing in our rear. We proceeded and encamped in advance of the small town of Hazaman. Here we learned that deserters from the French cavalry, above a hundred, had become brigands and pillaged the country around, Oau their Head-quarters. The Mayor of Hazaman, being redhot Republican, was deposed on our entering the country. He had given information the day before to those brigands that a small party of British were in the town. Accordingly the rascals came last night and made prisoners two officers, two paymasters, five hospital mates, 40 or 50 soldiers and all their baggage. The deposed Mayor made his escape when he saw us unexpectedly arrive.

March 19th
We waited the arrival of our two Companies left at Hazaman and preceded in a short time to San Savier. Headquarters having advanced, we found plenty of room, but not a bottle of the fine claret was to be had! His Lordship's staff had cleared every cellar.

March 20th
We had a long march to Barcelona where I was on guard. A large and good town; but we were surprised to find, in the grand square, or market place, a triangular gallows, affording accommodation to three malefactors at the same time! We were much astonished at this public offer of triple accommodation, never before having noticed any thing of that kind.

March 21st
Lieut. Harnet rejoined us this morning before we started. The Colonel had despatched him some days ago to ascertain where we could find our Division. He reported that they are seven leagues off and are daily advancing. This is a bad prospect for us, for, instead of a halt, our daily marches will be extended.

This morning was fine, but squalls of rain blew up; before they became heavy we reached Plaisance. A good town, well inhabited, and the market abundantly supplied with poultry at reasonable prices. Captain Chitty was billeted on the cure, where we dined. Our fowl was again roasted by a turnspit dog. The patron was very civil, gave us some excellent wine and apparently enjoyed our company. He has resided here since the year 1784.

March 23rd
We marched for Tournay, but when within a league of it met the paymaster of the Fusiliers, who informed us the Division had

altered its course this day. So we halted for the night in the village of Rouan. Our host was, at first, much alarmed, but soon came round and was very attentive to our little wants. He has a brother, prisoner in England, and received three letters from him. While talking with us, the servant girl of the house could only talk patois, a true child of nature, who had a peculiar delight in examining every article belonging to us, even the epaulettes on our shoulders.

March 24th
Our Paymaster mustered the Regiment and proceeded to Tarbes for money. We counter-marched and, passing through Trie, halted at Castelnau, both large towns.

March 25th
Again we found intolerable bad roads, equal to those of the 22nd. Halted at Boulogne. On our way met Pollock who went yesterday to Headquarters. He brought to us English letters. I received one from my father dated February 4th detailing the severe illness of my dear mother, and the death of many old friends, that when I came to a fire, I burnt it.

March 27th Sunday
The roads, bad enough in themselves, were rendered more intolerable by a brigade of Portuguese artillery forcing their way and crowding us to the confined banks and ditches. We passed Lord Wellington's Headquarters. Pursuing the road, we had a good sight of Toulouse. We then struck across the country to the very worst quarters I ever saw. And no orders issued for the morrow, we spent our evening in conjecturing how to make our hovel comfortable. We all proceeded, and encamped, about a mile and half north of Toulouse.

March 30th
An order for marching arrived, but by way of an *agreeable* prelude, we were first to attend a Brigade punishment. We remained under arms full two hours afterwards, then returned to our ground and again pitched our tents. How we are indebted on this, as well as many other occasions, to our *dearly beloved* Lieutenant General, for his great care and consideration for our comfort!!!! Received a letter from my brother Philip dated 28th February.

March 31st

This morning I repeated my visit to my sick friend. Also to Colonel Wilson; I found him alone. He promised to recommend my brother Edward to a commission in the 48th when he had an opportunity. A sudden order to march sent me back in double quick time. On reaching our tent, I found a letter from my sister Fanny and one from my cousin G. F. which by some mistake had been sent to the 53rd Regiment. We marched about a league and again encamped under orders to march to the attack of the bridge and all the formidable works before it at St Cyprien, W. S. west of Toulouse. It was half past two when we struck our tents, and it was sadly into the dark night before we were again settled.

Chapter Six

The Battle of Toulouse

Following Wellington's victory over the French at the Battle of Orthez on 27 February, his army, depleted by casualties and the draining effects of fatigue, failed to capitalize upon its initial victory. Instead, Marshal Soult was allowed to withdraw his beleaguered force virtually unchallenged. Steadily retreating towards Toulouse, Soult's troops moved relatively swiftly in comparison to Wellington's. Whereas Soult reached Toulouse on 24 March, having destroyed bridges to his rear, Wellington's army, laden down by the paraphernalia of siege, took a further four days.

Toulouse was a walled city interconnected by ancient towers located on the right bank of the River Garonne. To the east of the city lay the suburb of Saint Etienne, that of Saint Michael to the south. The canal of Languedoc ran to the east and north. Although sturdy, the defences were far less impressive than the ramparts of many previous cities which fell foul of Wellington's siege train in his relentless push through the Peninsula.

Marshal Soult, well aware of the inadequacies of trying to defend Toulouse as it was, set about constructing a series of defences in the limited time he had available. To this end he had trenches dug in the vicinity of the outlying suburb of Saint Cyprien, redoubts and breastworks positioned around the city and constructed a *têtes du pont* at all the bridges along the canal. Furthermore he ordered the remaining bridges across the River Ers destroyed.

Upon Wellington's arrival in the area, the first task undertaken was the construction of a pontoon, which would span the Garonne. Soult had determined the river, which flowed to the south of the city, was defence enough, given its width and the swiftness of the current. Wellington's first attempt to ford the river proved futile due to the waterlogged condition of the roads but a force consisting of the 4th and 6th Division, under Beresford, was eventually landed to the north of the city by means of a hastily constructed pontoon bridge. However, this almost proved disastrous due to a sudden rise in the height of the river. As a result Beresford was stranded on the right bank of the Garonne with a more numerically superior force of the enemy to his front and the flood-swollen Garonne to his rear. Retreat was impossible, the pontoon bridge having been removed for fear of being swept away.

However, Marshal Soult failed to capitalize on his good fortune, with the result that the 4th and 6th Divisions remained unopposed until the following day when, due to a drop in the level of the river, a Spanish corps under Frere was able to cross and reinforce their position.

By 10 April Hill's 2nd Division was located in front of Saint Cyprien, whilst Picton's 3rd and Alten's Light Division took positions in front of the canal of Languedoc to invest the north face of Toulouse. The lines were now drawn. Let Lieutenant Crowe set the mood.

April 1st
We were all ready at the appointed time, but received no order to march. We had, *par divertissement*, a drumhead court martial[1]. After which we waited a full hour, when the covering serjeants were ordered to the front and to accompany the Quartermaster to take up cantonments. Thus we found that the "broken-head fair",[2] was postponed *sine die*! We soon followed, left in front, a strong indication that any thing did go forward our regiment would come into full benefit! We proceeded a full league along the Rio Grande, or great road, to Toulouse. Halted more than an hour ere we could learn our destination. Our regiment took possession of a row of good houses, not far from the road, which were much he worse for the occupancy of French soldiers, and a Portuguese Brigade, which vacated this morning.

We instantly ordered fatigue parties to clear away the filth and soon made ourselves at home. The other part of the Brigade returned to the camp we had left. The Light Companies of our Brigade form the advanced picquet, and our regiment the in-lying picquet. They are stationed in two very fine châteaux, on an eminence, which affords an excellent view of the road broken up, the Faubourg of St Cyprien; the Telide Pont; the bridge itself, loaded with barriers of every description, with guns of heavy calibre, commanding the whole range.

After lunch, that is to say "breakfast", we visited these châteaux and were well pleased that we had not been sent to surmount such deadly impediments. The gardens of the châteaux were in very nice order and we found many herbs and esculents. I secured three seedling roots of celery, which greatly improved our ration soup at dinner. I ought to state the defences above alluded to were faced by two very strong blockhouses. While we were indulging our curious gaze a flag of truce advanced beyond the blockhouses, accompanied by some peasants. We ran down to the road on the tiptoe of expectation to learn its purport. But it was merely a request that two peasants with their horses might be allowed to return to their homes, which at once was granted.

A Light Company man of the 48th, posted as an advanced sentry, deserted to the enemy. Our quarters, easternmost of the cantonments, commanded a fine view of the city, and we wish we could proceed thither, without passing the *"broken-head fair!"*

There are some six thousand French on this side of the river and bridge. Their army on the other side were formed on the heights beyond the city, in open order, making the utmost show they can, but we feel confident they are not more than thirty or forty thousand strong, if so much.

April 2nd

We stood to arms before daylight. After which the provisional battalion relieved the Light Companies at their advanced picquet. Each regiment is to relieve daily in rotation. I walked to the extreme left of our sentries and obtained an admirable view of the bridge and the many works in its front. I was within a stone's throw of the French sentry and saw another beyond, very deliberately seated and lousing himself.

April 3rd, Sunday

At 6 o'clock a.m. we returned to encampment. The 40th Regiment took our cantonments and the 48th relieved the Provisionals. After breakfast we attended, with the rest of the Brigade not on duty, Divine Service, a base drum on end serving for reading desk and pulpit. I hope I shall never again be obliged to listen to such an incoherent address, a sermon.

April 4th

Agreeable to orders we were last night under arms at half past ten o'clock, and at eleven proceeded along the road to Grenade, with strict orders for the utmost silence to be observed. No man was to speak to his fellow, and every man to carry his musket firmly, so that it did not clap with another, all which was strictly complied with, for the night was as comfortless as might be. Rain began to fall when we started, then wind arose, and both continued till break of day. The night was extremely dark and I wonder how those at the head of the march could discern the road.

We behind followed of course, like ducks to a pond, and verily we had a very narrow escape from the water!! Our progress was very slow and, for myself, I must confess I was insensible to rain and wind, and the danger of our position. For being thoroughly worn out by painful anxiety and reflection, during the afternoon I marched along unconsciously, between the rear file of our Company, who kindly took me in tow. About three in the morning I was roused from my stupour by the Colonel's voice behind, demanding, "What officer is that?" When I replied, he said, "You are one of the very last I should have expected to pursue this road. What could induce you to come here? Here is the rapid Garonne on your right, and this broad canal on your left! If attacked how can you extricate yourselves?" I replied, "I hear the Garonne, and can imperfectly discern the chasm on our left, and admit that we are in a very awkward predicament, but know not why we came here. We have only followed the line of march."

The Colonel desired us to make room that he might proceed to the head of the regiment, for he was very anxious about this untoward circumstance. And well he might, for on discussing this circumstance subsequently with my compeers, I learnt that he had reconnoitred the road by daylight, and ought to have led the march, but this isolated road had escaped his wonted acute perception and he had left us to find our own way. We heard the rumbling of the pontoon carriages, on the other side of the canal, but could not imagine, not knowing the cause, what evil portended! About 4 o'clock a.m. the sky became more clear, and we were well pleased to find ourselves accompanied by friends. At break of day we met, short of . . . Blanca, where a rivulet diverted the course of the detestable canal, and afforded us egress from our dilemma.

Operations actively commenced. While regular working parties carried the Pontoons down the declivity to the Garonne, our artillery took up position on the bank, with lighted fuses. A boat, with a small party of Brunswick Oels, ferried across conveying a strong cord, by which, when landed, they hauled a hawser or cable. The communication being thus established, they resumed their rifles, and faced the enemy, of whom a strong close column mustered under cover of the numerous trees, on our right, watching us. Soon after they were visited by a general officer and his staff, who rode quickly about until he had fully reconnoitred our proceedings. It was now broad daylight, and, convinced that there was no abidance within point plank of our guns, the General sent his Aide de Camp to order the column of infantry to retire. He then took two more galloping views of our proceedings and disappeared, leaving a cavalry picquet, with videttes, to watch our operations. But they soon after withdrew, probably under the cover of the trees. At all events we saw no more of them. During all this, our working parties had been active and carried down everything requisite.

About 7 o'clock the first pontoon was moored, and progress now proceeded rapidly. And at 9½ o'clock proceeded by a brigade of hand rockets, our Brigade, left in front crossed the Garonne, our drums and fifes playing the Grenadier's March. Never had I stepped to time so proud a pace!!! When the whole of the Division had crossed, our artillery followed, with their matches still burning. But nothing obstructed our progress and we marched in a southern direction, followed by the 6th, the 3rd and the Light Divisions. At a late hour in the evening we were crammed into some miserable hovels, but the other Divisions bivouacked.

April 5th
We stood to arms long before daylight, then returned to our hovels, one half of our men remaining accoutred. At 11 o'clock came an order to march, but we only proceeded to camp near the village.

April 6th
Rain in abundance throughout the night, most obligingly ceased when we turned out at 4. a.m. In full expectation of being attacked, we were all day on the alert. The garrison had forced into the

swollen river trees and large beams of wood to sever our bridge of tin pontoons. But they all passed very harmlessly, for our engineers were equally alive to the circumstance, and opened the bridge to allow the flush of water to pass, and with it passed the trees and timber. Our force on this side of the Garonne consisted of 3rd, 4th and 6th and Light Divisions the 7th, 10th, 15th, 18th Hussars, the heavy German Cavalry, and three Regiments of heavy cavalry, under Colonel Vivian, three Brigades of Guns, one of Flying Artillery and one of hand rockets.

The 2nd Divisions is where we left them, before the bridge of St Cyprien, west of Toulouse, and keeps Marshal Soult in awe, or he would gladly avail himself of the separation of our Army. Should he have the temerity to make the attempt, he will assuredly find out his mistake for Lord Wellington has, most unquestionably, passed over the elite of his army. And the 2nd Division would quickly force their way across the bridge of St Cyprien.

April 7th

The 3rd Division is moving to the front this day. The fine weather will allow of all of us pushing on tomorrow. At 10 a.m. we moved our camp to the rear of the village. And 2 p.m. our Company was ordered forward as outlying picquet. It fell to my lot to be in advance; my furthest sentries were very near the French videttes[3] and had a good view of the town, its approach and defences.

April 8th

All was quiet during the night. I was relieved by Ensign Ovens for one hour to allow me to get breakfast. After mid-day the Division advanced, and had proceeded some way, before I received orders to withdraw my advance, that we had to scamper across he country to rejoin our Company and Division marching to the left. During the day we halted till our artillery could come up with us. We saw the enemy in position north-east of the city, on a range of hills, on which are some formidable fieldworks. We took up our camp ground at 6. p.m. Waiting for our baggage, we perceived the purport of our flanking movement, for on the rising ground to our left we saw our Hussars very busily engaged with the French cavalry. The declining sun was at the exact point to shine on their sabres and every cut was like a flash of lightning. We saw them drive away the foe. And they kept them at a good distance.

April 9th
We remained in hourly expectation of orders to march. Forty-three French prisoners, taken last night, passed our camp this morning. They were cut about their heads most desperately. One man's nose was clean cut off, another was deficit a cheek and an ear.

The last great battle of the Peninsular campaign was fought on Easter Sunday 10 April 1814. The 3rd Battalion the Inniskillings in conjunction with the 1/40th and 1/48th, formed Anson's Brigade as part of Lowry Cole's 4th Division. Early on the morning of 10 April 1814 Wellington's troops made a determined attack upon the eastern front of the city. Once the Bridge of Croix d'Orade had been secured by the 18th Hussars Beresford and Freire were able to move their men up the left bank of the Garonne and take up a position opposite the heights. Clinton's 6th Division occupied the centre with Lowry Cole's 4th Division on the left and Freire's Spaniards on the right. The cavalry under the command of Sir Stapleton Cotton and Lord Edward Somerset was formed up in support of the Allied left and centre, whilst Vivian's Brigade, now commanded by Arentchild, supported the left, with Ponsonby lending support to the right. Alten's Light Division, linked to Hill's Corps by means of the pontoon bridge, occupied the ground between the Garonne and the road to Croix d'Orade.

As the opening shots of the battle were fired, an assault was made on the heights as Hill, Picton and Alten attacked the French positions opposite their Corps. Meanwhile, Cole's 4th and Clinton's 6th Divisions moved diagonally against the French right and succeeded in taking the heights and overrunning a redoubt. The Spaniards under Freire advanced prematurely and, although initially successful, soon came up against stiff opposition. Subjected to heavy fire from the French batteries they were thrown back in confusion which soon became a disorganized rout as the French advanced and drove them off their position.

April 10th EASTER SUNDAY
We struck our tents soon after midnight and marched to support our Light Companies, at the bridge, Croix de Orade, across the Ers, N.E. of the City. As we were this day, left in front, our 8th Company was sent forward as Advanced Guard and proceeded to the bridge, barricaded with every description of wagons, carts and hurdles that could be procured.

We spent the remainder of the morning on the cold sloping approach to the bridge; this was our main approach. The French last night destroyed a bridge southward, but this leading to Croix de Orade was of too much consequence for us to part with. We were therefore sent to assist the Light Companies, to defend the barricade in front of the bridge, in case of a night attack. Waiting such an event, to leave the road open for the relief of the sentries beyond, we reclined on the grassy side of the bank, at the foot of which was a broad ditch of water. At about 8 o'clock our whole Division joined our post. A fatigue party cleaned the road of the barricading, while the Light Company rushed forward to, and above, the French picquets from a good country house or villa, with a spacious walled-in yard, eastward situate at the foot of the heights, on which were the enemy's grand fieldworks. And they instantly poured down an abundance of shots and shells of every size. Regardless of which, our Company was again sent to the support of the Light Company. It is quite marvellous how we passed through this tremendous pelting, with scarcely a casualty.

We found the two upper storeys of the house absolutely riddled by cannon balls! The Light Companies ensconced themselves in the basement but we were obliged to remain outside, with our backs to the wall of the house, and with care watch the busting of every shell!!! It is a curious notice, to mark how the splinters of the shells, influenced by internal combustion, still retained the forward impetus from the mortar! Chief of the fragments passed over, or through, the eastern wall of the courtyard, tearing the attached buildings and sheds into atoms.

Whilst we were thus *"agreeably"* engaged, our Division advanced in open column of Brigades over the morass, so soft that every general and field officer was compelled to march and have his horse led over. Our left Brigade skirted the bank of the River Ers. Our Portuguese took the centre of the morass and our Right Brigade proceeded nearer to the heights. The Division had made but small advance ere an Aide de Camp galloped into the courtyard and led the Light Companies to skirmish to the front, leaving orders for us, in ten minutes to follow and regain our post at the head of the Brigade. Not one of us looked at a watch to note the time!

As soon as the Light Bobs were gone, we quitted our uncomfortable abidance, but which in truth, now became the safest location, for the advance of the Division diverted the whole attention of the redoubts. When the enemy found we could and would pass the morass, in defiance of their heavy cannonading, they blew up the bridge over the Ers, south-west of their position and thereby impeded the approach of our artillery and cavalry. The three columns of our Division advanced sections in threes, to be as compact as possible, and at the same time to allow free passage for cannon balls, through our line of march, as chance could direct. Regardless of this precaution, some shots and shells swept down all before them.

When leaving courtyard, Captain Chitty ordered me to bring up the rear as closely as possible as he would lead the Company, helter-skelter as fast as he could run. I had no difficulty with the order; every man scampered off as briskly as he could. My progress was arrested by a most heart-rending scene!! An infernal shell of large calibre had struck our regiment in the centre as it passed! I knew not how many men were killed or wounded by the explosion, but in the midst lay Lieutenant Gough[4], nephew of the hero of China and India, supporting himself on the ridge of a furrow by his hands! The internal of his right thigh was torn more open than the leaves of this book, the bone was skijored into atoms, the femoral artery jetting out his life's blood in a most awful manner!!! I stopped and condoled with him. He thanked me, but urged my departure! "Run forward, my dear friend! This is not a place for anyone to tarry in!!"

"But Gough can I render you any service? What of your baggage?" "My kind friend, in a very short time baggage, and everything in this world, will be of no consequence to me. Do pray run forward and escape from this dreadful fire! Your stay causes me painful apprehension." And thus I left the poor fellow to his fate.

Our kind-hearted assistant surgeon, Harry Franklin, visited him very soon after, but mortal aid was futile! Our Light Companies scoured the base of the enemy's position, and left the valley free. By hard running I overtook my company just as they took the head of the line of march, opposite the second redoubt, right of the French position, from which we experienced no firing. Having passed the extreme of their position, some three hundred yards, we brought forward our left shoulders, and ascended to the summit of the French position and works, completely outflanking the enemy.

110

The acclivity was great, and our progress consequently slow, during which I was much amused by a trait in the field of a grand battle! Our commander Lieutenant General Cole, (who, when Lieutenant Colonel commanded our Regiment) anxious for the success of the movement of his Division, had followed on foot, and gaining the pivot flank of our leading Company, endeavoured to encourage our exertions. "Bravo! Enniskilleners!! I always knew you were the lads to depend on at a sharp pinch!"

Our men had not had time to regain their breath after their sharp run over the morass when they had to ascend the heights, about which Sir Lowry Cole, had all the colloquy. At length old Dan Sullivan, the veteran of our Company could not restrain himself. "Och! Ge lar o' that Lawry! Sure now don't I remember how you would always blackguard and bully us on parade? And now you want us to have our heads broken by these cursed vicra balls you come tipping us the Blarney! Ge lar o' that Lawry, and we will prove ourselves soldiers!"

More pleased than offended at the freedom of the response, for he well knew he had struck the right chord of an Irish harp, or heart, Sir Lowry looked towards the enemy until he could re-compose his countenance. As the first and second redoubts were vacated we had flattered ourselves that on crowning the height, we should get into a quiet position. Very far from that! The Division spanning the height, in open column of Brigades, attracted a tre-mendous cannonading! And immediately on our left was a strong muster of French cavalry, threatening our position and watching our Light Companies skirmishing, in our front. Very deliberately General Cole despatched an Aide de Camp, who very shortly returned, accompanied by two artillerymen with hand rockets.

General Cole welcomed their arrival by saying, "Come lads, drive away those cavalry!" The reply was, "Leave them to us, General, and we will punish them!" The staff of the first rocket slightly touched the mound, which caused it to pass in front of the squadron under the noses of their horses and drove them off helter-skelter! After a while they reformed on the same ground. "Now then," said the artilleryman, "I will have you!" and he was as good as his promise! The second rocket passed through the bodies of the first horse, the second man and the head of the third, or drove it from the shoulders. The precision of this aim was admirable and had the desired effect, for our unwelcome visitors did not again

111

make their appearance. One drunken trooper reappeared in the lower ground immediately in front of our skirmishers, evidently a good horseman, although he could not sit steadily in his saddle. He kept his steed well in hand, and with his flourishing sword appeared to offer single combat to any one. Our skirmishers heard his vociferation and replied by their muskets. Multitudes of shots were fired at this drunken charlatan. But as he kept in constant motion not one was immediately fatal, although we could see his clothes and face were bloody. Our sympathy was for the sober horse, who, stung by repeated bullets, at length galloped off in spite of all restraint and bore his torn[5] of a rider out of our sight. During all this, to compete with this demonstration of cavalry, our regiment was ordered into close column.

The enemy marked this movement and, as we thus offered a prominent mark, directed two of their nine pounders against us. The first shots fell short and harmless, but one spent ball came whizzing along the ground to the front of the column. A young Grenadier jocularly said to it, "Get out of that, old chap. We don't want you here!" And gave the ball a kick, the centrifugal force whipping off his foot! This even caused an uneasiness amongst our men, for it was evident that the enemy had measured the range, and the cavalry having taken themselves off, we were unnecessarily exposed to danger. Captain Chitty ordered me to pace in rear of the column and command silence. About the centre I was calling some men to order when I found great difficulty in keeping myself from falling, so many men falling against me. I turned my eyes right and saw a chasm in the column like a V. An unfortunate but well directed ball struck the breast of the front Grenadier and, in passing, killed and wounded eleven men! Many men knocked down in the confusion had difficulty in convincing themselves that they were not personally injured. I felt obliged to rouse them from their horror and urge them back to their posts.

A recruit belonging to our Company was driven twice his own length from the ranks. When risen, the poor fellow trembled like an aspen leaf. "Come my good chap get into your rank." "Oh Sir," he replied, "that's where the ball passed!" "Well then," I rejoined, "that is the place you should take, for we know that no two balls strike in the same spot!!" "What! Don't they, Sir?" and the brave fellow resumed his post. Leading this recruit back, I called Dan Sullivan, before mentioned, who was picking up his musket,

Dan gave me one of his quaint side glances, adding, "Och sure, you are a cool hand! For didn't that ball pace between your own legs, sure!!" "Then give over your Blarney, Master Dan! Get into place!!" Dan resumed his place, grumbling, "Och! Och! Sure you were always a cool hand!!!"

The cavalry having departed, we now formed line over the height and sat down by our arms. Thus deprived of a point blank aim, the French fired ricochet shots, which passed us, and passing to the rear Brigades did very little mischief. During all this time we heard a great deal was going on. The 6th Division who followed us, defiled, and attacked the centre redoubt. Here was some desperate fighting. General Pack was wounded at the head of his Brigade but was able to continue in the field. This assault outflanked the right of the enemy's position.

Our skirmishers had been equally active, and fought their way over the height to a small two-floored house south-west of our left, westward of which was a garden, enclosed by a clay wall about seven feet high, through which they cut loopholes to fire on the enemy, ensconced in a sunken road, parallel with our position and the small house. By the house was a small by-road, passing the hollow road, at a right-angle. We had also a by-road, about two hundred yards below the left of our line, in the same direction. Both of these roads we had to defend, and in the exposed field between them very many officers and men were wounded and killed, for they were exposed on an open plain, without any shelter, to the deliberate fire of the enemy, who were not to be seen until they popped up their heads to take aim.

This desultory warfare exasperated our men excessively! They called for orders to advance, pledging themselves to take the city!!! We had the utmost difficulty to allay their excitement. Beyond all question, our advance would have achieved all this! And we did not learn for some days why we were detained in such a perilous and tantalising position! Lord Wellington knew of Bonaparte's retreat from Russia and sent, by flag of truce, the intelligence to Marshal Soult, who replied that he had not received such from his own government and could not accept it from an enemy! The citizens, aware of this, sent an earnest request to Lord Wellington to save the city! Which he promised! Thus we were kept, as the post has said, "to be popped at, like pigeons, for sixpence per day!" In such matters soldiers are not consulted; they are required to be at their post! And I will resume mine by taking up the thread of my narrative. Our Company, the 8th, was ordered to take post in the by-road below the heights. This was in direct line from a bridge on the Languedoc Canal, on which the French placed a cannon, which raked our post.

We laid down on the bank, beside the road, but our red jackets afforded a glimpse of our locality. And the balls most uncomfortably furrowed the road, scattering the gravel over us with such fury that we were compelled to lie on our faces. I now felt myself totally worn out, by the violent pain in my head, and the want of sleep, and went and laid myself down on the rising bank on the other side. The enemy marked me and destroyed my slumber by directing their fire at me. I was in such agony that I was totally indifferent about life!!! Some of the balls fell so close to me that I was dusted all over. Captain Chitty kindly exerted his authority and ordered me back to my post. An event occurred to arouse us and divert the tedium of our situation. Captain Bignold's lurcher-dog, Doxy, ever restless, crossed the road and, by a slight turn of the head, acknowledged my call. She proceeded to the open plain, and hunted about. Bignold noticed his dog and sprang up exclaiming, "Doxy is scenting a hare!" Away he ran with his blackthorn stick, a regular shillala, in hand, for Frank had no sword, having carelessly left it behind some day. It was a long course, but Bignold actively pursued. The hare being hard-pressed ran very close under the fire of the French in the hollow road, who tried hard to punish Bignold for his rashness. He secured the game and triumphantly brought it back on his shillala and presented it to our Brigadier, Major General Anson.

In less than three hours poor Frank received his death-wound very near to the spot where the hare was killed. The French cavalry mustered in rear of their nine pounder gun, on the bridge apparently with an intent to charge along one of the two roads. The 6th Company had relieved the 7th in the field between us and the house, occupied by the Light Companies, and requiring relief, having lost many men, and nearly expended their ammunition, requested Captain Chitty to report it to our Colonel. Chitty despatched me and the Colonel ordered me to hunt up Captain Bignold and desire him with the 5th Company to relieve the 6th.

After a long march, I found poor Bignold, with cap off and jacket open, with Pollock and Radcliffe, seated behind a sand-bank, in rear, some way off the Regiment enjoying such food as they could muster. Bignold promptly obeyed the order and I saw him no more until late in the evening when I found the poor fellow in the château in rear of our right, to which the wounded had been conveyed. He had received a musket ball in his right temple, which forced out the eye, and lodged behind the left eye, destroying all but its sight. Another shot had fractured his left arm, a little below the shoulder. And in his attempting to rise, it had left a bloody mark on the surface of the room.

Being ordered late in the evening to take command of the 5th Company, I sent poor Frank's servant down with his rations, and soon after was able to go myself to render him any assistance, but nothing could be done. Poor Frank was too delirious to recognise my salutations, taking the morsels of boiled beef from his servant, rubbing each on the sole of his shoe, and holding each piece up to his left eye before putting it in his mouth! All the time calling for his dear mother! He continued in this restless state until near 8 o'clock next morning when his existence and suffering ceased. My painful recollections of my good, kind-hearted comrade have drawn my pen from the field of battle, but I must return to my post.

The 7th Company had gone down to support the Light Companies at the house and had returned. But the French made a sudden and violent effort to dislodge our Light Bobs. On which we were ordered from our raking, gravel road to go down to their support. Captain Chitty on receiving the order, came to me, and said, "Truly my friend this is no joke of a job! We must run through the fire of this reinforcement of French skirmishers. I shall order the Company to scamper widely over the fields, for we shall be within point-blank shot. And you must bring up the rear as well as you can. Anyway we went helter-skelter, passed over the field without a single casualty and arrived at the gate on the west side fortunately, but it was so small that only one could enter. The French well knew the locality and fired over the eastern wall in the hope of hitting us in the ingress.

We found we were sent to relieve a Company of our Portuguese, a recruit in which caused great danger to himself and me while placing our men at the loop holes. He fired before he could take his aim, the ball recoiled and passed close to my face, for I felt the wind. The enemy's reinforcement quickly expended their ammunition and retired. When we had more deliberately expended ours we were relieved. But on retiring we had again to run the gauntlet. The enemy was relieved shortly before, and they noticed our relief, played the same trick as when we retired, the balls whizzing very close. Captain Chitty saw the danger and ordered me to force the men out at the doorway as quickly as possible.

All but four or five were gone, and I was urging them to be active, and clapped my hand on the knapsack of the rearmost, a smart young soldier who had not long joined us with whom we were much pleased. At that juncture I felt the wind of a ball on my right ear; it pierced the head of the young fellow, who fell dead across my path! I felt excessively grieved! The only kindness I could now render was to drag his corpse aside, that it might not be trampled on! This delayed me a short while, and when I got out I found all our men clear ahead of me, and I could go my own pace over the field.

I moved too briskly to offer any aim, but looked about as I trotted along and saw my good old friend Captain Reid of the 48th placing his Company for skirmishing. The old veteran had been often wounded and his usual ill luck awaited him here, for he very soon received a shot on his ribs, which glided off causing two wounds. He kept his post for some time encouraging and directing his men where to fire with most effect. Another shot struck and brought him to the ground making two more wounds. Finding himself growing faint from loss of blood, he resolved to crawl on his hands and knees towards the house. Some of his men came to assist him, but he ordered them back to their posts, as he could still take care of himself. He was lying in the lower room, when a cannon ball passed through the room above him, in which were assembled all the Light Company officers, watching the proceedings of the enemy.

The arrival of such an unwelcome visitor, although no one was wounded, caused a great commotion among the occupants. The pressure was so great that my worthy friend Val Blomfield, Lieutenant 48th, who was by the south window, jumped out and alighted in the garden below, mid-leg deep in the mould. He called out to his comrades, "I am very safe and comfortable, hope you are all the same?" The Honourable Lieutenant Browne of the 40th Light Company ran downstairs, his face and jacket covered with fragments of the white wall. Old Reid laughingly said, "Why, Sir, you are in a forlorn plight and you soon frightened!"

The Honourable tartlet[6] replied, "Sir, your remarks are very inappropriate. Had you been in the room above you would not have thought it an occasion for joking and I consider your laughing as excessively unfeeling!"

"Darn it, Sir," rejoined the veteran, "I consider that when a man has four holes in his body he has a right to laugh if he can!"

Our Company again occupied the gravel road and, while receiving a supply of ammunition, were molested by more ricochet shots, which pelted us with stones and gravel.

We found our Division guns silent for want of ammunition, having expended all that they could bring with them over the hastily repaired bridge. We found it very heart-sickening to continue in our comfortless, inactive position and see our brother officers pass, badly wounded. Captain Geddes[7] was carried by, wounded in the thigh, which crippled him for life! Lieutenants Harnett and Burns, and Ensign Arnett were supported past us, after our return. The wind was behind us, but between the gusts we could hear distinctly the heavy firing near the bridge from which we sallied in the morning. It was late in the evening when we received orders to rejoin the Regiment. And right glad we were to quit our vile station, and stretch our legs. Night, welcome night, put an end to the bloody conflict!! We took up position in segment of a circle, our left opposite and close to the extreme redoubt occupied by the Portuguese, our right tending to the further redoubt held by the 6th Division. These redoubts were constructed with large casks, the staves of which supplied us with firewood for the night.

I borrowed a blanket, sucked a bone of chicken, the remains of provisions we had brought, ate some bread with lemons, drank some ordinary country wine, then took my couch in an adjoining furrow, and slept, without *rocking*!

After we had taken up our position I went, as I have before related, to visit poor Captain Bignold having been ordered to take the command of the 5th Company. Near the château I met that excellent fellow, Harry Franklin, our assistant surgeon, looking spiritless and oppressed, and I gave him a cheerful salutation, which roused him from his melancholy. Harry replied, "I am rejoiced to see you, my dear fellow, safe after this dreadful battle! All day have I been in that house, no one to speak to but my poor wounded comrades whom I have been cutting and slashing, until

117

I am gorged with gore! Sick unto death!! I must go and seek for something to eat and drink. I have performed (my memory cannot now recall the great number) operations or rather amputations, and that nice fellow, corporal of your 5th Company distresses me exceedingly! He bears his suffering with heroic fortitude! He lost so much blood in the field that there is no chance for his recovery but I must perform my painful duty and amputate both legs above the knee. It is the only chance for life, but I do not think he can survive it! I wish my good friend, you could attend me!" I responded, "Well, well! Harry, for yours and the poor fellows' sake I will attend you, with the hope of being a comfort to either or both, but truly I am not ambitious of the occasion, for really I have had enough this day!" I saw no more of my friend Harry that evening, and was right glad to escape from such a painful scene! Next morning I learnt the poor corporal did not survive the operation two hours. When entering the château to visit poor Bignold I saw, in the ante-room, a pile of arms and legs, fully corroborating Harry Franklin's remark! It was a sight to take the shine out of my aspirant for military glory! And in the room with poor Frank Bignold were ten or a dozen poor fellows, looking most death-like! I was glad to hurry away from such a spot!

I have omitted to state that, after we reoccupied our position in the gravel road and were receiving a fresh supply of ammunition, our Colonel rode past us to reconnoitre the post of the Light Corps. from whence we had returned. In his wonted manner, he would not hurry "the poor beast", his horse, for it was a remarkable sight even to see him trot. He passed down without scathe, but, returning, was shot through his bridle-wrist. Like a true Scotsman, our colonel never bothered himself with a pocket-handkerchief. On my noticing his wound he asked me to lend him one! It was a most unfortunate application; the small one I had was in constant requisition by my poor oozing head and totally unfit for a fresh wound. I was compelled to say I had not one. I find in an old letter we had two officers, above 100 men killed, four officers wounded.

It is difficult nowadays to fully appreciate the carnage, devastation and sheer horror of such a battle. How can we possibly visualize the scale, magnitude and ferocity of such a battle with our twenty-first century perception of modern warfare? Indeed, we can follow the movements of various Regiments and Divisions as they move to and fro across the battlefield, sometimes making slight advances, at other times making hasty retreats. Battles of this era resembled games of chess; move and countermove played out against a timescale of hours, maybe even days. We know the facts, figures and outcome of such battles. We even know the scale of casualties, represented as statistics and percentages, but what do we know of the suffering and individual cost of such a battle or campaign?

In the diary accounts of Lieutenant Charles Crowe we are given a privileged glimpse, albeit an abridged version, of the highs, lows and the mundane. Through his writings we get a privileged first hand account of the terrible price often paid by soldiers of that period.

What shines through in his diary, however, is the overwhelming humanity displayed by all. Generals have a sense of humour, soldiers express their emotions, surgeons show their feelings, whilst men are prepared to die for a cause they know little of. The old perception that officers stood aloof from their men may hold true in some instances, but Lieutenant Crowe demonstrates a concern and humanity towards his men which we fail to perceive in mere history books.

His superiors may not have judged the incident in which he drags the body of a young soldier to one side in order that it may not be trampled under foot as prudent, given that it temporarily distracted him from the job in hand. However, such an action displays a high degree of respect for a fallen comrade, even though he was surrounded by dead and dying on all sides. Above all, Lieutenant Crowe comes across as a man of conviction, someone who appreciates life and abhors needless waste, as in the case of his friend Frank Bignold and the Corporal who lost his life on the operating table. Even though belonging to a profession in which one assumes life is cheap, he can nevertheless loathe the misery and horror which surrounds him.

April 11th

We were under arms long before daylight. When the sun arose, not a responsive smile could we find in all our ranks! The zeal of the fight had sunk with the shades of the past evening. And this morning the recollection of the horrors of the day past, and anticipation of what this day might produce, could not awaken cheerfulness in any countenance.

119

We piled arms and renewed our fires. We there roasted some beefcakes on a couple of ram-rods and, with some salt pork, given by one of our men, made a tolerable breakfast, although our store of bread was very small, "tea, coffee, and eggs not to be mentioned!" No orders arrived and we remained in an irksome suspense.

At length Lieutenant Batty and I ventured to visit and inspect the right of our position. Stationed as we were, at the extreme right of the French works, forming an extended crescent, or as it is called in fortification, a half moon, we did not feel satisfied with the result of the great sacrifice on the past day. The morass over which we scampered yesterday in fearful haste we deliberately re-passed and found it furrowed by the innumerable shots and shells from the French, especially in front of the third redoubt, from the right, which was stormed and carried by our gallant companions the 6th Division, under Lieutenant General Sir H. Clinton, who accompanied us yesterday over the bridge. Here was sufficient to assure us that, whatever we had suffered, others partook of the hard knocks.

When we reached the road from Toulouse, over the bridge to Croix d'Olade, the numerous graves on each side made our hearts ache! A Grenadier of the 42nd Regiment was mournfully wandering about, but quickly raised his head, showing the big tears, which streamed down his fine manly countenance, glad to relieve his grief, by responding to our kind enquiry, "Who are buried here?" "Oh!" he replied. "We had a fine gallant Company yesterday, but, alas, here they lie! There are only two beside myself left to tell the tale! Our right wing was ordered to lead General Freire's Spaniards to carry this approach to the city. We made such good progress that the French pushed the Spaniards hard and the rascals turned tail, leaving us to bear the brunt. We fought every inch of ground but could not stand against such numbers!! Oh! My curse on those cowardly Dons!! Our left wing and the 12th Regiment of Portuguese came to our assistance. They were soon followed by the Light Division, and the enemy was effectively beaten." We reached the parapet of the fifth redoubt, from which more especially they blazed at us so unceasingly yesterday, for its position caught us point-blank on the morass over which we scampered in dreadful haste and we marvelled at our escaping so well.

We were proceeding to inspect the 6th and 7th redoubts, or left of the French position, but an alarm was given and the advance

120

and the in-lying picquets and guards were instantly under arms. We deemed it prudent to hasten back to our posts to be ready for any event.

So far from alarm, our soldiers were employed to seek for and deposit in the 1st and 2nd redoubts all the cannon balls they could find. The men imagined they were to receive sixpence for each ball, but I never heard of their being paid, altho' it was said they collected *four thousand*! The real purport was full accomplished by giving employment; they were kept from knowing about or slinking into the city. I went down to the hospital, and chatted some time with Captains Geddes and Reid. Poor Bignold was still alive and continued all night in the distressing restless state in which I left him last evening.

The French have been in motion all day; we see them very busy on the other side of the canal. They are evidently moving off. We shall not see any of them on the morrow. Late in the evening our baggage came, and we pitched our camp on the side of the hill, out of sight. Colonel Maclean's[8] wound obliged him to leave the Regiment, and go into the village beyond the hospital, whither the slightly wounded were conveyed. Before leaving he issued orders for Major Thomas to take command of the Regiment, Lieutenant Batty of the 3rd Company, Boyle of the 4th and I of the 5th. From poor Bignold's dislike to and consequently neglect of accounts I much fear I shall have a very ruffled skein[9] to unravel! But if my head will allow me to accomplish the task, I shall reap the emolument, until our other Battalions join us.

April 12th
When we turned out this morning we discovered some large buildings in Toulouse burning furiously, which convinced us that the enemy was gone, and when daylight came, not a French soldier was to be seen. Our picquet advanced and quietly took possession of the city. We returned to our tents, but before we could finish breakfast came an order for us to march immediately. We soon gained a large road and, after four leagues' march, halted near Le Bastide. I went out with a foraging party and found that the French soldiers, even in their own country, pillaged every portable thing.

Lieutenant Crowe's observations were quite correct. On 11 April Marshal Soult made preparations to abandon the city that very night. As his troops retreated in the direction of Carcassonne, sections of the town were put to the torch, thus, as Lieutenant Crowe witnessed on the morning of 12 April, much of the town was ablaze.

Never was a bloodier battle fought so needlessly. Few victories have ever been so costly in terms of human life; the casualties on both sides could be counted in the thousands. Yet it need never have happened. The entire battle was a fruitless waste of life. Had Marshal Soult taken heed of Wellington's communiqué on 10 April concerning Napoleon's retreat from Russia, events may have been different. The war was all but over yet both parties were ignorant of the full facts. On the evening of 12 April a British and French field officer, Colonels Cooke and St Simon arrived at Wellington's Headquarters with news of Napoleon's abdication which had taken place on 6 April 1814, a full four days prior to the Battle of Toulouse. However, it was not until the evening of the following day, 13 April, that Marshal Soult finally accepted that Napoleon had abdicated and the war was at an end.

Although Soult accepted that Napoleon's reign had indeed come to an end, he refused to pledge allegiance to the Bourbons, thus placing Wellington in the position of having to order the pursuit and interception of the French Marshal's remaining troops. It wasn't until a second official communication arrived that Marshal Soult finally agreed and accepted the inevitable.

April 13th
Breakfasted in full expectation of another order for marching. But about noon came permission for officers to visit Toulouse. Captains Chitty and Lynch went. Our halt has given rise to numerous reports and conjectures. The Horse Artillery are come to the rear. We are assured that Paris has proclaimed Louis 18th and the preliminaries of peace were published in the theatre at Toulouse.

The surgeons have pronounced my poor head to be healing, and I may be able to wait till the regiment goes to England. "Long life to the honours for I have long since set them at naught!!"

April 14th
I employed the whole day with the Accounts of the 5th Company and find my anticipation realised. I shall find a great deficiency.

Captain Chitty returned to dinner, and confirms the rumours respecting peace, and the death of poor Bignold.

April 15th

Ensign Ireland of the 5th Company (late our Serjeant Major) had assisted me in inspecting poor Bignold's wardrobe and effects, and we discovered plain proof that poor Frank had been most woefully plundered before the baggage came into our charge. From suspicion of the fact, we kept the whole within our sight. We found that Frank used to roll his surplus money for the Company into cartridges of twenty guineas each, but only one contained the correct number and some were sadly deficient. He kept these, with his wardrobe in a common pannier[10], covered with bullock's hide. There was a lock to it, but the bend in the lid proved that the contents had been often rifled. Agreeable to orders, we disposed of everything by cant,[11] the Quartermaster being the auctioneer. And under existing circumstances all sold well.

April 16th

Rode to Villenouvelle to see after the sutler of the 34th Regiment who owes me 66 dollars for my mule. He was gone to Toulouse, but returns tomorrow with the Paymaster.

We received another month's pay, this day. I found, on my return, my chums in the act of shifting our tent, more under cover from these troublesome high winds. On removing my bedding I discovered that for three nights I had been nurturing a numerous nest of reptiles, much resembling vipers. A flag of truce has been sent to Marshal Soult, but he refuses to coincide with the peace, until informed thereof by his own government; this is very prudent on his part! But in consequence we are ordered to advance tomorrow.

April 17th Sunday

We started at 6 a.m. and after a march of five leagues, over extremely rough cross-country roads arrived at St Felices. While our dinner was preparing, I had leisure to return thanks for spending this day differently from last Sunday! A little anecdote may diversify the monotony of my journal. Colonel Coke bore a flag of truce to Marshal Soult. A counsel of all the Generals was held. During their deliberations, a rumour ran amongst the French soldiers that an English officer had arrived with preliminaries of peace, and three hearty shouts rent the air. One General walked to the window to ascertain the cause, and turning round, coolly remarked, "It was only a hare started up, amongst the men!" Colonel Coke replied, "Yes! We have had many such hares, in the north!" Soult could not refrain from smiling.

April 18th
We were ordered to be ready to march, and continued in uncertainty till noon, when counter-orders arrived. A detachment of recruits for the 53rd and 48th Regiments arrived. With the latter came my old acquaintance Lieutenant Brotheridge, with whom I associated at Northampton, and who received me at his quarters at Santarem on my route from Lisbon.

April 19th
Rumour talks loudly that Soult has mounted the white cockade. Our inactivity rather confirms this. I persevered with my ruffled accounts.

April 20th
As Marshal Soult is now assured of the Peace, we, at 6 this morning, began to retrace our advance. And the French Army advanced from St Felices and occupied our post; this may be our last glimpse of our late mortal enemies. To be quite clear from them we had another tedious and rough march of five long leagues. And when we halted I was ordered for a foraging party. Luckily we had not to travel many miles to attain our object. In the evening when we sat down to dinner rain came down freely and continued.

The Peninsular War came to an end on 17 April 1814, after six long years of bloody battles, arduous marches, lengthy skirmishes and real hardships. As for Napoleon Bonaparte, he abdicated the French throne to be replaced by the Bourbon King, Louis XVIII. His final ignominy was to be banished from France, exiled upon the tiny island of Elba with many of his trusted Generals and advisers who willingly accompanied their leader.

As in all cases of conflict, once the fighting has ceased the politicians move in to reshape and rebuild. So too, the end of the

Peninsular campaign sounded the death knell for Wellington's victorious army. Over the next few months many of those triumphant regiments who fought with such valour and distinction would be re-located throughout the known world, whilst battalions so necessary for the conflict just ended would be disbanded and veterans returned to civilian life.

April 21st
We marched along a narrow road, which at length proved to be the one on our left, on the 10th inst. which we so resolutely defended. While approaching, and passing the house where the Light Companies had been posted, a solemn silence pervaded the whole line of march. A silent monitor said, "How many of our brave comrades fell here!" When we saw the hollow road of which the French availed themselves we were surprised that our loss was not even more severe. In our progress we crossed the bridge over that truly grand national work, the canal, which connects the trade of the Mediterranean with that of the Atlantic Sea.

We entered Toulouse with fixed bayonets but supported arms; the floating fragments of our Colours proudly told the natives whence we came and what we had been doing. The utmost regularity was preserved in our line of march. On quitting the city and crossing the noble bridge over the Garonne we found the breastworks sufficiently removed to make a free passage, but enough remained to prove how many men must have lost their lives in attempting to force such a very formidable position.

When the Brigade had far passed the City I obtained leave to return to visit the Colonel and other wounded friends, not forgetting poor Captain Geddes, whom I found in great pain, also my very good friend Captain Reid of the 48th Regiment. I met my strange, quondam[12] friend Rawlings of the 4th Regiment cashiered by sentence of a General Court Martial, for not being to be found, when called to some duty unexpectedly, while he was galloping over the country as Acting Commissary, in consequence of some seniors being on the sick list. According to his own statement, his is a very peculiar and very severe case. And under his conviction he is about to accompany the Proceedings of the court martial to England and plead his own cause before the Prince Regent. He has stated many strong points in bar of sentence and he is not the chap to let such rest. I should not be surprised if he be reinstated.

125

April 23rd

We marched right in front along the great road, but my feet still suffered from my forced march on Friday, that for more than two leagues I hobbled woefully; the interesting appearance of the fine town of Auch beguiled my sufferings; the approach, with the lofty cathedral towering above, was very interesting, and as we expected to encamp not far beyond, we all anticipated a pleasing ramble in the afternoon, and only two or three officers obtained leave to diverge from the line of march. We found our error when too late, and our comrades informed us the cathedral retained its wonted grandeur, having been saved from spoliation by the residence of the Archbishop. That the extensive barracks, which we noticed, will amply accommodate the 6th Division, and our Portuguese Brigade, marching in our rear, for this town has been a depot for ten thousand men, being a central point to Bayonne, Bordeaux, Toulouse and the interior of the country. From what we hear, it may be that the 4th Division will never meet again. Report says our Portuguese will halt here till they march next month for Portugal, that our left Brigade will march tomorrow for Condom and we for Valence. Our Paymaster is not yet arrived from Toulouse.

April 24th

I was on baggage-guard and on my arrival found that the town had proved too small for our Brigade. The 48th Regiment was sent to a village on our left, and we went to houses in the adjacent country, that our cantonment must have compassed five square miles. Had we been before an enemy, we should have been ordered to make ourselves comfortable under canvas in some ploughed field. My 5th Company were well off, nor more than four men in a house, and the natives treated them most hospitably to bread and wine.

My host had been a soldier at Vitoria, Pamplona, San Sebastian. Although we had been thus opposed as bitter foes, "now all the wars are over." "Should friend or foe henceforth appear, we gaily live on clover, and will greet him with a welcome cheer, now that the wars are over," and this brave fellow received me with the hospitality of a warm friend. Wine, bread, eggs, fowls, marmalade were fully produced, ere I could express a wish!!! The worthy fellow's eyes glistened with tears of gratitude when I congratulated him on having escaped the perils of the service and been able to return to the blessings of domestic life.

Hostilities at an end, both Crowe and his French host found they shared a common bond, their experiences as opposing soldiers. They could appreciate that, although once enemies who had faced each other on the battlefield, they now had put those experiences and their enmity behind them. However, unable to cope with the oppressive nature of his new-found friend's continual and overwhelming attention, Crowe was forced to make his excuses and find another billet.

So too, with the war at an end, life for Crowe became more mundane. In contrast to the highs and lows of campaign life, when the course of the war could change from day to day, he had to settle down to more general, run-of-the-mill duties which are part and parcel of military life. In some instances those duties were quite harrowing but there were also those of a more humorous nature, even though, they did contain their very own element of danger! The case of a certain Mrs Fisher, a camp follower, is one such incident!

May 2nd
This morning at sunrise one of our drummers received the deserts of his good behaviour, according to the sentence of a General Court Martial. One thousand lashes was his award but he escaped with only eight hundred. The event also excited the curiosity of the inhabitants, but very, very few waited for the end. They were much shocked by the severity of our punishment, but admitted the good effect, not a single complaint having been made against any man since we entered the town, which would not have been the case with their own soldiers. The drummer's misdemeanour had been committed long before we came hither. The daughter of the gentleman where Major Thomas was quartered, a very fine woman about 26 years of age, and very high-spirited, intimated her desire to witness the punishment. The Major flattered himself that his strong remonstrations had prevailed, but the young lady crept to the scene just as the blood was trickling down the culprit's back but was quickly carried away, totally insensible.

It was rather singular that another punishment occurred this day, in which I was judge and juror and, if not executioner, I directed the process. The guardhouse afforded no accommodation for an officer, and a strong serjeant's guard was responsible to the

127

officer of the day. As this was my duty, I kept close quarters, in case I should be called for. Early in the afternoon the serjeant of my 5th Company came and earnestly requested me to go and quiet the woman Fisher, wife of our fifer, for she was mad with excessive drink and her most outrageous conduct had so frightened the inhabitants that they had fastened up all the houses! I instantly ordered him to give her in charge of the guard. But he had assured me that he had thrice done so, and she had forced her way out. I sent him for the fifer to met me in the guardhouse. On my way thither I was quite astonished to observe the great consternation which this beast of a woman had occasioned! My wonder however ceased when I met the frantic demon. I never witnessed anything so atrocious!! I desired the husband to control her but he declared his incapability for she had knocked him about like a ninepin. And the poor fellow's face and cloths confirmed his assertions. He begged me to quiet her if I could anyhow, but that he would not go near her. It was very evident that something must be done, but I knew not what.

Thinking my rank and authority would check the fiend's fury, I tried to reason with her, but she showed fight and made such desperate blows at me, that I was compelled to beat them off with my sheathed sword in my left hand. I then fixed a stern and steady look at her and by my orders some soldiers closed around her and forced her into the guardhouse. I made the drummer take the sling from his drum and unbraid it. I very soon wound the cord around and secured the woman's legs, carried it up and tied her hands behind her, but could not affix it to her tongue, her yells and vociferation were quite deafening! To stop this nuisance I was obliged to put a drumstick across her mouth and bound it behind her head. In this state she was placed on the inclined plane or guard bed. I walked about outside, until the "dear creature's dulcet notes became pianissimo," and the serjeant of the guard informed me that she was nearly asleep. I gave order to remove the drumstick when she was sound asleep. And if, on her waking she became quiet, to release her. About three hours after I received a report that Mrs Fisher was gone to her billet quite subdued.

The natives had narrowly watched my proceedings with this horrible monster and on my way home gave me many salutes. I was rejoiced to find their confidence fully restored. Necessity is said to be the mother of invention, and such must have the case in the above expedient, for otherwise, I know not how I could think of it. Had I not stopped the nuisance I should have incurred censure, for I stood in double responsibility as Officer of the Day and Officer of the Company to which the witch belonged. Our discipline and the good conduct of our men were the admiration of every inhabitant, and the greatest cordiality subsisted in every rank. It was not to be endured that a vile drunken woman should thus disgrace us!

This Mrs Fisher is the identical Fifer's wife who purchased Madame Soult's satin slippers, at the cant the day after the Battle of Vitoria! Every one in the regiment, not even excepting her own husband, was rejoiced at my having abashed the dauntless Mrs Fisher, well known to be as desperate a marauder as ever followed an Army.

By all accounts women such as Mrs Fisher were more difficult to control than many of the actual soldiers themselves. "Camp followers", by the very nature of the life they led, the relationships they had with the troops, whether it was through marriage or not, were tough, hardy individuals who experienced the horrors and deprivation of life in the field with the added strain of actually bringing children in tow. Life for such women was a squalid affair, constantly on the move, trying as best they might to make a 'home' wherever the regiment found itself, constantly in danger of losing their partners and family whether in battle or as the result of disease. Such women were part and parcel of an army and, although often troublesome as in the case of Mrs Fisher, they nevertheless provided a vital service and a much needed morale boost for the beleaguered troops.

However, the term "camp follower" extended far beyond simply the role of family members. The term was applied on a much wider base to include all those who provided any vital element in support of the army. Merchants, contractors and all elements of support staff came under the umbrella of "camp follower".

The whole incident of the notorious Mrs Fisher was not lost upon Lieutenant Crowe's Commanding Officer, as he was soon to find out.

May 3rd
Our Commanding Officer, Major Thomas, surprised me much this morning on parade. He came direct up to me, and with a grave face

enquired, "Did you not receive a message from me last evening?" Really I did not Major! "You are positive you did not receive any message?" I am positive, Major! "Sir, I can tell you that I have a most serious complaint laid against you." But the Major could not carry on the farce, he burst into a violent fit of laughter, then stated, "The truth is that vile woman Mrs Fisher came to complain of your treatment of her yesterday. I did not know how to keep a serious countenance before the baggage, for I thought there never was anything better done. And I am very, very much obliged by your admirable expedient! She stated her complaint most fully. I replied, and did he actually so treat you? Oh yes your Honour, with dozens of courtesies, that he did! Then do you go to him. Oh Yes! Your Honour, that I will. Give him my best regards and best thanks and tell him I hope he will always serve you in like manner, whenever you are so beastly drunk and disgrace the Regiment and your country."!!! Again the worthy Major laughed heartily and added, "I did not imagine that you would receive my message, but I am truly rejoiced that someone has succeeded in shaming that brute of a woman."

May 4th
We learn that our 1st and 2nd Battalions are marching to meet us at Bordeaux. Should such be the case, it will be a most unprecedented event that ever occurred in the British Army, to say no more, for three battalions of one regiment to meet on foreign service! We hear rumours of our proceeding on our march, but I hope not yet. Colonel Maclean visited us today, en route to Bordeaux, to wait the arrival of our comrades.

It was evident to Lieutenant Crowe and his fellow officers that now the war in the Peninsula was at an end, something new was in the wind. The fact that a significant number of regiments had been ordered to converge on Bordeaux was, to them, a clear indication that, as they suspected, America beckoned. Over the next few days their assumption would be proved right.

May 13th
Early this morning an order arrived for us to send our best tents to the 40th Regiment, ordered to America. We considered this as a plain indication that we shall not go there. To my great surprise

130

my friend Captain Chitty rejoined us, accompanied by Lieutenant Harnet, who dined with me. Chitty's renovated health made him full of spirits on again joining us. In one instance to my annoyance, for I had requested the landlord to let me have some of his oldest and best wine.

Well knowing the plain matter-of-fact character of my servant Barney Bradley, Chitty asked, on his entering carefully with a bottle, "Did you shake the bottle Barney?" "No Sir!" "Then shake it well Barney!" No sooner said than done! All remonstrance was vain!! So we laughed heartily at sturdy Barney's solemn and prompt obedience of orders.

Chitty informs me that 13 regiments formed into 6 Brigades, or 2 Divisions, are to be sent from this country to America without loss of time.

Chapter Seven

Across the Atlantic

Following the abdication of Napoleon Bonaparte in April 1814 Britain was now free to turn her attention to the pressing problem of American incursions across the Canadian borders. As a result of the break-up of Wellington's victorious army of the Peninsula, the 27th Inniskillings became one of a number of regiments to be relocated around the globe. In the case of the 1st and 3rd Battalions the Inniskillings Fusiliers, they were among those regiments to cross the Atlantic bound for Canada.

Greatly overshadowed by events of Europe, the hostilities between America and Canada had been ongoing since 1812. Ontario and Quebec had frequently been the target of United States incursions on to Canadian soil and the decision was taken to strengthen the garrisons along the frontier. The small British contingent already located there, aided by the Canadian Militia, was therefore to be strengthened by a force of sixteen thousand Peninsular veterans under the command of General Sir George Prevost.

The events which followed in the next few months proved a less than glorious chapter in the history of the 27th Inniskillings, though what transpired was not of their own making.

The 1st Battalion set sail from Bordeaux in June 1814 and arrived at St John's, New Brunswick, on 25 August of the same year. Their arrival was less than auspicious. It was their misfortune to be placed under the command of a mediocre General, an officer whose criticism, though partially justified, significantly failed to recognize the worth of hardened veterans of the Napoleonic Wars. Contrary to Wellington's explicit orders during the Peninsular campaign, many officers had adopted the practice of wearing irregular forms of dress. Grey replaced regulation blue jackets, while overalls of every conceivable colour were worn with differing braids and ornamentation, with little or no distinguishing rank insignia. Such lack of discipline infuriated General Prevost who commented in a General Order:

> The commander of the forces has observed in the dress of several officers of corps and departments, lately added to this army from that of Field-Marshal the Duke of Wellington, a fanciful variety inconsistent with the rules of the service, and in some cases without comfort or convenience, and to the prejudice of the service, by removing essential distinctions of rank and description of service.
>
> His Excellency deems it expedient to direct that general officers in charge of divisions and brigades do uphold His Majesty's commands in that respect, and only admit of such deviations from them as may be justified by particular causes of service and climate, and even then their uniformity is to be retained.
>
> Commanding officers are held responsible that the established uniform of their corps is strictly observed by the officers under their command.[1]

General Prevost's ill-conceived and ill-timed comments smacked of a soldier whose lack of understanding and tact denoted a lack of practical experience on the field of battle. His preoccupation with strict codes of military dress and etiquette, though understandable, failed to appreciate the conditions under which those newly arrived men and officers had served for the past six years. Wellington, though explicit in his orders regarding the same, had the foresight and experience to know a soldier's worth was proven on the battlefield and not by his choice of tailor!

Not only were General Prevost's comments ill-conceived but they served to alienate many of those recently placed under his command. Widespread resentment amongst veterans of the Peninsula, who had served with such distinction under the Iron Duke, led to a lack of confidence in Prevost's ability as both a soldier and commanding officer, an assumption which subsequent events would prove correct. A leading Canadian historian summed up the situation precisely when he commented:

> It created great dissatisfaction in all ranks that soldiers who had fought under the great Duke in the Peninsula, and had come to Canada to take part in the war, should receive such a reproof from General Prevost. The proceeding destroyed all confidence in his

133

capacity. It is a common feeling that they had passed from the command of one who had won belief in his genius, and had lead them forward to victory, to be under an officer who in no way deserved their consideration, and under whom they must go into the field with little faith in his military experience and ability, and without reliance on his good feeling towards them. Plattsburg only too soon proved the truth of this sentiment.[2]

As Kingford so rightly commented, General George Prevost soon showed his true colours. As a part of a much larger force, the 1st and 3rd Battalions took part in an attack on American forces situated on the southern shores of Lake Champlain. This stretch of inland water was strategically vital to the overall security of Canada. An American military presence in the region threatened Montreal, which, if the St Lawrence were to come under American domination, would put at risk settlements on Lakes Erie and Ontario, cutting them off from the sea and thus jeopardizing Canada's very existence.

As a result, on 11 September the Inniskillings took part in their first action, if action it could be called, at Plattsburg[3]. Due to the nature and strategic location of Lake Champlain the Americans, besides having a military garrison, also possessed a formidable naval presence. The British attempted to match like with like, and had built up a small fleet consisting of a frigate, three brigs and twelve gunboats. The plan of attack, as Prevost saw it, was for the British Navy[4] to attack the American fleet as it lay at anchor, whilst being supported on land by an attack on Plattsburg by the infantry. However, true to form, Prevost proved America's greatest asset! Not only did he alienate the British Navy through a combination of crass ignorance and rank stupidity, he committed them to the battle when they were least prepared. The outcome was the annihilation of the small force within hours.

However, rather than attempt to push the attack forward, much to the dismay of his officers, Prevost ordered a general retreat and returned to Montreal leaving behind both wounded and supplies to a numerically inferior American force. Thus ended the ignominious Battle of Plattsburg. However, as luck would have it the Americans failed to take full advantage of the situation. Knowing the tenacity of the British soldier as they did, it seemed inconceivable that they should retreat so readily. Presuming it a *ruse de guerre* the American forces held their position.

As for Prevost, he died before he could be brought to task and thus avoided the ignominy of trial by court martial and its obvious repercussions. However, prior to his death he selected the 1st Battalion the Inniskilling Fusiliers to take part in a British expeditionary force, which was to operate against the southern coast of the United States. So began a series of voyages which were to have a profound effect upon the fortunes of this battalion.

On 5 November 1814 the battalion, nine hundred and fifty strong, embarked at Montreal. Lieutenant-Colonel Neynoe[5], whom Crowe held in the highest disregard, and his staff, plus three companies of the 27th embarked on the *British Hero*, while the remaining seven companies occupied quarters on several transports viz. *Clarendon*, *Bacton*, *Doncaster* and *Mary*. Destined for Halifax, Nova Scotia, the small, unprotected convoy became separated en route but successfully reached their intended destination by 10 December. After just over a week in port, they left Halifax bound for Bermuda, there to await further orders.

It was this phase of the voyage that was to prove so fateful for some of the 1st Battalion and guide them to a destiny that would become one of the most significant events in the history of the regiment to date.

In mid-Atlantic the small convoy ran into trouble. Encountering ferocious gales, the ships became temporarily separated. Riding out the storm as best they could, they waited for the storm to abate, only to find that their command ship, the *British Hero*, was nowhere to be found. Under the circumstances it was eventually deemed prudent to continue their voyage to Bermuda and assume the *British Hero* would do likewise. However, this assumption proved incorrect. The vessel was blown so far off her intended course that she eventually reached Barbados some time during February 1815.

Little more is known of the *British Hero* until 29 June 1815 when at the island of St Thomas she tagged along with a convoy of seventy-eight vessels escorted by HMS *Crescent* bound for England. The *British Hero* eventually parted company with the convoy on 8 August off the Needles, en route to Portsmouth, thus arriving too late to take part in the Battle of Waterloo.

Meanwhile the 2nd Battalion, which had also left Bordeaux in late May 1814 en route to Ireland, had then proceeded to barracks at Gosport.

The seven companies of the 1st Battalion which had parted

company with their headquarters ship the *British Hero* eventually arrived at Bermuda in January 1815. However, by 18 February they were once more back at sea on board HMS *Statira* conducting operations along the coast of Cuba.

In near perfect conditions the ship ran aground on uncharted rocks off the coast of Cuba on 27 February and, despite the best efforts of the troops and crew, the ship foundered. However, it did not sink immediately, affording the troops and crew time to transfer to the transports which accompanied them. The convoy anchored off Port Royal, Jamaica, on 2 March.

By 5 March the troops were once more on the high seas, this time bound for Mobile, arriving there on 14 March 1815. On their arrival they were refused permission to land, peace having been declared between Great Britain and the United States. Unable to go ashore, they sailed the next day for Bermuda.

In the interim events in Europe had taken an unexpected turn. Napoleon Bonaparte's brief exile on the Isle of Elba came to an end as he sailed for France, intent upon dethroning Louis XVIII and taking control of his Empire once more. It was the closing act in a brilliant career, culminating in the final battle of the Napoleonic Wars, the Battle of Waterloo. Furthermore, it was the only occasion on which the Duke of Wellington and Napoleon Bonaparte actually faced each other on the field of battle.

Wellington found himself in the awkward position of having had his victorious veterans of the Peninsular War scattered throughout the globe. Many of those who had fought their way through the Iberian Peninsula had retired from the service and settled back to civilian life. The problem now facing him was assembling a force not only strong enough numerically but also experienced enough to take on Napoleon and his rejuvenated French army, the majority of whom eagerly anticipated the return of the Emperor.

Leaving Elba on 26 February 1815, Bonaparte landed at Var in France on 1 March. His landing was unopposed and enthusiastic crowds greeted him. Troops, demoralized by defeat, rallied to his flag. By 20 March he had entered Paris and the palace of Fontainebleau, as Louis XVIII abandoned his capital on hearing of the approach of Napoleon, who was once more offered the Empire and accepted.

From the outset Napoleon was aware his return would be unacceptable to both the British and their allies. Accordingly he set about reorganizing his once great army. His impressive Imperial Guard was re-established, his cavalry strengthened and his artillery, for many years the backbone of his army, enlarged and re-equipped.

Wellington, now faced with the growing prospect of having to face his old adversary once more, was under extreme pressure to gather a force strong enough to curb Napoleon's new-found virility. With the majority of his old regiments unavailable, he had to content himself with an army in which the British contingent was greatly out-numbered. This new, relatively inexperienced, army now consisted of Germans, Hanoverians, Brunswickers, Belgians, Dutch and Nassauers. Although good troops, seasoned they were not, something which drove Wellington to comment, "an infamous army, very weak and ill equipped".

With time of the essence, many regiments were recalled under instruction to make all possible haste for Europe. As a result, the 1st Battalion the 27th Inniskillings sailed from Bermuda bound for Portsmouth, arriving there on 9 May 1815.

However, even though the regiment was a veteran of the Peninsula, its troops were not. The greater part of the battle-hardened veterans had left the 27th at the cessation of hostilities, which now consisted mostly of young raw recruits.

To make matters worse, the strain of such a long sea voyage compounded the problem, as many of those that landed at Portsmouth were physically unfit to continue on to France. In all, it was necessary to take a draft of two hundred and eighty men from the ranks of the 2nd Battalion to replace those unfit for active service. Within a week of their arrival, however, the 1st Battalion set sail once more, bound for Ostend.

At this point Crowe has some interesting remarks to make about the 1st Battalion.

Seven Companies of our 1st Battalion arrived from America, having encountered tremendous weather in the Atlantic, where they lost sight of the Headquarters ship, with the other three Companies on board, and all were supposed to have gone to the bottom. It was really disgusting to hear the levity of remarks, on the chance of such an event proving true, and the great promotion resulting made with unblushing front by some individuals. So I will proceed. The arrival was reported to the War Office. And in reply an order arrived that seven companies were not to disembark, but be completed to one hundred men in each Company from our ranks, i.e. the 2nd Battalion were to proceed as quickly as possible to France. This order came sharp on us, for as Adjutant I was obliged to part with my servant, old Carter, to complete the number of effective men.

I cannot but mention the old man's career (for he was above 60 and more fitted for discharge than active service). He had been long in the regiment, but being a good bricklayer and mason, had all along been detained with the depot by Major Neynoe who found him a very useful tool in building Castle Neynoe, a white-bricked house, some twenty miles from Enniskillen, an excellent specimen, this, of "Irish Jobbing" even in military terms!!! Old Carter took leave of me with streaming eyes and a firm presage of his fate. In vain did I recount the many perils I had escaped, but I could not rally the poor fellow's spirits, and his premonition was but too true for a cannon-ball cut him in twain!

Although we did manage to furnish the number of men required, there was deficiency in officers, only sixteen instead of twenty-one. And no one with us belonged to the 1st Battalion. I volunteered my services, and requested my Colonel to sanction it. His reply was more than usually laconic. "Nonsense! You have seen enough; you will only get your head knocked off. You are my Adjutant and I shall not part with you!" Thus I was prevented from whitening the field of Waterloo with my bones! By the nip on the brow on Sir John Maclean, that there was strong resolve working in my mind. After some silence, in a firm resolute tone, he said "Go and send Lieutenant McLeod to me, then proceed to the Orderly Room and forward the embarkation returns as much as possible, for we have no time to lose. Yet leave the list of subalterns open till you hear from me by my Orderly." I obeyed. And McLeod embarked with the seven companies. Never was a greater act of justice done in the service! Sir John and the Lieutenant were both Scotch men. McLeod had married the sister of Major Neynoe, and by him had been kept at the depot throughout the war, as Paymaster, while others were fighting for his promotion.

As regards the 3rd Battalion, which had accompanied the 1st Inniskillings to St John's, it parted company with the 1st and moved on to quarters at Chambly, near Montreal, following the abortive action at Plattsburg. It wasn't until several weeks after the Battle of

Waterloo that the battalion arrived back in England. It also marked the return of Lieutenant-Colonel Neynoe, whose arrogance and pomposity made him instantly disagreeable in the eyes of Charles Crowe and many of his fellow officers.

About a fortnight after the seven companies had sailed for France, our 3rd Battalion also returned from America. And orders from the War Office, for us to transfer a stated number of men, cleared off every drill squad to whom I had given arms. Many of them had not fired off a musket. This event brought me into disagreeable collision with the great and pompous Major, now Lieutenant-Colonel Neynoe. He was continually obtruding my Orderly Room, giving orders about the intricate and troublesome embarkation returns, rejecting some more and nominating others. My clerks were puzzled and could not fulfil my orders. After he had caused me much delay, I was fortunately present when he repeated his officious visits and ordered me to make a variety of alterations. I listened to all his bluster, and quaintly replied, "Colonel Neynoe, this is the Orderly Room of the Second Battalion and I am acting under the orders of Sir John Maclean, without whose authority I cannot make any alterations. I must therefore refer you to him!" This was a decided closer! My clerks could proceed with the returns, for the self-important man never troubled them again. Nor would he, during our short stay, even speak to, or look at me! Sir John was greatly amused when I recounted the circumstances.

Although Crowe's dislike of the overbearing Neynoe is obvious, it adequately demonstrates that he was a man who did not suffer fools gladly. He was a man who had the ability to discern between those who earned respect and those who demanded it. Likewise, although a professional soldier, he was a deeply religious individual who could combine the rigours his profession demanded with a deep sense of compassion.

A very painful duty devolved to me, when embarking these raw soldiers. Most of them had brought young wives from Ireland. The War Office order granted only three wives per company. And the number actually on board the transports, according to the official returns was too great to allow many embarking. Sir John had to

139

draw lots for every company. I was obliged to have a serjeant's guard at the approach of the jetty from whence the men descended into boats to row off to Spithead. I was deeply engaged at the extreme of the jetty when a shout of horror made me look to the rear. A lovely young woman with a baby in her arms, had forced through the guard, and was rushing with the frenzy of desperation to throw herself and babe into the boat below to her husband! She was not ten yards distant, but instantly I ran and grasped her in my arms and having given myself a rotatory motion to check her impetus, the woman, baby and Adjutant were sprawling on the jetty! In this interval the boat had shoved off and the wretched lovely woman had no alternative but to return to Ireland with the government allowance per mile, with her numerous and equally disconsolate companions.

Chapter Eight

Arrival in Belgium

Without doubt all three battalions of the 27th (Inniskilling) Foot acquitted themselves admirably throughout the Peninsular and Napoleonic Wars, though it was to be the 1st Battalion which would forever earn itself a place in British military history as a direct consequence of its engagement in the final battle of the Napoleonic Wars, the Battle of Waterloo.

No sooner had the 1st Battalion arrived in Belgium on 24 May 1815 than they immediately took up their duties as part of the 10th (British) Infantry Brigade under the command of Major-General Sir John Lambert, KCB.[1] In doing so they joined the 1st/4th (King's Own), 2nd/81st Foot and the 1st/40th (Somersetshire), which, as the 10th Infantry Brigade, made up a section of General the Hon. Sir Lowry Cole's 6th English Division. Lowry Cole, however, was not present at the Battle of Waterloo as he had returned to England and was married on 15 June 1815.

Having just returned from America with all the deprivations and discomforts of a prolonged sea voyage, the Regiment was glad of a period of respite before being thrown into battle. The first duty assigned to the 27th was, as part of the 10th Infantry Brigade, to provide a guard for Louis XVIII[2], the recently unseated King of France, who, on being informed of Napoleon's advance on Paris, had fled to Belgium.

Billeted at Ghent in the days leading up to the decisive battle at Waterloo, the Regiment waited for orders to move out. At this point the strength of the 1st Battalion numbered in total 746, comprised of:

- Two captains.
- Fifteen subalterns.

141

- Thirty-four sergeants.
- Eight drummers.
- Six hundred and eighty-seven other ranks.

Now once more enthroned in his capital, Napoleon made the bold decision to make a pre-emptive strike upon the Anglo-Allied Army, as the troops under the Duke of Wellington were collectively known, on 15 June. It was his intention to make a swift and speedy assault upon Wellington's army before the Russians, who were yet a few days off, could join the main force.

Crossing the Belgian border with the intention of taking on the Anglo-Allied army before it had a chance to muster, he first set about attacking Quatre Bras, which at the time was held by a very under-strength garrison. Initially, Napoleon had a certain modicum of success but this was short-lived due to reinforcements arriving from Brussels, having been dispatched post-haste by Wellington.

However, Napoleon's second attempt brought more success. Ligny, which was held by the Prussians under the command of Field-Marshal von Blücher, Prince of Wahlstadt, fell to the French after a fierce battle. Nonetheless, his victory was hollow. Misinterpreting the situation, Napoleon wrongly assumed that the Prussians were a spent force and could be taken out of the equation.

Unfortunately Napoleon's miscalculation was further compounded by his desire to finish off the retreating Prussians. Dispatching Grouchy[3] in pursuit with the 3rd and 4th Corps and the cavalry of Excelman and Pajol, Bonaparte effectively balanced the equation by denying himself the use of these troops at a vital point in the battle, which was yet to come. This miscalculation would shortly return to haunt him on the battlefield of Waterloo.

Concerned at this turn of events, Wellington summoned Blücher and informed him that the Anglo-Allied troops under his command would fall back from Quatre Bras and hold a position near the village of Waterloo until the Prussians could rejoin him. Wellington had decided Waterloo would be the make or break venue for both armies.

As Wellington's troops retreated from Quatre Bras their rearguard was constantly harried at every opportunity by French cavalry. Although several attempts made by the 7th Hussars and the 23rd Light Dragoons proved ineffectual it wasn't until the Life Guards under the command of Lord Uxbridge were ordered into action, that the French were repulsed.

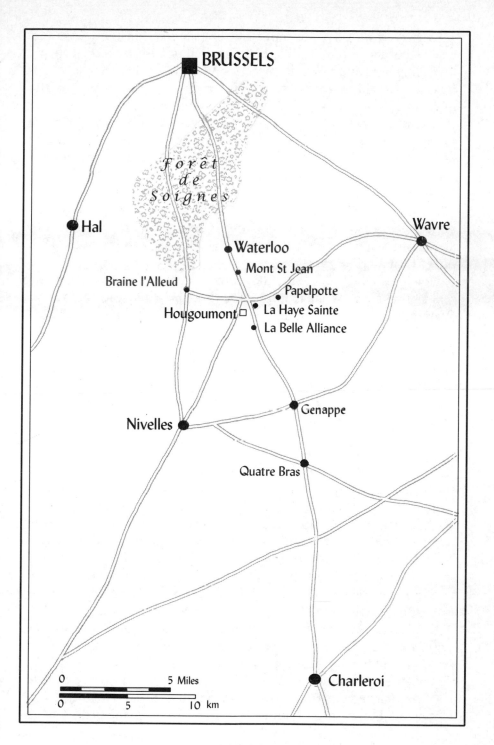

BRUSSELS

Forêt de Soignes

Hal

Wavre

Waterloo

Mont St Jean

Braine l'Alleud

Papelpotte

Hougoumont

La Haye Sainte

La Belle Alliance

Genappe

Nivelles

Quatre Bras

0   5 Miles

0   5   10 km

Charleroi

143

On the same day, 15 June, Major-General Sir John Lambert received orders from Wellington to move his 10th Infantry Brigade up from Ghent and make all speed for Waterloo, where it was to join forces with the main body of the army in preparation for the impending battle.

According to official papers and records held by the Regiment, there is a difference of opinion regarding the precise route the Inniskillings took on their road to Waterloo. According to one source, they marched from Ghent on 16 June, passing through Brussels on their way to Waterloo. Another source states that the 10th Infantry Brigade left Ghent on 15 June and first moved to Assche where they received a dispatch from Quatre Bras directing them to Genappe from where they force-marched on the morning of the 18th direct to Waterloo.

However, whichever route they took to arrive at Waterloo is of no real significance. What is important though is that they arrived at Waterloo in time to make such a contribution to Wellington's overall victory. There is one indisputable fact of which we can be certain: the Inniskillings were forced to make lengthy forced-marches over extremely awkward terrain, in atrocious weather conditions to reach their objective. Severe thunder and lightning storms combined with torrential rain, turned the Belgian chaussée into an almost impassable quagmire, making the passage of the troops all that more tedious.

As if that were not sufficient, the roads leading to Waterloo were littered with the paraphernalia of war. Carts, requisitioned by the army from local country-folk, slowed down the passage of the column. Laden down with provisions and ammunition for the troops, these carts churned up the already swamp-like conditions even further. Such congestion only went to exacerbate an already overused road system, blocking the main thoroughfares, whilst retreating locals also added to the mayhem by abandoning many of their own carts and belongings on hearing of the advance of the troops and the impending battle.

Realizing how important the roads were as a vital lifeline for the army and the success of the battle, Major-General Sir John Lambert set his men about the task of clearing a path which was to be kept clear before marching the 27th through the village in order to take up their assigned position on the extreme left of the Anglo-Allied line. However, before they could take up this position, orders were

144

received to proceed north of the farm of Mont St Jean. There, in a hollow, the brigade formed up in columns of companies, piled arms and settled down to rest and await further orders.

However, a major problem for any regiment out of the line was that they were subjected to the noise and thunder of battle whilst actually taking no active part. So, too, the 27th Inniskillings as they rested in the hollow, were confronted with the depressing vision of shell-shocked stragglers and wounded as they made their way to the rear, in the sure knowledge that their turn was soon to come.

The following poem by General T. Carlton Smith from his book entitled *Rude Rymes* gives a glimpse of what it must have been like for pratically every soldier on the eve of battle.

> Mysterious Power! Since Thou alone canst pour
> Blessings or sorrows on this mortal frame,
> O! Grant Thy servant's boon, he asks no more,
> Than such as sinners from Thy grace may claim.
>
> If doom'd to welter in my dying gore,
> Then sudden be the blow and short the pain:
> If blest with life, though bruis'd and mangled o'er,
> Grant Thou no ball may rend my limbs in twain.
>
> For thus to live were but to live in vain,
> With fate to murmur, and with grief to pine.
> Nor ask I life, if death Thou should'st ordain,
> Let short and instantaneous death be mine.
> Yet I'm resign'd to all, or good, or ill;
> Whate'er it prove, O! be Thou near me still![4]

A sober, rather melancholy poem it may be, yet one that voices the sentiment of every soldier on the eve of battle. If death was ordained then it was hoped it would be swift and clean. To be so badly mauled or mutilated as to be severely disabled for the remainder of their lives was not an option! However, the author of this particular poem may have had more preying on his mind than the average soldier!

Having served in the Royal Navy and been wounded three times before transferring to the 27th Inniskillings in 1813 may have had some bearing on his frame of mind at the time. As a point of interest, he was wounded yet again, in the leg, while serving with the Regiment as an Ensign at Waterloo and later through the trunk of the body during a duel, yet incredibly lived to the ripe old age of eighty-nine, an extremely lucky individual to say the least, considering the medical techniques in vogue in the early nineteenth century.

However, as the battle approached the following is a brief topographical description of the battlefield in relation to Wellington's army. It is an extract from the regimental history of the Royal Inniskilling Fusiliers and gives us a brief understanding of the lie of the land in which the battle was to be fought.

In a storm of thunder and rain, the common prelude to his victories in the peninsula, Wellington on the evening of the 17th had taken up a position along a narrow plateau, on a ridge about a mile and a half long. It formed the boundary of a gentle valley, at its broadest but fifteen hundred yards in width.

The main road from Charleroi and Genappe to Brussels ran from south to north across the valley, and cut through the position, dividing it into two almost equal portions. Behind the plateau, the ground sank gently to the farm of Mont St Jean, where Lambert's Brigade was halted. To the north (in rear) of this farm was the village of Waterloo, and behind it, still further to the northward, was the forest of Soignes, which lay athwart the high-road to Brussels.

Along the crest line of the ridge occupied by Wellington ran a sunken road, which crossed the highway at right angles. This sunken road varied in depth from six to ten feet; hedges grew on both its banks; its general direction was east and west, but on the left of the cross-roads it receded northward, and on the right it tended to the south.

Thus from the French or southern side of the valley Wellington's right appeared thrown forward, his centre straight, his left drawn back. Three advanced posts covered the front of the Duke's position. On the right, about four hundred yards from the main line, was the farm-house of Hougoumont, strongly built, surrounded by walls which enclosed an orchard, and screened from direct artillery fire by a wood, now cut down, extending about a quarter of a mile south of the building.

On the left the hamlet of Smohain and the farm of Papelotte served as outworks, about five hundred yards in advance of the main line. In the centre and near the cross-roads and less than three

146

hundred yards from the sunken road, the farm-house of La Haye Sainte stood on a hollow on the western edge of the chaussée; from is southern wall a large orchard sloped towards the French, and a garden, encircled by hedges, lay between its northern buildings and the British position. Almost opposite the farmhouse, but rather nearer the sunken road, were a gravel-pit and a bank or mound of earth, both important to the history of the Inniskillings.[5]

Chapter Nine

Waterloo

18 June 1815 had been preceded by several days of torrential rain and severe thunderstorms. Such was the relentless deterioration in the weather that the area in and around Waterloo had been turned into a seemingly impassable quagmire. The morning of the battle itself was dull and wet, as the Anglo-Allied troops took on the role of impassive onlookers as the French broke camp. Through the haze of early morning mist, which shrouded the landscape, the French could be observed moving into position on the opposite side of the valley in eleven massive columns. Their precision and conduct were viewed somewhat in awe by Wellington's army. Whereas the Allied Army, especially the British contingent, had taken up their assigned positions with their customary cool determination in the face of what might be their final battle, the French on the other hand were actually in a buoyant mood, fired no doubt by their recent engagements at Quatre Bras and Ligny, not to mention the impassioned exhortations of their newly returned Emperor.

To the fore two lines of infantry formed their first line of attack. Behind were positioned two lines of heavy cavalry. To their rear a reserve number of both cavalry and infantry stood in column behind the centre, whilst the extreme rear was manned by the pride of the French army, the Imperial Guard. These men were the cream of Napoleon's army, toughened veterans of the Peninsular War who stood in readiness to step in and turn the tide of battle if all else failed. Their presence was both a source of pride and encouragement to the remainder of the French Army, whilst intimidating to the Allied troops, not just the raw recruits, of which there were many, but even the most hardened veterans.

As for Wellington's troops, they were drawn up very much in a

148

similar formation to the French, though not so exposed. Two lines of infantry occupied a position on the plateau, though many were sheltered from direct fire because of the nature of the sunken road. Along the crest of the plateau Wellington had positioned his artillery and the cavalry occupied the third line of attack behind the infantry. To the rear of the left centre of the line were drawn up the 27th Inniskillings as part of Major-General Sir John Lambert's 10th Brigade, while a corps of Brunswickers was assembled in reserve.

At that moment both armies must have provided an awesome spectacle, resplendent in their vivid colours, breastplates gleaming, flags and banners held high. It was a sombre, if sobering thought that such a magnificent display of colour and precision would soon degenerate into a resemblance of Dante's inferno.

It has often been said that the Battle of Waterloo resembled a drama in five acts, each stage independent yet inextricably linked and dependent upon the next. This analogy is quite fitting, though it also resembled a game of chess with blood, two 'Kings' battling for supremacy with the infantrymen the expendable pawns. Each move throughout the day was in direct response to the opponent's counter-move.

Given the nature of the terrain in which the battle was to be contested, the key positions of advantage were the farmhouses. However, whilst most of those held by the Allied armies were well strengthened and fortified, one, La Haye Sainte, had been over-looked, with the result that it was totally unsuited to the needs of the Rifle Battalion of the King's German Legion assigned to occupy it, an opinion voiced by an officer expressing his concern at its lack of loop-holes and general readiness.

Three great apertures, which we made with difficulty when we were told in the morning that we were to defend the farm. Our pioneers had been sent to Hougoumont the night before.[1]

To appreciate fully the task entrusted to the 27th Inniskillings it is first necessary to understand something of the disposition of Wellington's troops. The following is an extract from the regimental history of the Royal Inniskilling Fusiliers, which graphically details the positions held by the various regiments at the outset of the battle.

149

It will be remembered that the high-road ran through Wellington's position from north to south, intersected at right angles, about three hundred yards to the south of the farm of La Haye Sainte, by the sunken road, the Allies' main line of resistance. In the northeastern angle, formed by the crossing of the roads, stood the Fifth Division, commanded by Lieutenant-General Sir Thomas Picton, GCB. His right brigade (Kempt's) rested on the chaussée; next came Pack's Brigade, but at a considerable distance from the left of Kempt's command; two Hanoverian brigades prolonged the line to the left, their outer flank covered by Vivian's and Vandeleur's cavalry brigades. In front of this part of the line, a brigade of Dutch-Belgians was posted on the southern slope of the ridge held by the Allies. In the north-west angle of the cross-roads was the left (Ompteda's) brigade of the King's German Legion, part of Alten's Division; to the right of Ompteda was Kielmansegge's Brigade of the same legion; and still further to the right was Halkett's[2] Brigade of British troops. It will thus be seen that Picton's right and Alten's left were alike charged with the duty of barring the approach to the road through the Allies' position.[3]

By examining the positioning of these brigades, the importance of the farm at La Haye Sainte and the cross-roads is obvious. If the French were to break through at this point, the whole of Wellington's line could be bisected. Thus, it was clear that this position had to be held at all costs. To allow the French to break through the Allied line could well have dictated the outcome of the battle.

In the course of the day when both General Sir James Kempt's[4] Brigade and Baron von Ompteda's[5] Brigade of the King's German Legion were both severely depleted, the 27th were drafted in to hold the key position at the cross-roads. This was to be their most costly action to date in terms of both men killed and wounded. Nevertheless it was also to go down in history as one of the Regiment's, if not the British Army's, most courageous stands.

11.30 a.m., 18 June 1815

The battle itself began at approximately 11.30 a.m. with a fierce French fusillade upon the Allied line of both cannon and musketry fire. No sooner had the barrage ceased, and before the smoke dissipated, than it was followed up by a fierce cavalry charge. Such would be the nature of the battle throughout the day – bombardments followed by charge after charge.

As previously stated, the Battle of Waterloo has been likened to a play in five acts, the first four consisting of fierce artillery barrages targeted upon various sections of the Anglo-Allied line, during which the infantry and cavalry remained dormant. These were instantaneously followed up by fierce charges upon those points in the Allied line already decimated by the artillery. The fifth and final act of this drama took the form of a last ditch all-out assault on Wellington's entire line.

For the purpose of clarification I will attempt to deal with each of these 'Acts' as they occurred. However, the following bullet points detail the events in a more abridged fashion:

- The first of the French assaults by General Honoré Reille[6], which began at 11.30 in the morning and continued all day, targeted the farm of Hougoumont. At the same time as this was taking place Napoleon ordered Marshal Ney to launch an assault on the left and left centre of the Allied line in the hope that by doing so they would break through to the rear of La Haye Sainte and thus occupy a commanding position on the road to Brussels.
- The next phase, which occurred around 2 p.m. in the afternoon, was an attempt by Count Drouet D'Erlon to turn the left flank and dislodge General Sir Thomas Picton's Division from the position it was assigned to hold on the left centre. However, whilst this was taking place and as Ney[7] organized this offensive, an advanced guard of Prussians was observed emerging from the woods on the extreme right of the French position. In an attempt to counteract this new threat to his line Napoleon detailed two cavalry divisions, numbering nearly ten thousand men, to engage the Prussians, thus effectively taking them out of the assault on Wellington's line.
- The third stage of the battle occurred between the hours of four and six in the afternoon. This took the form of a series of French cavalry charges on the Allied infantry squares. Napoleon ordered Reille to continue his vigorous attack on the farmhouse at Hougoumont, whilst two columns of General Donzelot's infantry division assaulted the Anglo-Allied army's weak point, La Haye Sainte. As if to compound

151

matters even further, it was also about this time that the Prussians, under Marshal Blücher, arrived on the battlefield to link up with Wellington's British troops on the extreme left of the line.

- The fourth episode occurred with Marshal Ney's attack on the centre of Wellington's line. It was also around this time, 6 p.m., that the farmhouse of La Haye Sainte fell to the French.
- The final phase and concluding act of the drama occurred about 7.30 p.m. when Napoleon risked everything in an all-out assault along the entire length of Wellington's line. In a last-ditch throw of the dice to try to win the day, Napoleon committed his elite force, the Imperial Guard, which until then had been held in reserve. This hardened band of Peninsular War veterans was seemingly invincible and on their shoulders rested the future of Napoleon himself.

1.30 p.m., 18 June 1815

Napoleon considered the fall of the farmhouse of La Haye Sainte crucial to his overall strategy. Thus, early in the day while Reille assaulted the château at Hougoumont, Marshal Ney prepared a force of some sixteen thousand men to attack the left and centre of Wellington's line. As Ney organized this huge force of four massive columns, each twenty-four ranks deep, orders were given for the French artillery to lay down a barrage on the Allied line. As a result seventy-four French artillery pieces were advanced to a raised area between the two armies. The French guns thus held a commanding position within three hundred yards of La Haye Sainte and six hundred from the Anglo-Allied line. These strategically placed French guns wreaked havoc on the Allies as they lent covering support to Marshal Ney's advancing columns.

As the French infantry columns advanced they encountered little opposition from the Dutch-Belgians who retreated before them, thus exposing the British left centre held by two brigades of Sir Thomas Picton's Division. The commitment of these Dutch-Belgian troops had long been suspect in the eyes of Wellington, as it was known that many, as close neighbours of the French were, if not open supporters of Napoleon, at least indifferent.

152

A corps of nearly eighteen thousand Dutch-Belgians swelled the numbers, but diminished the efficiency of the army, for the rank and file were in sympathy with the French, and on the battlefield, with a few exceptions, they proved worse than useless.[8]

Wellington's displeasure with the conduct of such troops in the face of the enemy was barely concealed in a communiqué to the entire army after the battle.

Two days after the battle the Duke issued a General Order of thanks to the troops couched in such ambiguous terms that it is clear he was thinking as much of the misconduct of some of the foreign contingents as of the noble behaviour of his fellow countrymen. "The Field Marshal takes this opportunity of returning thanks to the army for their conduct in the glorious action fought on the 18th inst.; he will not fail to report his sense of their conduct in the terms which it deserves, to their several sovereigns." Wellington expressed his view in such unmistakable clearness to at least one crowned head that he added a request that certain paragraphs in his despatch might not be published.[9]

As a direct result of such a lack of enthusiasm for the fight displayed by the Dutch-Belgians, Picton's two brigades under the command of Kempt and Pack were severely outnumbered by approximately four to one, having lost many of their men at Quatre Bras in the prelude to Waterloo. Even though they made a valiant attempt to stem the flow of the advancing French, there was very little they could do in the face of such overwhelming strength. In an effort to launch a counter-strike, Picton, while rallying his troops, was shot through the head and killed. Nevertheless his troops were successful in holding the right. Unfortunately, the rest of the line was not so successful, as General Allix's brigade made a breakthrough dissecting the Allied line with almost disastrous repercussions.

Had it not been for the timely intervention of Sir William Ponsonby's Union Brigade of cavalry, consisting of the Royals, the Scots Greys and the 6th Inniskilling Dragoons, the consequences could have been dire. A blood-curdling charge by Ponsonby's[10] cavalry overwhelmed Napoleon's mass of artillery but unfortunately, whether as a result of their enthusiasm or the heat of the battle, or both, they were taken by surprise by two French Infantry regiments, thereby suffering heavy casualties. Numbered amongst those lost was their commander, Sir William Ponsonby. At the same instant Lord Edward Somerset led the Household Brigade of cavalry against those French troops who threatened the chaussée.

With the advance of Ponsonby's cavalry to drive out Allix's Brigade the 27th Inniskillings, as part of Lambert's 10th Brigade, were brought up to occupy a position on the left of the road to Brussels. At this time they were placed in the rear in support of Picton's Division, but it wasn't long before Lambert was called upon to reinforce this division, it having passed under the command of Kempt when Picton was killed.

At this point in the battle, while the 27th were kept in reserve, there appears an interesting observation recorded in the Regimental History. It was made by Captain E. W. Drewe who served at Waterloo with the 27th as a young subaltern and who was severely wounded during the action.

> Many of the Regiment went to sleep, unconscious and apparently careless of the part they were about to take. Several of them were wounded by a few straggling shots that passed from the enemy over and through our advanced lines, and a few were killed. At about a quarter past three o'clock, the welcome and anxiously sought for tidings of advance reached us; every man grasped his firelock and moved forward with a decided, firm and confident step, passing close to and by the left of the farm of Mont St Jean, crossing the short valley, and proceeded to ascend the gradually rising ground on the left of the Brussels road and close to the cross-road leading to Wavre. On reaching this station we formed columns of companies at quarter distance, left flank to the enemy, the Fourth regiment on the right, the Fortieth on the right, and both considerably in the rear of the Twenty-Seventh, which accounts for the few casualties in these corps, comparatively speaking, with the Twenty-Seventh, as they were in great measure covered by the rising ground in front, while the Twenty-Seventh was exposed, from being on the high ground, to all that came.[11]

Such letters, unfortunately, are rare. As the Regimental History rightly comments, letters that were obviously in existence in the weeks and months following the battle have unfortunately not come

154

into the hands of the Regiment. What we must rely upon when cataloguing the events which surrounded the Regiment on 18 June 1815 is corroborating testimonies recorded by individuals belonging to other regiments who witnessed the fate of the 27th Inniskillings that day.

Chapter Ten

The 27th Square

The Duke of Wellington and Napoleon Bonaparte, whilst both brilliant commanders, differed greatly in the quality and perception of their tactics and abilities.

Whereas Wellington was the epitome of the steady, dependable, thorough tactician, Napoleon was the charismatic leader of men who believed solely in his own ability and the power he possessed over men to have them follow him unquestioningly, even when the outcome was anything but clear.

Thus we have in the Duke of Wellington a man whose principle in this instance was one of caution. He was prepared to set his stall out, so to speak, as one of initial all-out defence while patiently waiting and relying upon his opponent's reputation as an all-out protagonist to manifest itself. Therefore, while the Allied forces under Wellington laid the ground and waited, all the actual moves were made by Napoleon. Wellington was happy to bide his time and allow Napoleon to come to him. In the end this more than anything settled the outcome of the Battle of Waterloo.

Throughout the course of 18 June 1815 the 27th were sometime in reserve, sometime displaced throughout the entire line and sometime formed up in square.

Although it is recorded that Lambert's 10th Brigade was not actually subjected to the brunt of the French cavalry charges, the 27th were nevertheless subjected to frequent cavalry attacks. As Major Mill of the 40th Foot, which also comprised part of Lambert's Brigade, can testify, the hours between four and six in the afternoon were especially horrendous.

A very tremendous cannonade was commenced by the French on our lines, and uninterruptedly continued. We lay down in square to escape as far as possible its destructive effects. Half the Inniskillings were mowed down in a similar position, without having the power or opportunity to return a shot. At one time the officer commanding the Twenty-Seventh, when there was temporary cessation from artillery, rode up to our major, and announced the fact of having barely an officer left to command each company. Major Browne offered to lend him some from the Fortieth. This, however, was imperatively declined. "The sergeants of the regiment," he said, "liked to command the companies, and he would be loathe to deprive them of the honour." Whenever there was an intermission in this fire, it was to find ourselves surrounded and beset by hordes of horsemen, who were slashing and cutting at our kneeling ranks. The file firing of our standing ranks, being concentrated and constant, was very effectual against their attacks, and both horse and rider were to be constantly discerned rolling over on to the plain, and the remainder flying back in disorder to their own lines.[1]

A cynic could possibly interpret Major Mills' statement in a totally different light from that intended. He could voice the opinion that there was no real courage displayed on the part of the 27th, given that so many were mown down before they even had the chance to realise what was about to take place. This is indeed true; many met their deaths within a very short time. However, with so many of their number killed and wounded, it must have taken extraordinary courage to stand fast and remain at their post in the face of such pressure. As their numbers dwindled due to death and wounding, so the courage required to stand their ground against wave after wave of French cavalry must have stretched the remainder to the limit.

To fully understand and appreciate the position of the 27th Foot on that day the above must be put into perspective. It must be remembered that the vast majority within the rank and file of the 27th Inniskillings were little more than raw recruits, who until that day had scarcely witnessed a shot fired in anger let alone been engaged in a battle of such significance. Indeed there were very few veterans of the Peninsular War to whom they could look for support or guidance. Add to that the fact that they had spent the previous few months at sea, and we have a picture of very inexperienced Fusiliers being thrown unprepared into the thick of the fight.

6 p.m., 18 June 1815

By 6 p.m., the ammunition supplies at the farmhouse of La Haye Sainte having been exhausted, it became clear that the post was now untenable and would have to be abandoned. It had withstood onslaught after onslaught throughout that long day, at a terrible cost in human life, but it was clear by late afternoon it could no longer hold out and that it would inevitably fall to the French. Thus the survivors of Major George Baring's Battalion of the King's German Legion were forced to evacuate the position. Having driven back units of Foy's[2] and Bachelu's Divisions the defenders of La Haye Sainte could no longer hold out as Ney entered the assault. Out of ammunition, Baring's troops were forced to abandon the position and fall back.

In doing so the French were quick to seize upon their departure and soon set about bolstering up the fortifications, knowing well the importance of the farmhouse to both protagonists and aware that a counter-attack before they could secure the position was imminent.

Subsequently, when General Sir James Kempt attempted to do precisely that, his efforts failed, mainly due to the fact that the battle had progressed to such a stage that troops could not be diverted into this action, given that every available man was already in the thick of the fight. He is recorded as having reported to Wellington that he was unable to get assistance from the 27th, stating that he

> requested Lambert to cross the great road with the Twenty-Seventh and retake La Haye Sainte, but at this period it was found to be impracticable, all the infantry in this part of the position being formed in squares, and the enemy's cavalry around them. I directed all the broken ground that offered the least cover to be completely lined with troops, but in addition to this I found it absolutely necessary to increase our fire by moving up the greater part of the Twenty-Seventh, which Lambert posted in as good a position as circumstances would permit, but it was unavoidably much exposed. The Regiment behaved nobly and suffered exceedingly.[3]

This was not a criticism, as one might assume, of Lambert or the 27th. Rather it was an honest appraisal of the situation as it appeared at the time. As can be observed from his despatch to Wellington, the

27th were under such excessive pressure already that it was impossible, if not down right foolhardy, to divert them from their position in the line. Theirs was the most exposed, most vulnerable and most vital of all the positions at that time, which had to be held at all costs.

One consequence of the fall of La Haye Sainte to the French was that the 27th suffered appalling casualties. French skirmishers were now in a position to occupy the high ground to the front and flank of the farmhouse from where they could inflict heavy losses on the static position held by the Inniskillings. This was to be very much the case right up until the general advance of Wellington's army later in the day, a period during which the 27th would be forced to stand and suffer a musketry onslaught with little hope of effective reply.

An officer with Halkett's Brigade which had closed in to the left of the 27th square is reported as saying:

> At about 6 o'clock I perceived some artillery trotting up the hill . . . I hardly mentioned this to a brother officer when two guns unlimbered within seventy paces of us and by their first discharge of grape blew seven men into the centre of the square. They immediately reloaded and kept up a constant and destructive fire. We would willingly have charged these guns, but had we deployed, the cavalry that flanked them would have made an example of us.[4]

An officer of the 95th Rifles commented on the scene:

> The French sharpshooters clustered thick in the sand pit and behind the knoll and bank of earth; the British manned the sunken road and the hedges which grew upon its banks. The distance between its firing lines was barely a hundred yards, and more than once parties of French tirailleurs sprang from the cover behind which they knelt and advanced towards the hedge, headed by their officers, with vehement gestures. But our fire was so very hot and steady that they almost instantly ran back behind the crest of the hill, always leaving a great many killed or disabled behind them. During this musketry contest, which I firmly believe was the closest and most protracted also ever witnessed, some apprehension was entertained that the French would endeavour to force their way along the chaussée and attack the rear of the troops lining the thorn hedge, and on a report of the kind being made to me by one of our officers, coupled with a suggestion that a part of the Ninety-fifth

Riflemen should be concentrated on the extreme right, so as to fire into the road, my reply was, "The Twenty-Seventh is in square in our rear, and that regiment must protect our rear, for the French are gathering so fast and thick in our front that we cannot spare a single man to detach to the right."[5]

The positioning of the 27th in such an exposed area, whilst perilous in the extreme for those concerned, was nevertheless becoming increasingly vital to the overall outcome of the day. As the afternoon progressed into early evening, the ground held so tenaciously by the Inniskillings came under increasingly severe pressure. Lambert's strategy, however, was sound. His reasoning in placing the Inniskillings more or less out on a limb was two-fold, reasons which would become only too apparent as the battle unfolded.

Positioned as they were with the right face of their square parallel to the chaussée, they were fully prepared to meet the advancing French should they succeed in breaking through at that point and forcing their way along the road. Similarly, should the French overwhelm what was left of Ompteda's brigade at the crossroads then the 27th were equally prepared to confront them with a flanking fire. Although prepared for any contingency, it was the second which the Inniskillings were called upon to carry out.

As the day wore on it became increasingly evident to Napoleon that if success were to be achieved then it was essential the French should take the cross-roads. Equally it was clear that, once taken, to secure such a key position it was imperative that the 27th should be dislodged from their position.

However, as circumstances ordained, it was the brigades on the right of the Inniskillings which broke formation and fell back under the weight of the French skirmishers. In doing so the Inniskillings were forced to hold their section of the Allied line entirely on their own. To have broken and fallen back at that particular moment would have spelt disaster for the Allied cause. Fortunately, by holding its position and formation, the 27th provided Wellington with a much-needed breathing space during which the King's German Legion and the Hanoverians had time to regroup and push the French back off the ground they had so recently acquired.

It is an undisputed fact that the entire line could have been breached with disastrous consequences had it not been for the steadfastness of the Inniskillings. By their valiant action they undoubtedly saved the day. However, more cynical commentators on the day's proceedings have suggested that the 27th hardly fired a shot throughout the entire battle.

The Regimental History refutes this slander emphatically and says that fresh ammunition was readily at hand in the pouches of the killed and wounded and that, indeed, fresh supplies were brought up later in the day. Common sense would dictate that no regiment could have withstood such a vicious onslaught by the French so resolutely without engaging the enemy. At this juncture the best comment comes from their commander in the field, General Lambert in a communiqué to his divisional commander pointing out specifically the 27th:

> The steady and gallant conduct of the Twenty-Seventh under Major Hare, unavoidably exposed for several hours to a galling fire, is well known to you, and much to be praised, and I should be much obliged to you to name him to the officer commanding the forces particularly.[6]

Again in letters to Captain William Siborne, author of *Waterloo Letters*, he states:

> After the enemy had got possession of La Haye Sainte, they kept constantly sending small detachments to a mound, close to the intersection of the Brussels road to Genappe, which forced the Hanoverian Brigade of the Sixth Division to fall back, and which would have allowed the enemy to advance, if it had not been for the square of the Twenty-Seventh, as its position will point out. This mound should appear, it strikes me, as it was so important in that part of the line, and so honourable and fatal to the Twenty-Seventh, which kept its formation and lost more men and officers than any regiment during the day, and would otherwise have afforded an opportunity to the enemy to have made an impression in a very serious part of the line.[7]

7 p.m., 18 June 1815

By seven o'clock in the evening it was apparent to all that the 27th had held what was an almost impossible position against horrendous odds. Even though they had suffered greatly from repeated French attacks the battle was far from over.

161

The following is an extract from *Adventurers in the Rifle Brigade* by Captain J. Kincaid which graphically depicts the scene of desolation on he battlefield at Waterloo around seven o'clock, just half an hour before Napoleon ordered his prized Imperial Guard into action in a last-ditch attempt to break Wellington's line. He was about to place the entire outcome of the battle, and the future of his empire for that matter, on these apparently invincible veterans.

I shall never forget the scene which the field of battle presented about seven in the evening. I felt weary and worn out, less from fatigue than anxiety. Our division, which had stood upwards of five thousand men at the commencement of the battle, had gradually dwindled down into a solitary line of skirmishers. The Twenty-Seventh regiment were lying literally dead, in square, a few yards behind us. My horse had received another shot through the leg, and one through the flap of the saddle, which lodged in his body, sending him a step beyond the pension list. The smoke still hung so thick about us that we could see nothing. I walked a little way to each flank to endeavour to get a glimpse of what was going on, but nothing met my eyes except the mangled remains of men and horses, and I was obliged to return to my post as wise as I went.

I have never yet heard of a battle in which everybody was killed, but this seemed likely to be an exception, as all were going by turns. We got excessively impatient under the tame similitude of the latter part of the process, and burned with desire to have a last thrust at our respective *vis-à-vis*; for, however desperate our affairs were, we had still the satisfaction of seeing that theirs were worse. Sir John Lambert continued to stand as our support, at the head of three good old regiments, one dead (the Twenty-Seventh) and two living ones; and we took the liberty of soliciting him to aid our views; but the Duke's orders on that head were so very particular that the gallant general had no choice.

Presently a cheer, which we knew to be British, commenced far to the right, and made every one prick up his ears; it was Lord Wellington's long-wished-for orders to advance; it gradually approached, growing louder as it grew near; we took it up by instinct, charged through the hedge down upon the old knoll, sending our adversaries flying at the point of the bayonet. Lord Wellington galloped up to us at the instant, and our men began to cheer him; but he called out, "No cheering, my lads, but forward, and complete your victory!"[8]

Although, according to this account of the final stage of the battle, such incidents occurred around seven o'clock in the evening, it is generally understood that Napoleon made his final attempt to divide Wellington's line around seven thirty; therefore the proceedings above must have occurred later. This is quite understandable, given the mayhem and confusion of battle. It is not always possible to judge correctly times, or even incidents, during the heat and confusion of battle.

Likewise it is an understandable exaggeration to insinuate that the entire strength of the 27th had been wiped out whilst standing in square. Considering the number of dead and wounded they did sustain, it is no small wonder Captain Kincaid assumed they had been entirely destroyed.

Chapter Eleven

Napoleon's Last Throw

As the day's gruesome proceedings drew to a close, Napoleon was keenly aware that time was running out. The longer he delayed a final push the more likely it was that Wellington would receive new impetus with the arrival of fresh troops.

Both armies had been decimated, as attack after attack took its toll of both the French and Allied troops alike throughout that long day. The scene on the battlefield was one of total devastation. The mangled remains of men and horses littered the field as the cries of pain from the wounded and dying mingled with the exhortations of the living. Cries of *"Vive l'Empereur"* were met with cheers from Wellington's line as his troops attempted to stem the seemingly unending flood of French.

As with a game of chess, each move of the opposing force was calculated either to gain an advantage or to ward off a disaster. The arrival of the Prussians commanded by Marshal Blücher heightened the pressure on Napoleon to act. It was now evident that the only thing that could win the day was success against the British or relief in the form of Grouchy and his troops.

7.30 p.m., 18 June 1815

Napoleon, realizing the day would most certainly be lost if he failed to act, and act decisively, ordered a general attack upon the entire Anglo-Allied line. The time had come for all or nothing. He was now prepared to play his trump card, the Imperial Guard. Reluctant to risk their participation at any earlier stage, it was now imperative that they act and, in doing so, fire his remaining troops with a renewed zeal and enthusiasm for the cause.

164

As the French General Foy is reputed to have said after the battle, concerning the conduct of the British infantry:

> Wounded, vehicles, reserve ammunition trains, auxiliary troops, were hurrying in confusion towards Brussels. The angel of death was ever before their eyes and busy in their ranks. Disgrace was behind them. In these terrible circumstances, neither the bullets of the Imperial Guard nor the victorious French cavalry could break the immovable British infantry. One could have inclined to believe that they had taken root in the ground, if the battalions had not, some minutes after sunset, moved forward in grand array.[1]

Such sentiments could well be applied to the behaviour of the 27th Inniskilling as they stood resolutely in square.

When the order to advance came, the pride of the French army, the Imperial Guard, under the command of Ney, moved forward, ten battalions strong, supported by every available man capable of wielding a weapon. While the Imperial Guard moved against Wellington's right centre between La Haye Sainte and Hougoumont, their advance was covered by a ferocious musketry fusillade from the tirailleurs against the 5th Division. Simultaneously huge columns of French infantry pressed forward in support of the Imperial Guard.

As these veterans of the Peninsular War went forward, they failed to appreciate the nature of the terrain. Pressing onwards towards the crest of the ridge on which Wellington had positioned his line they were constantly bombarded by the Allied artillery, which wreaked havoc among their ranks with canister fire. But yet they pressed on.

On cresting the ridge they were unaware that the British Guards lay in wait. As the Imperial Guard reached the summit they were met by a fierce volley of musket fire as the Household Division of the British Guards were ordered forward to meet them. The result was a rout. The Imperial Guard broke ranks and retreated along the path upon which they had just come, straight into the Middle Guard who had been in their rear, causing confusion.

The ensuing retreat caused panic to spread among Napoleon's remaining troops. If the Imperial Guard, whom they had come to believe were invincible, were routed, what possible chance had they now? As the 27th, as part of Lambert's 10th British Infantry Brigade, followed up the retreating French a general cry of *sauve qui peut* was taken up throughout the French army.

As Napoleon's troops retreated in disarray Wellington's line closed in from the extreme points at Merbe Braine and Braine L'Alleud to form a half-crescent rather than their conventional line, thus roping in the retreating French. As the retreat turned into an all-out rout the 27th continued their advance as far as La Belle Alliance. The Prussian cavalry, however, more unforgiving of a defeated foe, continued to harass and slaughter the straggling French long into the night.

All was lost. Napoleon, on observing the defeat of his prized Imperial Guard and the rout of his army, is reported as saying before he left the field for Charleroi, "*A présent c'est fini! Sauvons nous.*"

The aftermath of the battle is difficult to visualize with our present day perception of twenty-first century warfare. Considering that the Battle of Waterloo lasted no more than eight or nine hours in total, the casualty figures are horrendous.

> Could the melancholy appearance of this scene of death be heightened, it would be by witnessing the researches of the living, amid its desolation, for the objects of their love. Mothers and wives and children for days were occupied in that mournful duty; and the confusion of the corpses, friend and foe intermingled as they were, often rendered the attempt at recognising individuals difficult, and, in some cases, impossible.
>
> In many places the dead lay four deep upon each other, marking the spot some British square [27th Inniskillings] had occupied, when exposed for hours to the murderous fire of a French battery. Outrider, lancer and cuirassier were scattered thickly on the earth. Madly attempting to force the serried bayonets of the British, they had fallen in the fruitless essay, by the musketry of the inner files. Farther on, you traced the spot where the cavalry of France and Britain had encountered. Chasseur and hussar were intermingled; and the heavy Norman horse of the Imperial Guard were interspersed with the grey chargers which had carried Albion's cavalry. Here the Highlander and tirailleur lay, side by side together; and the heavy dragoon, with "green Erin's" badge upon his helmet [6th Inniskilling Dragoons], was grappling in death with the Polish lancer.[2]

It is not the intention of this book to belittle the contribution and sacrifice exhibited by the numerous other British infantry or cavalry regiments during the battle, nor to apportion credit where it is not due. The sacrifice of the Allied forces is testimony enough of their bravery, bravery which is equally applicable to the French, adequately borne out by their persistent attempts to follow Bonaparte's orders to assault the Allied lines.

It must surely have been a sobering thought for all those who survived to hear their names called out by their sergeants as they took the final roll call that they should count themselves lucky not to be numbered among the dead and missing, considering the slaughter that had ensued.

If we take the position at the château of Hougoumont as a microcosm of the entire field of battle, the numbers killed and wounded in that one particular section of the field, over such a short period, is staggering.

> The attack against the position of Hougoumont lasted, on the whole, from twenty-five minutes before twelve until a little past seven at night. Within half an hour one thousand five hundred men were killed in the small orchard at Hougoumont, not exceeding four acres. The loss to the enemy was enormous. The division of General Foy alone lost about three thousand; and the total loss of the enemy in the attack of this position is estimated at ten thousand killed and wounded. About six thousand men of both armies perished in the farm of Hougoumont; six hundred British were killed in the wood; twenty-five in the garden; one thousand one hundred in the orchard and meadow; four hundred men near the farmer's garden; two thousand of both parties behind the great orchard. The bodies of three hundred British were buried opposite the gate of the château; and those of six hundred French were buried at the same place.[3]

The aftermath of such a hotly contested battle can only be imagined. Death and destruction were evident everywhere. The broken remains of military paraphernalia and bodies littered the churned-up earth as the rain continued to fall. The cries of the wounded and dying must surely have made many a sane man wonder at the absolute futility of the entire affair. What could justify such a field of carnage? Surely one man's pride and ambition could not warrant such misery.

167

The luxurious crop of ripe grain which had covered the field of battle was reduced to litter, and beaten into the earth; and the surface, trodden down by the cavalry, and furrowed deeply by the cannon wheels, strewn with many a relic of the fight. Helmets and cuirasses, shattered firearms and broken swords; all the variety of military ornamentation; lancer caps and Highland bonnets; uniforms of every colour, plume and pennon; musical instruments, the apparatus of artillery, drums, bugles; but good God! Why dwell on the harrowing picture of a "foughten field"? Each and every ruinous display bore mute testimony to the misery of such a battle.[4]

The casualty figures for the 1st Battalion the 27th Inniskillings bear silent witness to their participation. According to the regimental records there was a discrepancy in the number of killed and wounded recorded after the battle but this is quite understandable given the confusion which must have been apparent everywhere. The final casualty figures were not settled upon until 13 April 1816. According to that report the disposition of the casualties is as follows:

- Eighty-three were killed in action.
- Thirty-four died of wounds.
- Sixteen underwent amputations.
- Forty-eight were discharged as unfit for further service.
- Nine were transferred to invalid battalions.
- One remained in hospital at that time.
- Two hundred and thirty-six had recovered from their wounds and returned to the colours.

As a result of the findings of this report it has been ascertained that out of a total complement of seven hundred and twenty-nine other ranks engaged in the Battle of Waterloo four hundred and twenty-seven were either killed or wounded.

The casualties suffered by the commissioned ranks of the Inniskillings were no better. Out of a total of eighteen officers present two were killed and fifteen wounded, but again there is a discrepancy. According to the Regiment at the time, the figures recorded on the "morning state" gave a complement of twenty-two, while Colonel Lemuel Warren's report dated 19 November 1816 gives the names of eighteen surviving officers with two additional reported as killed, which gives a total of twenty and a discrepancy of one. Unfortunately the "morning state" does not record the names of those officers present on the field of battle on the morning of 18 June 1815.

According to the Army List for 1827 Lieutenant Andrew Gardiner had joined the 27th Inniskillings prior to 1815 but for some inexplicable reason the letter "W", signifying his participation in the Battle of Waterloo, was omitted from the Army List until 1822. It is generally accepted however, that Lieutenant Gardiner remained behind to clear the road north of the village and thus was unable to take his place in the square. According to the regimental records, as there is no evidence that this officer was extra-regimentally employed during the battle, his name has been included in the number present, twenty-one in total, and been recorded as such in Appendix I.

In percentage terms the numbers of the 27th Inniskillings recorded as both killed and wounded are staggering. The percentage of casualties among the rank and file numbered fifty-nine per cent, while the percentage among officers was seventy-one. No other single British regiment suffered casualties to the same extent as the 27th, in total an overall percentage of sixty-eight.

All in all, the casualties sustained by the British troops excluding the German Legion and the Hanoverians amounted to four hundred and sixty officers killed or wounded and six thousand and sixty-four other ranks. The total in all amounted to six thousand, five hundred and twenty-four either killed in action, died of wounds or wounded.

An officer in Picton's Division gives us a sombre insight into conditions on the battlefield on the morning of 19 June 1815, especially the area in which the Inniskillings held their square:

I then bent my steps to the spot on the great road which had been so fiercely contested the day before – I mean the ground above the small pass formed by the chaussée, running up the slope and cut through it. Every circumstance confirmed the idea which had previously formed of the noble devotion of the combatants on both sides. The killed and wounded of the British consisted chiefly of the 27th, 40th, 23rd, and 33rd, and they were neither few nor far between. I stood looking over an old grey-haired veteran of the 27th, who lay on his face (if face it could be called – for half of it, with the upper portion of the skull, had been carried away by a round shot); here was the cup of glory filled to the brim! The above regiments, or rather perhaps the detachments advanced from

169

them, had no breastwork, whereas the enemy had some shelter from the shape of the ground. I proceeded to the brow, and there lay the brave fellows of the advance, who made so gallant a resistance, many of them with their flintlocks in their hands, their fingers on the guard, just as they died, all within a few paces of their equally gallant antagonists . . . Sir John Lambert posted them in the road, saying he had given them the post of honour. They died fighting almost muzzle to muzzle. The brave, the gallant 27th! The ground was strewn with your dead.[5]

Chapter Twelve

A Raw Deal

The recognition and acknowledgement of the heroic deeds performed by the 27th at the Battle of Waterloo is an issue which has been overlooked for far too long. It is an oversight which has been perpetuated by succeeding generations while, as previously stated, the lion's share of the credit has gone to more 'fashionable' regiments.

Although not present at Waterloo, Crowe rightly voices the opinion held by many at the time and since that the less fashionable regiments present on that day were given a raw deal. Bravery comes from the heart; it has absolutely nothing whatsoever to do with rank or position.

Six hundred and ninety men (for one man who had re-enlisted was absent without leave; drunkenly spending his Bounty in Isle of Wight) and seventeen officers sailed to bear their part at Waterloo. Formed in square in the centre of the British Army, endured the brunt of the whole day. Thrice did the Duke of Wellington ride up to the little square of the 27th Regiment, calling out – "Make room for me, lads!" I am very sorry I have no official returns from which I can recount the loss of this small corps on that bloody day, but it is very much greater, according to their numbers, than any other regiment in the field. Ensign Kater was on baggage guard, and of the sixteen officers present Lieutenant Betty was the only one unscathed! Chief of them killed or were wounded a second time. Lieutenant Miller lost the sight of his right eye by the wound of a musket ball. A bandage was applied and he returned to his post but a severe wound obliged him to return to the rear.

Ensign Ireland, a tall muscular Irishman, who as Serjeant Major of our 3rd Battalion had been through all the Peninsular War declared he had been in many a hard-fought battle, but this was the worst he had ever witnessed, to stand still all day to be shot at was most irksome and trying! Within the next half hour this poor fellow was killed! Everyone who has been in the field of battle will accord to poor Ireland's remark. But the little gallant band of Enniskilleners is only mentioned by their desperate loss in killed and wounded, whereas, in reading the history of the Battle of Waterloo, a civilian is led to imagine the Guards and Hussars fought the whole of the hard fight!!! "Palmam qui meruit ferat" and here I will leave this topic, or I shall be drawn into remarks about the invidious distribution of *Medals*!

Clearly, as a member of the Inniskillings, Crowe harboured a barely concealed sense of indignation that the sacrifice of his regiment should have been demeaned to such an extent, that credit was not accorded where credit was surely due.

Even as news slowly filtered back to England the outcome of the battle was uncertain.

At the early morning's drill our Quartermaster's Serjeant, returning from Portsmouth, told me the account he had read of the battle and that the English Army was in full retreat on Brussels. At post hour, I imparted to the Colonel the news as I had heard it. With a significant shake of his head, he replied, "I can readily imagine there has been a hard-fought battle, but I must have better authority than the paper you quote ere I can believe that the British Army is beaten! Go you to the Orderly Room and test these documents and I will go to the mess room and examine the newspapers." It was the only instance that I saw Sir John in the square before parade.

In the evening after dinner, when we fully discussed the important news of the day, Sir John fixed his eyes on me and quaintly said, "Yes, truly, such a fight could not but be attended with heavy loss of life. Our seven companies have suffered woefully! Yet a friend of ours, present, was half angry with me, because I would not allow him to go to this broken-head fair! In all probability he would not now have had a smile on his countenance!" With a broad grin, I bowed my assent to the Colonel's remark.

In a similar vein, the following is a copy of a letter from a W. C. Tremble to the editor of the *Army and Navy Gazette* as late as

22 May 1885 prior to the seventieth anniversary of the Battle of Waterloo. The letter is self-explanatory and needs little clarification.

My dear Sir, – I observed that when presenting the new colours to the Duke of Cornwall's Light Infantry yesterday, the Prince of Wales said that the Regiment had at Quatre Bras and Waterloo lost more than any other one corps engaged. His Royal Highness is, I venture to say, slightly in error. The 27th Inniskillings, now the 27th Inniskilling Fusiliers, lost more men. This fact has been wedded to romance and story by Lever and other writers. According to the Regimental returns of killed and wounded in the 27th's square on the memorable 15th of June [*sic*] – officers killed 2, wounded 13, rank and file killed 203, wounded 260, total 478; which was more than two thirds of the Regiment. [The numbers here are incorrect.] More than one writer has referred to the "Irish Howl of the Inniskillings".

If ever the Sovereign gave them another motto, it should be "Muzzle to Muzzle," for so they fought at Waterloo. I may be permitted briefly to indicate the nature of their cruel position on that occasion by quoting the words of Charles Lever, when writing of his own countrymen –

"Milhaud's Cuirassiers, armed with their long straight swords, swept down on the 27th, and a line of impassable bayonets, living "chevaux de frise", of the true blood of Briton, stood firm and motionless before the shock. At length the word 'Fire' was heard within the square, and the bullets at pistol range rattled upon them, the cuirass afforded them no defence against the death volley; men and horses rolled indiscriminately upon the earth."

A military writer, Major-General Charles Beckwith one of the oldest staff officers of the Peninsula, thus describes the conduct of the Battalion at one period of the day, only 600 strong, and all young soldiers who had not previously witnessed a shot fired in anger:

'I have seen many proofs of the intrepidity of the British soldier, but the conduct of the Battalion of the 27th Regiment at Waterloo was the most extraordinary I ever beheld. They were placed in column, under the fire of several batteries, and there, without forming a line or firing a shot in return, the bullets ploughed through their men until nearly two-thirds went down, and the survivors, as fearing their own nerves might give way, but resolved

173

not to go back, pressed their heads and shoulders inwards, forming a solid ring, and thus leaning together, and striving, as it were, to push all to the centre, moved round and round like men in a mill, apparently frantic with horror and excitement, yet firm in the resolution to overcome nature and fall to the last; continued their tramp, closing in, lessening their glorious ring, as the crashing flights of metal continued to tear through the living mass!'

This was the way in which the young Inniskillings obeyed the order of the Duke of Wellington. That sooner than yield a foot of ground to the enemy, His Grace expected every British soldier would prefer dying on the spot on which he then stood. If His Royal Highness or any officer of the Duke of Cornwall's Regiment can show that their corps had as many as 478 out of 600 struck down at Waterloo, I will yield the palm to them, but till then a humble individual like myself must claim it for the Inniskillings,

I am, my dear Sir, very truly yours,
W. C. TREMBLE.[1]

Although the figures may be somewhat incorrect, the sentiment is very much one of proud indignation that the very monarchy for whom those Inniskillings died should attribute the significance of their deaths to another regiment. According to *British Battles & Medals* produced by Spink the casualty roll of the 32nd Foot (Duke of Cornwall's Light Infantry) number 370 out of a total complement of 662, significantly less than the Inniskillings.

Again, as published in the Inniskillings' Regimental magazine, *The Sprig of Shillelagh*[2] the following verse is very appropriate as it remembers those infantry regiments that gave their all at Waterloo. The quality of the poetry may not be of the highest standard, but it is not seriously intended as such.

Infantry Regiments at Waterloo

O' the Waterloo fight! Would you know who were there,
The English "Foot Guards" to whom none can compare,
The "Royal Scots" followed and made monsieurs prance   (1st)
The "4th or King's Own" taught them better to dance   (4th)
The "Buckingham Lads" told them all with their jeers,   (14th)
They'd be driven like goats by the "Welsh Fusiliers".   (23rd)

The "Inniskilling Foot" the French never could please,   (27th)
The "North Gloster" boys cut them down like old Cheese. (28th)
The "Cambridgeshire Students" tho' French
    they don't speak,   (30th)
Made the "Cornwall Boys" hug them and forced
    them to squeak.   (32nd)
The "Yorkshire Men" gave 'em a taste of
    their stingo,   (33rd & 51st)
The "Somerset" youths tipp'd them some of their lingo.   40th)
The "Brave Royal Highlanders" had their full share,   (42nd)
And the "East Essex" calves proved for them but bad fare. (44th)
The "Oxonians" told them of Blenheim of old,   52nd)
And the "Berkshire" youths proved fully as bold.   (66th)
The "Highland Light Infantry" caused them to run,   (71st)
While "Old Mangalores" re-enjoyed their old fun.   (73rd)
"Camerons" came next, swore they care not a fig,   (79th)
"Gordon Highlanders" forced them to learn a new jig.   (92nd)
The Artillery closed up with their guns great and small,
And "Riflemen" always cock sure of their ball.   (95th)
Other regiments panted to join in the fray,
But these are the whole that engaged on that day.[4]

Chapter Thirteen

The 6th Inniskilling Dragoon Guards

Finally one must acknowledge the presence of the 6th Inniskilling Dragoon Guards on the field of Waterloo.

Unlike her sister Regiment the 27th Inniskilling Fusiliers, the Dragoons took no part in the Peninsular War in Spain and Portugal. April 1815 found the 6th Inniskilling Dragoons dispersed among several barracks throughout Britain when orders were received to assemble at Northampton in preparation for their impending departure for Belgium. At that time, the Inniskilling Dragoons had only three squadrons of cavalry available, consisting of two troops commanded by Captain Madox and Captain Browne under Brevet Lieutenant-Colonel Miller. A further squadron remained in Ipswich detailed as a depot Squadron under the command of Brevet Lieutenant-Colonel Ellice.

Each troop of cavalry at that time consisted of a complement of:

- 1 Captain
- 2 Subalterns
- 1 Sergeant-Major
- 3 Sergeants
- 3 Corporals
- 1 Trumpeter
- 63 Privates
- 70 Horses

By 11 April 1815 orders were received augmenting the Regimental strength to:

- 51 Officers (including staff)
- 95 NCOs
- 800 Trumpeters and ORs
- 775 Horses

So it was that on 23 April 1815 six troops, numbering 450 men, of the 6th Inniskilling Dragoons embarked at Gravesend for Belgium under the command of Lieutenant-Colonel Miller, to join Wellington's Army. Arriving at Ostend on the evening of 24 April the Dragoons marched through the night passing through Bruges on 25 April and arriving in Oostaker the following day. A change in command took place on 30 April 1815 when Colonel Mutter took over as Commanding Officer.

The weeks following their arrival in Belgium were spent in relative inactivity. However, before very long the Regiment was ordered to Herzeele, where on 12 May it joined with the Royals and Scots Greys to form the 2nd Brigade of Heavy Cavalry. This Brigade was more commonly known as the Union Brigade, under the command of Sir William Ponsonby.

During the coming weeks the Regiment rested up, during which time the commander of the cavalry, the Earl of Uxbridge, inspected it. A general review of the Cavalry and Horse Artillery was held on 29 May at Schildenbecke near Grammont, at which time the Duke of Wellington and Marshal Blücher carried out the inspection. However, the Regiment's period of inactivity drew to a close when orders were received on 16 June 1815 to march immediately for Enghien. It was patently obvious from the movement of numerous other cavalry and infantry regiments they encountered on the way that something major was afoot. Even as the Dragoons neared their destination fresh orders were received diverting the Regiment to Braine-le-Comte and then further to Nivelles. The Regiment finally rested for the night near the village of Genappe on the Brussels to Charleroi road.

As Wellington's Anglo-Allied army retired to Waterloo the cavalry units on hand covered their retreat and held the French at bay.

The next day Captain Madox was detached at 7 a.m. with three troops to Genappe to mount the wounded infantry (from Quatre Bras) on their horses and take them back to Brussels. (They arrived there on the same evening, and rejoined the regiment on the field of Waterloo at nine next morning.)

The army retired on the Waterloo position, the cavalry covering the movement, the two heavy cavalry brigades as main body of the rearguard, along the high road to Brussels, with Vandeleur's and

Vivian's Brigades on their left through Thuy, and Dörnberg's German Legion Cavalry, with whom were the 13th Hussars, on the right; and the 7th Hussars and 23rd Light Dragoons were detached to the heavy Cavalry, and skirmished between it and the enemy.

During the Battle of Waterloo the 6th Inniskilling Dragoons, like the 27th Inniskillings, played a crucial role in Wellington's overall victory. After a night of near monsoon conditions, the 6th Inniskilling Dragoons, as part of Ponsonby's 2nd Heavy Cavalry Brigade, took up their position to the rear of Mont St Jean on the left of the road to Brussels. In such a position they were directly to the rear and in support of Lieutenant-General Sir Thomas Picton's Division.

At approximately 1.30 p.m. when D'Erlon, under orders from Napoleon, advanced with twenty thousand cavalry, infantry and artillery against the Allied line, Colonel Mutter, under orders from Ponsonby, was to hold his cavalry in check until signalled to advance.

As D'Erlon's four divisions advanced Bylandt's Dutch-Belgian Brigade broke before the advancing French thus leaving the French to fill the gap in the Allied line. At this point the Union Brigade advanced and entered the battle for the first time. D'Erlon's four divisions had advanced in echelon from the left. Donzelot in command of the left and therefore the leading division, was engaged with La Haye Sainte. Allix's, the next, had passed on and was topping the ridge on the left of the 28th, Kempt's left-hand regiment, and coming into the gap left by the Dutch Belgians; and his rear brigade, of the 55th and 54th Infantry of the line, was moving out to its right in echelon, while on his right again Marcognet's Division was advancing, and, further still to the right, Durutte's.

With the retreat of the Dutch-Belgians before the advancing French, Picton's Division came under severe pressure. It was at this point that the 2nd Cavalry Brigade entered the fray. The French artillery having ceased firing, their troops advanced. With no time to lose the Union Brigade entered the battle. The Royals galloped directly into the leading brigade of Allix's Division, whilst on their left the 6th Inniskilling Dragoons took on the 54th and 55th Infantry. The Scots Greys for their part, on the left rear of the Inniskillings, charged Marcognet's Division.

There can be no doubt that the charge of the 2nd Heavy Cavalry Brigade was a decisive moment in the battle. Had the French been allowed to consolidate their position Wellington's line would have been dissected and possibly the whole outcome of the battle altered. As it was, D'Erlon's advance failed, with severe casualties inflicted upon the French Army.

However, the heat of the moment having overcome common sense and good judgement, the Union Brigade failed to check their advance and advanced further into the enemy's ranks than was entirely prudent. The result was a near disastrous mauling at the hands of the French Light Cavalry. The only thing to prevent their total annihilation was the timely intervention of Vandeleur's 11th, 12th and 16th Light Dragoons supported by Vivian's Brigade.

During the final stages of the battle when Ponsonby was killed in action, Colonel Mutter took over as commanding officer of the Union Brigade; the command of the 6th Inniskilling Dragoons then fell to Lieutenant-Colonel Miller.

Regrouped, the Brigade moved across the Charleroi road in support of the infantry who were in square and under severe attack from both French infantry and cavalry. It was only later in the afternoon that the remnants of both the 1st and 2nd Heavy Cavalry Brigades united under Somerset to disperse the advancing cuirassiers as they attempted to take the high ground.

At around 6.30 p.m. Colonel Mutter retired from the field wounded, handing over command of the Regiment to Captain Madox.

As in the case of the 27th Fusiliers, the 6th Dragoons suffered inordinately large casualties.

Appendix I

Officers killed and wounded in the Peninsula

The following is a list of officers of the 27th Inniskillings wounded, killed in action or died of wounds during the course of the Peninsular Campaign 1808–1814.

Ensign Robert Bakewell, as of 12 April 1810. Promoted Lieutenant in the 27th Regiment as of 22 October 1812. Resigned as a result of being incapacitated, resignation accepted by the Marquis of Hastings in January 1813.

Full pay as of 17 January 1815, half pay 'by reduction of the battalion' 24 May 1817. Wounded in the Peninsula. Not married and no 'legitimate children'.

Place of residence, Castle Donington, Leicestershire. (PRO: WO 25/750 f34)

Captain Francis Bignall, commissioned as a Lieutenant as of 3 June 1805. Captain as of 14 November 1811. Killed at Toulouse on 10 April 1814 while serving with the 3rd Battalion. At Vitoria on 21 June 1813 commanded two companies of the regiment when ordered forward to act as light infantry and command was delegated to one William Boyle (rank unknown) as Captain Bignall was unable to proceed due to suffering from fatigue. (PRO WO25-789-82)

Major John Birmingham, as of 30 April 1807, died as a result of wounds received during a sortie at Badajoz on 10 May 1811, 3rd Battalion? Died the following day. (PRO WO 25/2965) (Name also spelt Bermingham in some sources)

Ensign William Boyle was born at Brakely, County Tyrone on 10 May 1784. Enlisted in the Royal Tyrone Militia at age 22 years and granted an Ensign as of 10 January 1807. Ensign in the 27th

Regiment as of 22 July 1808, as a result of getting seventy-six men to volunteer for the line. Remained in this rank for an extended time due to the Regiment having three battalions.

Lieutenant as of 6 February 1812. Engaged at Busaco 27 September 1810 and carried the colours on the retreat to the lines of Torres Vedras. He was involved in the pursuit of Marshal Massena's army and in the Affair of Joz-de-Arnose on 15 March to 16 March in the 4th Division. Engaged at Campomayor 25 March and the siege and capture of Oliverea on 15 April. Seems to have served in practically all the engagements of the Peninsula. (See also **Bignall**)

The following is an extract from a magazine entitled *Deeds That Won The Empire*: "At the Battle of Vitoria on 21 June 1813, two companies of the Regiment were ordered to the front to deploy as skirmishers. Lieutenant Boyle was given command as Captain Bignall was suffering from chronic fatigue. As his command came across the French supply wagons it was only by great force of will that he persuaded them to desist from looting. Shortly after, the men were hastily formed into square and saw off a body of French cavalry that were attempting to recover the supply wagons."

1 August: Lieutenant Boyle along with Captain Butler and two companies of the 3rd Battalion were ordered to attack an enemy-occupied height adjoining the village of Lesaka in the Pyrenees. As the assault began Captain Butler was hit by enemy fire and severely wounded. As he was taken to the rear command devolved to Lieutenant Boyle who led a successful attack.

10 May 1811: Boyle had his cocked hat shot from his head and was slightly wounded in the right ear, during a skirmish with the French at Fort Saint Christoval.

28 July 1813: was wounded on the right side of the face and received four musket balls through his hat while skirmishing near the village of Sourarer, near Pamplona in the Pyrenees. He married Miss Letitia Harvey on 11 October 1827; no children are shown up to 1830. (PRO: WO 25/789 f82)

Captain John Brown was born on 1 October 1777 at Dulwich, Surrey. Entered the army at age seventeen and was made a Cornet in the 6th Dragoons as of 27 May 1795. Promoted to Lieutenant on 17 May 1796 and Captain 1 June 1796. He was a Captain in the 34th Foot as of 25 June 1807 and a Captain in the 8th Garrison Battalion on 10 November of the same year. Captain in the 27th Regiment on

17 August 1808 and promoted to Major of the Portuguese Staff as of 16 February 1809. Promoted to Lieutenant Colonel, Portuguese Staff as of 14 March 1811 and the same rank with the 46th Foot as of 13 August 1812.

He is listed as being a Lieutenant Colonel in the Greek Light Infantry as of 25 January 1813, the same rank in the 21st Light Dragoons as of 6 April 1815 and the 13th Light Dragoons as of 9 May 1820. His last listed rank was as a Colonel in the Army as of 19 July 1821; Served in Argentina with Whitelock 1807–08: ADC at Rolica and Vimiero; DAAG in 1808 and 1809; took part in the retreat to Corunna; DAAG in 1810.

In a surprise attack on French cavalry at Fuente-los-Cantos and the retreat to Badajoz, he came under the notice of Lieutenant General Mendizabel and was mentioned in Divisional Orders. In the retreat from Badajoz to Elvas he attempted to save a Spanish Brigade under the command of Lieutenant General Don Carlos D'Hispaaha, and for his conduct he received that General's written thanks.

He was wounded five times during the year 1811, receiving no pension, but in lieu a year's pay. He was made a Knight by Patent on the recommendation of His Grace the Duke of Wellington and General Lord Beresford. The King of Portugal for services in his army created him a Knight of the Tower and Sword. He was created a Knight of Charles III, by the King of Spain for service in Spain with the Spanish Army.

He married a Mrs Franks on 1 June 1801 at Bath.

Ensign/Adjutant Henry Burn was killed in action on 28 July 1813 in the Pyrenees, while serving in the 3rd Battalion. 1814 Army List.

Captain William Butler was aged eighteen on his first appointment in the Army. Ensign in the 27th Regiment as of 16 August 1804 and promoted to Lieutenant on 27 June 1805. Further promoted to Captain on 25 June 1812.

He was severely wounded during the attack on Lezaca on 1 August 1813. Received a pension of £100 per annum commencing on 1 August 1814. He married in London on 17 July 1827, wife's name not listed. His residence is listed as Ballybar House (no county). Source *London Gazette*.

Lieutenant Arthur Byrne was born in Ireland on 8 June 1784. He joined the army t sixteen years becoming a non-commissioned officer in the 7th Royal Fusiliers, with whom he served from 1799 to July 1811. He was appointed as an Ensign in the 27th Regiment as of

18 July 1811 and promoted to Lieutenant on 25 August 1815. He became Adjutant on 21 April 1814.

Served at Copenhagen as an NCO in the 7th Royal Fusiliers in 1807.

He was at the capture of Martinique in February 1809 also as an NCO. Served at Busaco, Albuhera, Badajoz, Carasal, Salamanca, Vitoria, Pyrenees, severely wounded, received one year's pay as Ensign; Nivelle, Orthez, Toulouse, severely wounded while commanding a company, received one year's pay as Captain. Plattsburg; capture of Paris. Permanent pension of £10 per annum as of 1824. Married Frances Doyle in Gibraltar on 5 August 1819. Source *London Gazette*.

Ensign Richard Clunes: Originally served with the 1st Foot as of 25 February 1813. Severely wounded in the Pyrenees on 28 July 1813, while serving with the 3rd Battalion 27th Regiment. Promoted to Lieutenant as of 11 August 1814. Source *London Gazette*.

Lieutenant Charles Crawford: A Lieutenant with the 27th Regiment as of 23 November 1809. Mortally wounded at the Pyrenees on 26 July 1813, while serving with the 3rd Battalion. Died the following day. Listed on a casualty return dated 'August 1813'.

Lieutenant Frederick Crewe: A Lieutenant with the 27th Regiment as of 13 February 1806. Severely wounded while serving in the Pyrenees with the 3rd Battalion on 28 July 1813.

Lieutenant/Adjutant James Davison: Lieutenant in the 27th Regiment as of 15 January 1807, severely wounded by a musket ball at the storming of Badajoz on 6 April 1812, while serving as Adjutant. He was killed at Salamanca on 18 July 1812. Source *London Gazette*, where his name is spelt Davidson.

Lieutenant William Dobbin: Commissioned as a Lieutenant in the 27th Regiment on St Patrick's Day 1808. He received a slight wound while in the trenches before Badajoz sometime between 8–15 May 1811, while serving with the 3rd Battalion. He was attached to the 3rd Cacadores as a Captain and was again wounded during the storming of Badajoz on 6 April 1812.

Was in Portuguese service from May 1811 to April 1814. He received a temporary pension of $100 per annum commencing on 7 April 1813 for a wound received at Badajoz. Source Pension Return and Challis, *History of the Portuguese Army*.

Ensign Daniel Donavan was appointed Ensign as of 13 May 1812. Served as a Lieutenant in the 14th Portuguese Line and was wounded at the Nive on 13 December 1813. Was in Portuguese service from May 1812 to April 1814. Source *London Gazette*.

Ensign Daniel Donovan: Appointed as an Ensign in the 6th Irish Brigade in 1796, by virtue of raising men at his own expense for that corps. Served with the Brigade for between nine and twelve months. Sailed for North America and was shipwrecked, his life being saved by a frigate, but in the process losing his commission and all personal papers. Served as a Lieutenant in the 35th Regiment from about 1799 until 1803, when he retired from the service. During his time with the 35th Regiment he sailed from Malta in 1801 and was captured in the Gulf of Lyons and conveyed to Languedoc where he was a prisoner for eight months.

In 1809 he was recommended by the Duke of Wellington for a commission in the 27th Regiment. Ensigncy dated 13 May 1812, and promotion to Lieutenant as of 9 February 1814.

Enlisted in Portuguese service under Beresford in 1810. Wounded slightly at Salamanca while serving in the 12th Portuguese Line and again at Nive/Nivelle by a severe wound from a musket ball on 13 December 1813. The ball hit him in the right thigh, striking the bone. Postwar he lived in Kilovinogue and was unmarried in 1820. Source PRO.

Lieutenant John Ringrove Drewe: Ensign as of 15 November 1810. Promoted to Lieutenant on 25 February 1813. He lost an arm at Pamplona in 1813 and was granted a pension of £100 per annum commencing on 29 July 1814. Source Pension Returns.

Lieutenant Bartholomew Thomas Duhigg: Lieutenant as of 9 November 1806. He was severely wounded at the battle of Castalla, 12–13 April 1813, whilst serving in the 2nd Battalion. Source *London Gazette*.

Major William Howe Erskine: In view of his father's service, the Duke of York granted him an Ensigncy in the 27th Regiment in 1794, while still only twelve years old. He became a Lieutenant in September 1795 and Captain in 1800. His Majority was granted in 1805 and he became a Brevet Lieutenant Colonel in 1812, as a result of a severe wound suffered during the assault and capture of Badajoz. He received no pension, but was granted a year's pay for the wound.

He married in London on 12 August 1812 and had two children by 1829. Post service he resided mostly in Aberdeenshire. (PRO WO 25/757 f107) *London Gazette*.

Assistant Surgeon Gerald Fitzgerald: Appointed as of 25 April 1811.

Slightly wounded at the Heights of Ordal on 12/13 September 1813, while serving with the 2nd Battalion. (Also served at Waterloo.) *London Gazette* of 23 October 1813 and regimental roll.

Ensign John Galbraith: Appointed as of 13 April 1813. He received a severe wound during the battle at Nivelle on 10 November 1813, while serving in the 3rd Battalion. Notice in the *London Gazette*.

Captain John Geddes was born on 30 October 1787 at Edinburgh. Entered the army at age seventeen years as an Ensign in the 72nd Regiment in August 1804. He became a Lieutenant in the 27th as of 25 October 1805, seeing service at Calabria in 1806. Captain in December 1808 and saw service at Procida in 1809 and Sicily in 1810. Served at Nivelle and Nive, Orthes and Toulouse, where he commanded four companies of the 3rd Battalion and was severely wounded by a musket ball on 10 April 1814. The wound resulted in a broken thigh close to the hip joint. He received one year's pay and a pension of £100 per annum. Promoted to Major on 25 February 1825. Sources, *London Gazette*, Pension Records.

Lieutenant Philip Gordon: Appointed as of 8 November 1806. Slightly wounded in the trenches before Badajoz sometime between 8–15 May 1811, while serving with the 3rd Battalion (*London Gazette*). He received another slight wound during the storming of the town on 6 April 1812. Wounded again at Salamanca on the 22 July 1812. Wounded for the fourth time, fatally, at Vitoria on 21 June 1813, dying of his wounds on 28 August 1813 (PRO WO 25/2965).

Lieutenant Hugh Gough: Appointed to the regiment on 18 July 1811. He was killed at the battle of Toulouse on 10 April 1814.

Captain Thomas Hamilton: Appointed as an Ensign to the 27th Regiment on 29 August 1804, at age twenty-four. Promoted to Lieutenant on 7 September 1805 and Captain on 24 September 1812. Wounded during the action at Pamplona; not granted a pension. He married at Queen Square Chapel, Bath, on 14 December 1815. Reduced to half pay as of May 1817, by reduction. Post-service he lived in Liverpool. PRO and *London Gazette*.

Ensign Fethuston Hanby: Appointed as an Ensign as of 26 February 1808, aged seventeen. Promoted to Lieutenant on 10 July 1811. Served at and was wounded at Badajoz, Pamplona and in the Pyrenees. Not granted a pension. Married at St Ann's Church, Dublin, on 15 August 1815. Examined by a medical board at Dublin and sent on half pay due to wounds received. Resided at Dumlish, County Longford, Newton Forbes, Williamstown and Dublin.

Ensign Frederick Harding was appointed as Ensign on 1 September 1808. Killed during the assault on San Sebastian on 31 August 1813. (Reported in the *London Gazette* as Lieutenant Hardinge).

Lieutenant John Crosbie Harnett was appointed as Ensign on 20 March 1806, at 'about seventeen years'. Promoted to Lieutenant on 27 October 1807. Severely wounded at Toulouse on 10 April 1814, but not granted a pension. Served in Canada, Flanders, West Indies, France. Went on to half pay on 21 January 1819, 'ill health caused by 12 years Service in foreign climate.' Married in Camp Haven Church on 31 January 1819 and had two children by 1829. His home was in Kinsale.

Lieutenant Joseph Hill was appointed as Ensign at age twenty-five, but unable to state exact date due to his commissions being lost from his baggage. (According to the *Army List* he was commissioned on 25 November 1808; promoted to Lieutenant on 14 May 1812. Lost his leg and thigh at Vitoria and was awarded a pension of £70, commencing in January 1813. Married in Dublin on 6 November 1816 and had three children by 1829. Lived in Mullingar. (According to the Pension Return he was awarded a pension of £70 per annum for 22 June 1814 for the loss of an arm at Vitoria.)

Ensign Samuel Ireland: Appointed as of 25 August 1815; severely wounded at Nivelle on 10 November 1813. Killed at Waterloo.

Lieutenant J.K. Jameson: Appointed as Lieutenant as of 12 September 1808. Slightly wounded at Castalla 12–13 April 1813. *London Gazette*.

Captain Thomas Jones: Appointed as Captain on 8 October 1806. Killed during the storming of Badajoz on 6 April 1812.

Volunteer George Kennion: Killed at San Sebastian, 31 August 1813.

Lieutenant Charles Levinge: Captain as of 14 September 1808. He was wounded during the repulse of a sortie from Badajoz on 10 May 1811. Killed during the storming of the city on 6 April 1812.

Ensign James McCoard: Fatally wounded during the repulse of a sortie from Badajoz on 10 May 1811, dying on 27 May 1811.

Appendix II

Roll of Officers
27th Foot (Inniskilling Fusiliers)
25 March – 24 June 1815

The majority of the men listed below saw action at the Battle of Waterloo on 18 June 1815.

Officers:

Brevet-Major Hare, John. He was slightly wounded at the Battle of Waterloo where he commanded the 27th Foot. He later attained the rank of Major General and was honoured with a C.B. He served as Governor of the Eastern District of the Cape of Good Hope. At the outset he served as an Ensign with the Tarbet Fencibles, then volunteered with 300 men for the regular army and joined the 69th Regiment. He embarked for Helder and served in that campaign under the command of the Duke of York. He also served under Abercrombie in Egypt. He had seen service in Naples, Sicily, Calabria and the Peninsular War. He was appointed Lieutenant-Colonel of the 27th Inniskillings on 31 March 1825 and died on the passage back to the United Kingdom from the Cape of Good Hope in March, 1847.

Captain Holmes, George. He was killed in action at the Battle of Waterloo.

Captain John Tucker was severely wounded at the Battle of Waterloo. His full name was John Montmorency Tucker. He transferred to the 8th Foot as a Captain on 23 May 1816 and eventually retired from the service before 1824. He died at Haggen's Asylum, Northfleet, Kent, 22 February 1852.

Lieutenant Betty, John.

Lieutenant Craddock, Thomas. Born on 6 October 1786 he was the seventh son of William Craddock of Loughborough, Leicester. He served with the 27th Inniskillings throughout the Peninsular War. At the Siege of Badajoz he entered the town in command of the 27th. He served at the attack on New Orleans in 1815 and was severely wounded at the Battle of Waterloo when a bullet passed through both cheeks and destroyed the roof of his mouth. Appointed a Knight of Windsor in 1842, he retired a Major and died 5 April 1851.

Lieutenant E. W. Drewe was severely wounded at the Battle of Waterloo.

Lieutenant Fortescue, William Faithful. Severely wounded, he died from wounds received at the Battle of Waterloo. He was the second son of John Fortescue who served with the 24th Foot and saw action at the taking of Quebec.

Lieutenant Gardiner, Andrew. He entered the army in 1811 and his commission dates are as an Ensign 14 November 1811 and as a Lieutenant 30 September 1813.

Lieutenant Handcock, Richard. Severely wounded at the Battle of Waterloo, he retired from the army on full pay as a Captain in 1837.

Lieutenant Henderson, William. He was severely wounded at the Battle of Waterloo and retired on half-pay 25 April 1816.

Lieutenant Manley, Charles. Having served throughout the Peninsular War, he was severely wounded in the thigh at Waterloo. He was promoted Captain in the 27th Inniskillings, 10 September 1829. When just seventeen days out of the Cape of Good Hope he died of an apoplectic fit on 5 November 1839 on board the SS *Barretta*.

Lieutenant Miller, John was severely wounded at the Battle of Waterloo.

Lieutenant Macdonald, George (Army List spelt McDonnell) later became General George Macdonald, Colonel-in-Chief of the 16th Foot and lived to be "Father of the British Army". He entered the Army in 1805, joined the Expedition to Hanover in 1805, the Army in Sicily in 1806, the Expedition to Naples, in 1810, and was present at the capture of Ischia and Procida. He returned to Sicily in 1811 and was posted to Spain. He was present at the Battle of Castalla and the Siege of Tarragona and afterwards served in Canada. His commission dates are as follows: Ensign, 5 September 1805; Lieutenant 25 July 1806; Captain, 17 August 1815; Major, 31 August 1830; Lieutenant-Colonel, 1837; Colonel, 1851; Major-General, 1863; General, 1871. He was severely wounded at the Battle of Waterloo, having been hit three times.

Ensign John Ditmas was slightly wounded at the Battle of Waterloo.
Ensign Edward Handcock (who also appears as Theobald or Tiobas) was severely wounded at the Battle of Waterloo.
Ensign Samuel Ireland was killed in action at the Battle of Waterloo.
Ensign Thomas Carlton Smith was still living on half-pay in 1874 as Lieutenant-General T.C. Smith, unattached. He entered the Army in 1813, served in the Peninsular War and was present at the Battle of Ordal. He was severely wounded at the Battle of Waterloo. Whilst serving in the Navy previous to taking a commission in the Army he was wounded no less than three times. His commission dates are as follows: Ensign, 24 June 1813; Lieutenant, 15 August 1819; Captain, 27 March 1835; Major, 30 September 1842; Lieutenant-Colonel, 15 September 1848; Colonel, 28 November 1854; Major-General, 21 December 1862; Lieutenant-General, 25 October 1871.

Appendix III

Roll of
Non-Commissioned Officers
& Other Ranks
who served with the 27th Foot
25 March – 24 June 1815

Although service numbers were not in vogue at the time of the Peninsular Wars, it is nevertheless of interest to have a record of those who lived, suffered and gave their lives in the face of such dangers. Their names may again be acknowledged as having taken part in one of the most memorable battles of all time. In a less historic, more romantic way, this roll acknowledges lives, lived and lost, which under normal circumstances would have lain dormant in some dusty archive, unacknowledged and unappreciated. It is an unfortunate fact that very few pay credit to, or record, the sacrifice of the 'Other Ranks'. They simply represent the cannon fodder of more renowned military careers: individuals who by nature of their birth and the deeds of 'little men' endure to be glorified by historians. By recounting the names contained within this roll I hope, in some small way, to have set that to rights.

The majority of the men listed below saw action at the Battle of Waterloo, 18 June 1815. Those killed in action or who died of wounds are denoted by bold print.

Rank

Sgt. Major J. Armstrong

Q. M. Sgt. J. Kennedy

P. M. Sgt. B. McMullin

Arm. Sgt. F. Papa

Drum Maj. R Wilson

Col. Sgt. W Connelly

Col. Sgt. L. Connell

Col. Sgt. J. Evans

Col. Sgt. S. Haughton

Col. Sgt. J. Keegan

Col. Sgt. H. McKay

Col. Sgt. C. McTrue

Col. Sgt. R. Mulcahy

Col. Sgt. D. Sullivan.

Col. Sgt. W. Turner

Col. Sgt. T. Walsh.

Sgt. T. Beatty

Sgt. F. Campbell

Sgt. W. Connolly

Sgt. I. Cook

Sgt. R. Crozier

Sgt. T. Cusack

Sgt. J. Doolan

Sgt. P. Dunne

Sgt. E. Early

Sgt. J. Fitzsimons

Sgt. R. Gales

Sgt. J. Gardner

Sgt. D. Graham

Sgt. H. Hughes

Sgt. J. Hughes

Sgt. F. Jawnson

Sgt. E. Kelly

Sgt. T. Kerrigan

Sgt. P. Kilday

Sgt. W. Lee

Sgt. M. Lewis

Sgt. J. Lock

Sgt. J. McCormick

Sgt. D. McDonald

Sgt. J. McGowan

Sgt. J. McLean

Sgt. D. Mahon

Sgt. T. Margatide

Sgt. A. Miller

Sgt. P. Montgomery

Sgt. T. Mulherron

Sgt. W. Oddy

Sgt. J. O'Hara

Sgt. R. Scott

Sgt. S. Shaw

Sgt. A. Staunton

Sgt. J. Stewart

Sgt. D. Shields

Sgt. J. Sutherland

Sgt. S. Taggart

Sgt. W. Taylor

Sgt. T. Thompson

Sgt. H. Torphey

Cpl. W. Adams

Cpl. H. Armstrong

Cpl. H. Arburthnot

Cpl. J. Barton

Cpl. S. Booth

Cpl. R. Boyle

Cpl. J. Bowman

Cpl. T. Brooks

Cpl. R. Buckley

Cpl. B. Burnes

Cpl. L. Calvey

(L. Caffery)

Cpl. A. Cavanagh

Cpl. J. Campbell

Cpl. J. Coady

Cpl. P. Conway

Cpl. J. Cosgrove

Cpl. J. Courtney

Cpl. M. Cox

Cpl. W. Crawford

Cpl. J. Crozier

Cpl. T. Deane

Cpl. M. Devlin

Cpl. B. Devine

Cpl. F. Donaghey

Cpl. P. Dunncy

Cpl. J. Elwood

Cpl. F. Faggott

Cpl. J. Fallon

Cpl. J. Fegan

Cpl. T. Fraser

Cpl. J. Gawt

Cpl. I. Graham

Cpl. J. Hancill

Cpl. J. Haywood

Cpl. J. Hogan

Cpl. M. Hourigan

Cpl. T. Jenkinson

Cpl. T. Johnston

Cpl. B. Keefe

Cpl. G. Kilday

Cpl. W. Lawler

Cpl. M. McCausland

Cpl. J. McClean

Cpl. P. McCormick

Cpl. J. McCourt

Cpl. G. McConnel

Cpl. P. McGuire

Cpl. A. McMahon

Cpl. M. Martin

Cpl. S. Minton

Cpl. B. Moore
Cpl. M. Moyland
Cpl. J. Mullins
Cpl. J. Olliver
Cpl. W. Parker
Cpl. W. Shanks
Cpl. D. Shea
Cpl. F. Short
Cpl. D. Stewart
Cpl. R. Strudgeon
Cpl. W. Swalthy
Cpl. T. Wild
Cpl. Worthington
Drummer & Fifer
J. Bunton
Drummer & Fifer
M. Carr
Drummer & Fifer
J. Dunlop
Drummer & Fifer
W. Kicks
Drummer & Fifer
J. Kershaw
Drummer & Fifer
J. McCall
Drummer & Fifer
M. Martin
Drummer & Fifer
W. Morgan
Drummer & Fifer
W. Quinn
Drummer & Fifer
J. Robinson
Drummer & Fifer
C. Stewart
Drummer & Fifer
J. Sullivan
Drummer & Fifer
T. Wright
Drummer & Fifer

T. Watterson
Pte. W. Abbott
Pte. T. Abraham
Pte. J. Adams
Pte. R. Adams
Pte. J. Alexander
Pte. D. Allen
Pte. J. Allen
Pte. W. Allen
Pte. H. Ample
Pte. J. Anderson
Pte. S. Anderson
Pte. H. Argue
Pte. A. Armstrong
Pte. E. Armstrong
Pte. J. Armstrong
Pte. J. Arnett
Pte. W. Baird
Pte. J. Ball
Pte. C. Bampton
Pte. S. Barber
Pte. J. Barnett
Pte. J. Barnett
Pte. P. Barrett
Pte. W. Barrett
Pte. C. Bell
Pte. G. Bell
Pte. E. Begley
Pte. P. Bennett
Pte. R. Bennett
Pte. J. Berry
Pte. F. Blake
Pte. W. Blowe
Pte. B. Bowes
Pte. J. Bowles
Pte. J. Boyde
Pte. M. Boyde
Pte. W. Boyde
Pte. W. Boylam
Pte. J. Boyle

Pte. M. Boyle
Pte. T. Boyle
Pte. W. Boyle
Pte. J. Bradley
Pte. J. Bradley
Pte. P. Bradley
Pte. P. Brahaney
Pte. J. Breadborrow
Pte. T. Burke
Pte. F. Breen
Pte. D. Breman
Pte. T. Breman
Pte. W. Bridgett
Pte. J. Brockley
Pte. D. Broadbent
Pte. J. Brooks
Pte. J. Brown
Pte. W. Brown
Pte. M. Bryan
Pte. W. Bullard
Pte. T. Bunn
Pte. E. Burke
Pte. M. Burke
Pte. P. Burke
Pte. P. Burke
Pte. D. Burnes
Pte. E. Burnes
Pte. H. Burnes
Pte. M. Byrne
Pte. M. Byrne
Pte. C. Burch
Pte. J. Cadden
Pte. T. Calanan
Pte. M. Calaghan
Pte. W. Calder
Pte. P. Callaghan
Pte. S. Callaghan
Pte. J. Callegan
Pte. J. Callegan
Pte. J. Campbell

Pte. J. Campbell
Pte. J. Campbell
Pte. P. Campbell
Pte. T. Campbell
Pte. W. Campbell
Pte. C. Cameron
Pte. M. Carabine
Pte. J. Carbery
Pte. J. Carlen
Pte. J. Carlin
Pte. D. Carmichall
Pte. R. Carmichall
Pte. P. Carraway
Pte. M. Carregan
Pte. F. Carrey
Pte. T. Carrigan
Pte. T. Carrigan
Pte. W. Carrigan
Pte. J. Carsons
Pte. M. Carsons
Pte. R. Carter
Pte. H. Cassidy
Pte. J. Cassidy
Pte. J. Cassidy
Pte. M. Cassidy
Pte. P. Cassidy
Pte. E. Caulfield
Pte. P. Caulfield
Pte. T. Caulfield
Pte. L. Cavanah
Pte. H. Chambers
Pte. P. Cheeky
Pte. F. Clarke
Pte. J. Clarke
Pte. P. Clarke
Pte. T. Clarke
Pte. J. Clancey
Pte. P. Clancey
Pte. J. Cleary
Pte. M. Cocheran

(**M. Corcoran**)
Pte. D. Coleman
Pte. L. Coleman
Pte. O. Collery
Pte. D. Collins
Pte. J. Collins
Pte. J. Collins
Pte. T. Collins
Pte. J. Collrey
Pte. J. Comiskey
(**J. Cummisky**)
Pte. W. Concannon
Pte. J. Concoran
Pte. T. Conlin
Pte. J. Connell
Pte. J. Connolly
Pte. P. Connolly
Pte. D. Conway
Pte. J. Cook
Pte. P. Corbett
Pte. G. Cornerford
Pte. G. Costello
Pte. G. Costello
Ptc. T. Costcllo
Pte. C. Coughlan
Pte. E. Coughlan
Pte. J. Coughrin
Pte. F. Coultin
Pte. H. Cowan
Pte. W. Cowan
Pte. P. Cox
Pte. T. Cox
Pte. W. Cox
Pte. E. Coyle
Pte. F. Coyle
Pte. H. Crawford
Pte. W. Cray
(**W. Craig**)
Pte. P. Creaton
Pte. P. Cregan

Pte. C. Cremore
Pte. P. Cromyan
Pte. G. Croskett
Pte. J. Crowe
Pte. E. Cullen
Pte. P. Cullen
Pte. C. Cunningham
Pte. J. Cunningham
Pte. P. Cunningham
Pte. W.
Cunningham
Pte. J. Curren
Pte. J. Curren
Pte. J. Curren
Pte. D. Curry
Pte. J. Dailey
Pte. D. Daily
Pte. J. Daily
Pte. J. Daily
Pte. P. Daily
Pte. J. Davis
Pte. J. Davis
Pte. N. Davis
Pte. J. Day
Pte. R. Dempsey
Pte. J. Devanny
(**J. Delaney**)
Pte. W. Dever
Pte. F. Devitt
Pte. A. Devlin
Pte. T. Devlin
Pte. T. Devlin
Pte. A. Dick
Pte. J. Diew
Pte. J. Dixon
Pte. F. Donaghey
Pte. W. Donaldson
Pte. J. Donnavan
Pte. H. Donnelly
Pte. J. Donnelly

Pte. *M. Doolan*
Pte. H. Dorman
Pte. J. Dougherty ?
Pte. P. Dougherty
Pte. T. Dougherty
Pte. W. Douglas
Pte. G. Douthard
Pte. H. Dovan
Pte. J. Dovan
Pte. P. Downs
Pte. J. Doyle
Pte. P. Doyle
Pte. J. Drum
Pte. J. Drum
Pte. S. Duffey
Pte. O. Duffy
Pte. M. Duffilty
Pte. G. Duffin
Pte. J. Dundas
Pte. T. Dunleavy
Pte. A. Dunlop
Pte. B. Dunne
Pte. B. Dunn
Pte. M. Dunnigan
Pte. J. Durning
Pte. T. Egan
Pte. R. Eagin
Pte. J. Eakins
Pte. A. Eiott
Pte. W. Ellis
Pte. J. English
Pte. R. Ennis.
Pte. J. Enright
Pte. W. Evans
Pte. J. Ewart
Pte. J. Fair
Pte. M. Farrell
Pte. T. Farrell
Pte. S. Farrell
(S. Fanell)

Pte. O. Fanney
Pte. T. Fargue
Pte. P. Feeney
Pte. M. Feeghary
(M. Feighrey)
Pte. R. Feehaly
Pte. M. Feeney
Pte. M. Feeney
Pte. J. Fearen
Pte. P. Fegan
Pte. J. Ferguson
Pte. J. Foy
Pte. P. Felan
Pte. L. Finnerly
Pte. M. Firman
Pte. T. Fisher
Pte. P. Flynn
Pte. P. Flynn
Pte. T. Flannagan
Pte. J. Flannaghay
Pte. D. Flynn
Pte. J. Fougherty
Pte. J. Forster
Pte. J. Fox
Pte. T. Fox
Pte. A. Fraser
Pte. J. Fullan
Pte. P. Fullard
Pte. J. Fulthy
Pte. J. Gales
Pte. P. Gaffney
Pte. S. Gaffney
Pte. J. Gallagher
Pte. T. Gallagher
Pte. J. Galley
Pte. T. Gallimore
Pte. P. Gann
Pte. E. Garvey
Pte. L. Gatha
Pte. T. Gavin

Pte. J. Gaynor
Pte. J. Geary
Pte. T. Geary
Pte. J. George
Pte. D. German
Pte. J. German
Pte. J. Gibbons
Pte. J. Gibbons
Pte. P. Gibbons
Pte. S. Gibson
Pte. P. Gillan
Pte. J. Gillespie
Pte. O. Gillside
Pte. G. Gilman
Pte. H. Gilmore
Pte. R. Goodwin
Pte. P. Gordon
Pte. W. Gordon
Pte. C. Gorley
Pte. J. Gorman
Pte. T. Goughan
Pte. C. Goughitty
Pte. B. Goulding
Pte. L. Goulding
Pte. A. Graham
Pte. F. Graham
Pte. J. Graham
Pte. T. Graham
Pte. J. Grant
Pte. M. Grant
Pte. A. Gray
Pte. P. Gray
Pte. O. Green
Pte. T. Green
Pte. P. Gunn
Pte. J. Gurley
Pte. D. Haggerty
Pte. W. Haisdale
Pte. R. Hall
Pte. R. Hall

Pte. O. Hallanan
Pte. G. Hamill
Pte. D. Hammil
Pte. J. Hamilton
Pte. J. Hamilton
Pte. W. Hamilton
Pte. R. Hammond
Pte. B. Hanlow
(B. Hanlan)
Pte. D. Hannah
Pte. J. Hannah
Pte. M. Hannah
Pte. T. Hannon
Pte. L. Harcourt
Pte. W. Hardenham
Pte. J. Hare
Pte. J. Hare
Pte. T. Harrican
(T. Hammican)
Pte. J. Harrigan
Pte. W. Harrison
Pte. J. Hart
Pte. W. Harwood
Pte. J. Howtheron
Pte. W. Haslet
(W. Heslett)
Pte. J. Healy
Pte. P. Heanry
(P. Heaney)
Pte. T. Hefferman
Pte. E. Helmes
Pte. J. Henderson
Pte. P. Henery
Pte. B. Henry
Pte. C. Henry
Pte. W. Henry
Pte. J. Herbert
Pte. H. Hewett
(H. Hewitt)
Pte. W. Hewett

Pte. C. Hickey
Pte. F. Higgins
Pte. P. Higgins
Pte. P. Higgins
Pte. P. Higgins
Pte. J. Hinds
Ptc. J. Hogan
Pte. J. Hogan
Pte. J. Hogan
Pte. M. Hogg
Pte. J. Holder
Pte. D. Holliday
Pte. J. Holliday
Pte. W. Hopkins
Pte. W. Howe
Pte. D. Howtheron
Pte. J. Houburn
Pte. D. Houghton
Pte. T. Hoyle
Pte. J. Huddelston
Pte. W. Hudson
Pte. J. Hudson
Pte. O. Hughes
Pte. T. Hughes
Pte. W. Hughes,
Pte. W. Hughes
Pte. C. Humphries
Pte. P. Hunt
Pte. J. Hutchinson
Pte. M. Hyland
Pte. J. Jackson
Pte. J. James
Pte. R. Jennings
Pte. E. Johnston
Pte. J. Johnston
Pte. N. Johnston
Pte. P. Johnston
Pte. W. Johnston
Pte. A. Johnstone
Pte. J. Jolly

Pte. C. Jones
Pte. H. Jones
Pte. J. Jones
Pte. T. Jordan
Pte. T. Judje
Pte. C. Kain
Pte. J. Kearnes
Pte. T. Kearnes
Pte. W. Kearns
Pte. E. Keegan
Pte. W. Keegan
Pte. T. Keegan
Pte. D. Kelly
Pte. G. Kelly
Pte. J. Kelly
Pte. P. Kelly
Pte. R. Kelly
Pte. T. Kelly
Pte. W. Kelly
Pte. D. Kelso
Pte. N. Kenan
Pte. P. Kennedy
Pte. P. Kenny
Pte. R. Kernan
Pte. W. Kerney
Pte. W. Kernegan
Pte. M. Korr
Pte. T. Kerwin
Pte. T. Kens
Pte. G. King
Pte. J. King
Pte. O. King
Pte. W. Kingley
(W. Kinley)
Pte. T. Kinnealy
Pte. J. Lackey
Pte. W. Lackey
Pte. D. Lacreef
Pte. P. Langan
Pte. H. Lappin

195

Pte. M. Lappin
Pte. P. Lappin
Pte. A. Larkin
Pte. P. Larkin
Pte. T. Lavery
Pte. M. Lavin
Pte. C. Law
Pte. W. Lawn
Pte. D. Leadin
Pte. R. Learson
Pte. J. Leary
Pte. H. Ledley
(H. Leadly)
Pte. J. Ledley
Pte. M. Lee
Pte. J. Leech
Pte. A. Legg
Pte. D. Leonard
Pte. J. Leonard
Pte. T. Leonard
Pte. M. Lerry
Pte. J. Leslie
Pte. J. Lewis
Pte. O. Lily
(O. Lilley)
Pte. T. Limmox
Pte. A. Little
Pte. P. Little
Pte. R. Little
Pte. J. Loughlin
Pte. J. Loughnes
Pte. H. Loughran
Pte. J. Loughran
Pte. H. Lunny
Pte. L. Lunny
Pte. J. Lynch
Pte. J. Lynch
Pte. L. Lynch
Pte. J. Lyons
Pte. T. Lyons

Pte. I. McAlister
Pte. P. McAnulty
Pte. H. McAvenny
Pte. J. McAvenny
Pte. J. McBride
Pte. S. McBride
Pte. J. McCabe
Pte. J. McCabe
Pte. T. McCabe
Pte. B. McCabrey
Pte. J. McCafrey
Pte. B. McCaffrey
Pte. P. McCann
Pte. E. McCardle
Pte. C. McCarron
Pte. J. McCarter
Pte. C. McCarthy
Pte. F. McCarthy
Pte. J. McCaulay
(J. McCawley)
Pte. A. McDonald
Pte. T. McDonald
Pte. J. McEntire
Pte. T. McEwin
Pte. M. McFarlane
Pte. T. McGavey
Pte. J. McGaw
Pte. B. McGee
Pte. B. McGee
Pte. M. McGee
Pte. P. McGee
Pte. B. McGill
Pte. F. McGinn
Pte. F. McGinnett
Pte. E. McGinnis
Pte. P. McGinnis
Pte. J. McGiveron
Pte. J. McGlore
Pte. P. McGoldrick
Pte. M. McGrath

Pte. P. McCready
Pte. B. McGuire
Pte. J. McGuire
Pte. P. McGuire
Pte. P. McGuire
Pte. J. McHugh
Pte. J. McHugh
Pte. N. McHugh
Pte. T. McHugh
Pte. W. McKenny
Pte. M. McKeowen
Pte. J. McKibbon
Pte. T. McKinley
Pte. M. McLoughlin
Pte. F. McMahon
Pte. H. McManus
Pte. H. McManus
Pte. H. McNally
Pte. J. McNearney
Pte. M. Malanify
Pte. J. Marks
Pte. C. Mathews
Pte. P. Meath
Pte. D. Moran
Pte. P. Mulligan
Pte. J. Murray
Pte. P. O'Boyle
Pte. F. O'Brien
Pte. D. O'Bryan
Pte. B. O'Donald
Pte. H. O'Donnell
Pte. D. O'Hara
Pte. H. O'Hara
Pte. L. O'Hara
Pte. T. O'Hara
Pte. E. O'Hare
Pte. J. O'Mara
Pte. T. O'Mara
Pte. B. O'Neill
Pte. C. O'Neill

Pte. C. O'Neill
Pte. J. O'Neill
Pte. O. O'Neill
Pte. D. Orr
Pte. A. Owens
Pte. B. Owens
Pte. R. Owens
Pte. T. Oliphan
Pte. J. Palmer
Pte. P. Parriman
Pte. W. Parsley
Pte. W. Peoples
Pte. J. Pepper
Pte. J. Perkin
Pte. J. Perry
Pte. J. Petty
Pte. R. Phillips
Pte. J. Pollard
Pte. T. Price
Pte. G. Ponsonby
Pte. J. Proctor
Pte. C. Quigley
Pte. R. Quigley
Pte. E. Quinn
Pte. H. Quinn
Pte. J. Quinn
Pte. P. Quinn
Pte. J. Quinnis
Pte. J. Quirk
Pte. F. Rafferty
Pte. J. Rafferty
Pte. E. Reade
Pte. P. Reade
Pte. T. Reade
Pte. G Regan
Pte. P. Regan
Pte. W. Regan
Pte. B. Reilly
Pte. C. Reilly
Pte. J. Reilly

Pte. M. Reilly
Pte. O. Reilly
Pte. W. Reilly
Pte. J. Reily
Pte. P. Reily
Pte. J. Reynolds
Pte. M. Rice
Pte. J. Richmond
Pte. P. Roche
Pte. A. Roden
Pte. J. Rooney
Pte. P. Rooney
Pte. W. Rooney
Pte. P. Roper
Pte. G. Ross
Pte. J. Rourke
Pte. M. Rourke
Pte. O. Rourke
Pte. P. Rourke
Pte. J. Rowe
Pte. M. Russell
Ptc. Λ. Rutlcdgc
Pte. J. Ryan
Pte. J. Ryan
Pte. J. Ryan
Pte. T. Ryan
Pte. W. Ryan
Pte. W. Ryan
Pte. J. Savile
Pte. E. Saunderson
Pte. D. Sauntry
Pte. J. Savage
Pte. J. Scott
Pte. R. Scott
Pte. B. Scully
Pte. J. Sea
Pte. M. Sharkey
Pte. J. Shaughnasay
Pte. P. Shaughnasay
Pte. J. Shaw

Pte. P. Shaw
Pte. W. Sheerwood
Pte. T. Sherlock
Pte. J. Shields
Pte. P. Shields
Pte. T. Sholer
Pte. A. Short
Pte. E. Simpson
Pte. J. Simpson
Pte. W. Simpson
Pte. J. Skelly
Pte. D. Skillen
Pte. R. Slaugherry
Pte. A. Slayne
Pte. A. Slaytor
Pte. B. Smith
Pte. C. Smith
Pte. J. Smith
Pte. J. Smith
Pte. J. Smith
Pte. P. Smith
Ptc. R. Smith
Pte. S. Smith
Pte. T. Smith
Pte. T. Smith
Pte. W. Smith
Pte. W. Smith
Pte. J. Spence
Pte. J. Spiers
Pte. S. Stephenson
Pte. T. Stephenson
Pte. J. Stevens
Pte. D. Stewart
Pte. R. Stewat
Pte. R. Stewart
Pte. S. Stewart
Pte. W. Stibbbens
Pte. D. Strain
Pte. C. Strudgeon
Pte. J. Sullivan

Pte. O. Sullivan
Pte. H. Sutherland
Pte. A. Swarbig
Pte. J. Sweeney
Pte. M. Sweeney
Pte. J. Swift
Pte. B. Swords
Pte. S. Swords
Pte. R. Tarlenton
Pte. D. Tarpe
Pte. J. Taylor
Pte. P. Taylor

Pte. A. Tener
Pte. G. Thackeray
Pte. J. Thackeray
Pte. J. Thomas
Pte. J. Thompson
Pte. J. Thompson
Pte. T. Tierney
Pte. A. Toole
Pte. J. Toole
Pte. P. Toole
Pte. T. Toole
Pte. T. Toole

Pte. J. Toy
Pte. A. Traynor
Pte. P. Traynor
Pte. J. Treadway
Pte. C. Trotter
Pte. J. Turner
Pte. J. Tysdayle
Pte. J. Walsh
Pte. L. Walsh
Pte. A. Walters

Bibliography

Army List.

Harris, R. G., *The Irish Regiments 1683–1999*, Spellmount Ltd., The Old Rectory, Staplehurst, Kent, 1999.

Blackwood, R. M., *The Battles of the British Army*, Simpkin, Marshall, Hamilton, Kent & Co., London.

Fletcher, I., *Wellington's Regiments*, Spellmount Ltd., The Old Rectory, Staplehurst, Kent, 1994.

Cole, Maud Lowry, *Memoirs of Sir Lowry Cole*, Macillan & Co. Ltd., St. Martin's Street, London, 1943.

Regimental Diary/Memoirs of Lieutenant Charles Crowe, 27th Foot.

Regimental Historical Records Committee, *The Royal Inniskilling Fusiliers from December 1688 to July 1914*, Constable & Company Ltd., London, 1934.

Jackson, E. S., *The Inniskilling Dragoons, The Records of an Old Heavy Cavalry Regiment*, Arthur L. Humphries, 1909.

Tranie, J., *Napoleon's War in Spain, The French Peninsular Campaigns, 1807–1814*, Arms and Armour Press, London, 1982.

Joslin, E. C., *British Battles & Medals*, Spink, London, 1988.

Sprig of Shillelagh, June 1 1891 No. 9. Vol. I: The monthly Journal of the 27th Inniskillings.

Sprig of Shillelagh, July 1 1891;

Sprig of Shillelagh, December 1 1891;

Sprig of Shillelagh, January 1 1892 No. 9. Vol. 1;

Sprig of Shillelagh, March 1 1893;

Sprig of Shillelagh, April 1 1892 No. 19. Vol. II;

Sprig of Shillelagh, April 1 1894;

Sprig of Shillelagh, July 1 1894;

Sprig of Shillelagh, June 1 1896;

Notes

Chapter One

1. The Peace of Amiens was signed in March 1802, temporarily bringing to an end hostilities between Britain and France.
2. The Treaty of Tilsit was signed in July 1807 between Napoleon Bonaparte, Alexander I of Russia and Frederick William III of Prussia.
3. The Continental Blockade was a factor in the Treaty of Tilsit by which Prussia and Russia agreed not to enter into trade with Britain.
4. Sir David Baird commanded the 1st Division and was seriously wounded at the Battle of Corunna, 16 January 1809, having taken over command of the Allied Army following the death of Sir John Moore during the battle.
5. Sir John Moore commanded the Allied army at the Battle of Corunna, 16 January 1809, but died as the result of a musket shot which shattered his collarbone.
6. Lieutenant General Sir John Cradock (later Lord Howden) commanded the British Forces in the Peninsula following the Battle of Corunna.
7. The Battle of Corunna, 16 January 1809, was a bitter affair concentrated on the strategic heights of Monte Mero and the village of Elvina.
8. Major-General Alexander Mackenzie commanded the 3rd Division, comprising Mackenzie's Brigade of the 2/24th, 2/31st & 1/45th, plus Donkin's Brigade of the 2/7th, 2/53rd & 5/60th at the Battle of Talavera, 27/28 July 1809.
9. Sir Galbraith Lowry Cole was born on 1 May 1772, in Dublin, the second son of William Willoughby Cole, first Earl of Enniskillen and his wife Anne, the daughter of Galbraith Lowry Corry of Ahenis, County Tipperary. He joined the 12th Light Dragoons (12th Lancers) as a Cornet on 31 March 1787, aged 15 years. He was promoted Lieutenant in the 5th Dragoon

Guards on 31 May 1791, Captain in the 60th 30 November 1792 and Major in the 102nd 31 October 1793. He was present during the operations at Martinique, St. Lucia and Guadeloupe. He was promoted Lieutenant Colonel in the Hon Robert Ward's Regiment of Foot (the Downshire Regiment, disbanded in 1795). In 1796 he was appointed Deputy-Adjutant-General in Ireland and the following year Aide-de-Camp to Lord Carhampton, Commander-in-Chief in Ireland. Returned as M.P. for Enniskillen in the Irish House of Commons in 1798, he appears as a Lieutenant Colonel in Villette's Regiment, a corps of Albanians, in 1799. He received his Colonelcy on 1 January 1801. He transferred to the 3rd Foot Guards (Scots Guards) as a Captain and later Lieutenant Colonel, 25 May 1803. On 4 August 1804 he transferred to the 27th Foot (Inniskilling Fusiliers) and took command of the 1st Battalion in Malta in 1805. Elected M.P. for Fermanagh in the House of Commons in 1803, a seat he held for twenty years, he was promoted Major General 25 April 1808, and commanded the 4th Division in the Peninsula the following year. His marriage to Lady Frances Harris, second daughter of the Earl of Malmesbury, on 15 June 1815, prevented him from being present at the Battle of Waterloo, though he did command the 2nd Division in France during the subsequent occupation. He died suddenly on 4 October 1842 at Highfield Park in Hampshire, England.

10. Marshal André Masséna, Duke of Rivoli and Prince of Essling.
11. General William Carr Beresford, Marshal and Commander-in-Chief of the Portuguese Army.
12. *The Royal Inniskilling Fusiliers* pp. 188–190.
13. Wrottesley's *Life of Field-Marshal Sir John Burgoyne*, Vol. 1. p. 130.
14. Marshal Nicolas Jean-de-Dieu Soult, Duke of Dalmatia (1769–1851) commanded the II Corps of the Army of Spain, 26 September 1809, Commander-in-Chief of the Army of the South in Spain, 14 July 1810, Lieutenant General and Commander-in-Chief of the armies in Spain and the Pyrenees, 1 July 1813.
15. Ian Fletcher, *Wellington's Regiments,* p. 149.

Chapter Two

1. Lieutenant General Sir Thomas Picton commanded the 3rd Infantry Division.
2. Major General Sir James Leith commanded the 5th Division.
3. Baron General Armand Philippon was the officer commanding the French garrison at Badajoz.
4. Glacis: a bank sloping down from a fort which exposes attackers to the defenders' missiles.
5. Ravelin: an outwork comprised of two faces forming a salient angle, constructed beyond the main ditch and in front of the curtain.
6. *The Royal Inniskilling Fusiliers*, p.193.
7. Napier's *History of the Peninsular War*, Book XVI, Chapter V.
8. *The Royal Inniskilling Fusiliers*, p.196.
9. Marshal Marmont, Duke of Ragusa, took command of the Army of Portugal on 7 May 1811, replacing Masséna.
10. Hermanito; little brother in Spanish; however, in this instance it refers to a group of small hills or raised ground occupied by both French and Allied forces.
11. *The Royal Inniskilling Fusiliers*, p.201.
12. Ibid, p.202.

Chapter Three

1. Suchet, Marshal Louis Gabriel, Duke of Albufera, (1770–1826). Commanded the 1st Division of the 5th Corps (Army of Spain) 1809, commanded the 3rd Corps 1811, commanded Army of Aragon 1813. In 1813 he was appointed Colonel-General of the Imperial Guard and in 1814 Commander-in-Chief of the Army of the South.
2. Lieutenant Colonel George James Reeves. Ensign in the 8th Foot 9 February1791; Lieutenant 29 June 1793; Captain-Lieutenant and adjutant 21 December 1796; Captain in the 18th Foot 20 August 1801; Major in the 27th Foot 10 October 1805; Brevet Lieutenant Colonel 1 January 1812; Inspecting Field Officer of a recruiting District 1815; placed on half pay in the 27th Foot 25 December 1816. He was appointed Governor of Placentia 14 June 1819, a position he held until his death. He was promoted

Colonel 22 July 1830; Major General, 28 June 1838. He died in London 14 March 1845. He was made a Commander of the Bath and in 1824 a Knight of the Hanoverian Guelphic Order. Although he initially joined the 3rd Battalion he did not see service in the Peninsula with it. He commanded the 2nd Battalion in South-Eastern Spain, was present at Castalla and Tarragona and was seriously wounded at the Battle of Ordal.

3. John Hare began his service in the Tarbet Fencibles, which was commanded by Sir Edward Leslie. He joined the 27th Foot as an Ensign 29 October 1799; Lieutenant 17 May 1800; Captain 9 September 1805; Brevet Major 17 June 1813; Brevet Lieutenant-Colonel 18 June 1815; Major 30 July 1818; Colonel 10 January 1837; went on half-pay 28 February 1840. He was appointed Major General 9 November 1846 and died the following month, 10 December 1846. In 1799 he served in the expedition to Holland whilst attached to the 69th Regiment. He served with the 27th Foot in Egypt 1801; at Maida 1806; with the 2nd Battalion in South-Eastern Spain 1813–14 at Castalla and Tarragona. He took over command of the Inniskillings when Reeves was wounded at Ordal and was present at the siege of Barcelona. He commanded the 1st Battalion at the Battle of Waterloo for which he was made a Commander of the Bath, Knight of Hanover and Knight of St Vladimir. He commanded the 27th Inniskillings for fifteen years and was appointed Lieutenant Governor of the Cape of Good Hope 1 December 1839. He held this post until his death.

4. *The Royal Inniskilling Fusiliers*, pp. 206–7.
5. Maugre – in spite of, notwithstanding.
6. Napier's *History of the Peninsular War*, Book XX, Chapter IV.
7. *The Royal Inniskilling Fusiliers*, p. 208.
8. Ibid., p. 210.
9. Ibid., pp. 217–8.
10. Ibid., p. 217.

Chapter Four

1. *Chevaux de frise* – a defence made of concrete pillars to stop advancing horsemen, similar to dragon's teeth.
2. Certes – assuredly.

3. The "Forlorn Hope" – those troops designated to head an attack. In such a position their chances of survival were minimal.
4. Coxcomb – a dandy or fop.
5. General Miguel de Alava was the Spanish liaison officer with whom Wellington was in contact as a representative of the Spanish army.
6. Halbert, also halberd – a weapon which was a combination of spear and battle-axe, consisting of a sharp-edged blade and a spearhead ending in a point on a pole, not unlike a pikestaff.
7. *The Royal Inniskilling Fusiliers*, pp. 212–3.
8. The Brunswick Oels were the infantry of the Duchy of Brunswick. Also known as the "Black Legion", they were largely made up of prisoners and foreign soldiers. They arrived in Portugal in 1810.
9. Valise – this refers to an item of horse furniture (so called) and is defined as "a tubular container of cloth and leather strapped behind the saddle, usually bearing regimental devices on the circular ends. Valises were usually hollowed in the centre to prevent pressure on the horse's back. They were discarded completely in the 1890s." *British Cavalry Equipment* 1800–1941.
10. Gabion – a wicker basket of cylindrical form usually open at both ends, intended to be filled with earth, for use in fortification or engineering.
11. Barbette – a platform or mound of earth within a fortification on which guns are raised so that they can be fired over a parapet.
12. Pisan – a piece of armour to protect the upper chest or neck.
13. Flam – a liar or untrustworthy person.
14. Bat – bat-money was an allowance for carrying baggage in the field. It also applies to money paid as forage allowance.
15. Arms: to collect ammunition and weapons.
16. Sutler: a person who provides merchandise and supplies to troops.
17. Vascuence – the dialect spoken in the Basque area of Spain.
18. Pledget – a piece of lint or cloth, often soaked in medication, applied to a wound or sore.
19. Robert Melvin Blackwood, *The Battles of the British Army*, p. 158.
20. Tandem – a two wheeled carriage pulled by horses, often one before the other.
21. Bumbailiff – a bailiff who is close on the heels of someone.

Chapter Five

1. Morillo, General Pablo (1777–1838). He later fought in South America where he was defeated by Simon Bolivar.
2. Harispe, General Jean Isidore (1768–1855) commanded the 2nd Division of the III Corps at the sieges of Tarragona and Lerida.
3. Scapegrace – one who escapes the grace of God; a rascal.
4. Abernethy – a reference to John Abernethy (1764–1831), an English surgeon famous at the time for his lectures on anatomy.
5. Monotype – the one and only type, especially a sole species which constitutes a genus or family.
6. Shaves, on bits – pieces of gossip.
7. Scrumpled – hesitated or refused.
8. Rib – wife, as in Adam's rib.
9. Caldera – cauldron made of copper; *caldera de vapor*, steam boiler or ketttle.
10. Poniard – a dagger or small sword.
11. General Sir George Ramsay, 9th Earl of Dalhousie (1770–1838).
12. General Charles Doyle commanded the Portuguese brigades, which comprised the 7th Division, i.e. the 7th and 19th Line Regiment and the 2nd Caçadores.
13. Battles on 27, 28, 29 January 1814. This could possibly refer to Napoleon's attack on the Russians at St Dizier (27 January 1814) or the capture by the French of Brienne (29 January 1814).
14. Physiognomist – one who reads character or disposition from the face.
15. Capataztaza – foreman.
16. Lieutenant General Sir John Hope, 4th Earl of Hopetoun (1785–1823) replaced Sir David Baird as commander of the army when the latter was wounded at the Battle of Corunna. He in turn had taken over command following the death of Sir John Moore.
17. General Rowland Hill (1772–1842) commanded the 2nd Division of Infantry which comprised Tilson's and Stewart's brigades at the Battle of Talavera, 28 July 1809.
18. Marshal Jean-Baptiste Drouet, Count d'Erlon (1765–1844) was Commander-in-Chief of the Army of the Centre.
19. Light Bobs – a soldier of a light infantry company.
20. Deals – timber planks.
21. Quiz – an odd or eccentric-looking person.
22. See Chapter 6, Note 1.

Chapter Six

1. Drumhead Court Martial – a Court Martial convened for the summary trial of an offence committed during field operations. So called because it was sometimes held around a drumhead.
2. Broken-head fair – the auctioning off of a soldier's belongings after his death.
3. Videttes – mounted sentries placed in advance of the outposts of an army to observe the movements of the enemy.
4. Lieutenant Gough: nephew of Sir Hugh Gough who was the son of a Lieutenant Colonel in the Limerick city militia. He commanded the Royal Irish Fusiliers in Portugal and Spain during the Peninsular War, was severely wounded at the Battle of Talavera and captured the baton of Marshal Jean-Baptiste Jourdan at Vitoria (1813). As a Major General he commanded the British forces in Mysore, India, in 1837 and headed an expedition to China during the first Opium War (1839–42). Appointed Commander-in-Chief in India in 1843, he defeated the Sikhs in both the first and second Sikh Wars (1845–46 and 1848–49).
5. Torn – unruly or disorderly person.
6. Tartlet – a sour character.
7. John Geddes obtained his Ensigncy in the 27th on 22 December 1804 and was promoted Lieutenant 23 October 1805 and Captain 1 December 1806. He served with the 27th Inniskillings in Calabria and was present at the Battle of Maida 4 July 1806. He served in Sicily until 1810 at which point he joined the 3rd Battalion of the 27th in the Peninsula and took part in the battles of Nivelle, Nive, Orthez and Toulouse, where he was severely wounded. He was promoted Major 24 February 1825, Lieutenant Colonel 11 November 1831, at which point he went on half-pay. He was made a Knight of the Royal Hanoverian Guelphic Order in 1836; promoted Colonel 9 November 1846; Major General 20 June 1854, and appointed Colonel of the 27th Inniskillings 24 April 1860. He was promoted Lieutenant General 23 March 1861 and died in Edinburgh 28 April 1864.
8. The son of John Maclean of Pitmain, Badenoch, he entered the army as an Ensign in the 1st Foot (Royal Scots) 30 April 1794.

He was promoted Lieutenant 1 May 1794 in the 100th Regiment with whom he served in Gibraltar until June 1795. He was promoted Captain 15 June 1797 and served in Ireland during the rebellion of 1798. He served in the expedition to Holland in 1799 and the following year joined Sir Ralph Abercomby's expedition to the Mediterranean. He served on the Quartermaster-General's staff in Egypt and Malta March 1801–August 1802. He was present at the landing in Aboukir and took part in all the operations in Egypt in 1801. He was promoted Major 2 August 1804 and transferred to the 27th Inniskillings; served on the Adjutant-General's staff in Dublin from 1803 until 1805; on the Quartermaster General's staff in the expedition to Hanover October 1805 until February 1806; on the Adjutant-General's staff at Horse Guards from February 1896 until April 1808; on the Quartermaster-General's staff in the expedition to Sweden April to July 1808 under Sir John Moore. Promoted Lieutenant Colonel 9 June 1808, he took command of the 3rd Battalion the 27th Inniskillings in August of the same year and served with them through the entire Peninsular campaign. Among his awards he received the Gold Cross with two clasps and the Order of the Tower and Sword of Portugal, and in 1815 was made a Knight Commander of the Order of the Bath. He was promoted Brevet Lieutenant Colonel 4 June 1814 and commanded the 2nd Battalion of the 27th in England from August 1814 until July 1815, at which point he joined the 3rd Battalion on their return from America and accompanied them to France. In 1816 he brought the 3rd Battalion home to be disbanded and took command of the 2nd Battalion until they too were disbanded the following year. He was appointed Colonel of the 60th Regiment 7 January 1835; Lieutenant General 28 June 1838; transferred to the Colonelcy of the 27th Inniskillings 2 November 1842. He died 31 January 1848.

9. Skein: a term used in connection with thread or yarn, to unravel a series of knots.
10. Pannier – a basket carried on the back.
11. Cant – the share-out or division of spoils.
12. Quondam – at one time, formerly.

Chapter Seven

1. *The Royal Inniskilling Fusiliers*, 245.
2. *The History of Canada*, William Kingford, Vol. VIII, p. 531.
3. The Battle of Plattsburg was fought on 11 September 1814.
4. The small Royal Navy flotilla, commanded by Captain Downie, consisted of a thirty-six-gun frigate, the *Confiance*, three brigs and twelve gunboats.
5. William Brydges Neynoe joined the 39th Foot as an Ensign on 31 May 1792. He was promoted Lieutenant in 1793; Captain-Lieutenant in the 180th Foot 22 August 1794. When the 180th Foot was disbanded he joined the 34th Foot. He was promoted Captain 3 September 1795; Major in the 27th Foot 7 September 1804 and Brevet Lieutenant-Colonel 4 June 1811. He went on half-pay 25 February 1816; promoted Colonel 27 May 1825 and died in 1835.

Chapter Eight

1. Major-General Sir John Lambert, K.C.B. commanded the 10th (British) Infantry Brigade in Belgium.
2. Louis XVIII, brother of the guillotined Louis XVI, entered Paris on 3 May 1814 following the defeat of Napoleon and the armistice between France and the Allies dated 23 April 1814.
3. Grouchy, Marquis Emmanuel de (1766–1847). During the Peninsular War he commanded the cavalry of the Army of Spain and later spent time as Governor of Madrid.
4. *The Sprig of Shillelagh*, 1 July 1894, p. 210.
5. *The Royal Inniskilling Fusiliers*, pp. 254–256.

Chapter Nine

1. *The Royal Inniskilling Fusiliers*, p. 25, Siborne's *Waterloo Letters*, Major Graeme, p. 407.
2. General Sir Colin Halkett (1774–1856) commanded the 7th Brigade at the Battle of Salamanca and the 5th British Brigade of the 3rd British Division at the Battle of Waterloo.

3. *The Royal Inniskilling Fusiliers*, pp. 258–259.
4. General Sir James Kempt commanded the 8th British Brigade of Picton's 5th British Division at the Battle of Waterloo.
5. Baron Von Ompteda commanded the 2nd King's German Legion Brigade of the 3rd British Division at the Battle of Waterloo.
6. Reille, Count Honoré Charles Michel Joseph, (1775–1860) was Commander-in-Chief of the French Army in Portugal during the Peninsular War.
7. Ney, Marshal Michel, Duke of Elchingen (1769–1815) commanded the VI Corps of the Army of Portugal during the Peninsular War.
8. *The Royal Inniskilling Fusiliers*, p. 257.
9. Ibid., pp. 271–272.
10. Major-General Sir William Ponsonby (1772–1815) commanded the 2nd British Cavalry Brigade (Union Brigade) of Lord Uxbridge's British and Hanoverian Cavalry, comprising the 1st Dragoons (Royals), 2nd Dragoons (Scots Greys) and the 6th Dragoons (Inniskillings).
11. *The Royal Inniskilling Fusiliers*, p. 261. Siborne's *Waterloo Letters*, pp. 395–396.

Chapter Ten

1. *The Royal Inniskilling Fusiliers*, p. 263.
2. Foy, General Maximilien Sébastien (1775–1825). He was seriously wounded at the Battle of Busaco, 27 September 1810.
3. *The Royal Inniskilling Fusiliers*, pp. 263–264.
4. James Lawford, *Napoleon The Last Campaigns 1813–15*, Roxby Press Productions Limited 1977, p.146.
5. *The Royal Inniskilling Fusiliers*, pp. 264–265 Lieutenant-Colonel J. Leach, C.B., Siborne's *Waterloo Letters*, p.365.
6. *The Royal Inniskilling Fusiliers*, p. 266.
7. *The Royal Inniskilling Fusiliers*, p. 267; Siborne's *Waterloo Letters*, p. 392.
8. *The Sprig of Shillelagh*, I January 1892, p. 68. Extract taken from *Adventures in the Rifle Brigade*, by Captain J. Kincaid.

Chapter Eleven

1. *The Royal Inniskilling Fusiliers*, p. 268.
2. Robert Melvin Blackwood, *The Battles of the British Army*, pp. 190–191.
3. Ibid., p. 183.
4. Ibid., p. 190.
5. *The Sprig of Shillelagh*, 1 December 1891, p. 44. Extract from the Memoirs of an Officer of the 5th or Picton's Division, in the Campaign of Waterloo.

Chapter Twelve

1. *The Sprig of Shillelagh*, 1 April 1894, p. 144.
2. Ibid., 1 March 1893, p. 129.

Index

Adams, 14, 30, 191, 192
Albuhera, 183
Alcalda, 25, 48, 75
Alcoy, 13
Alicante, 13, 16, 17
Alten, 103, 108, 150
America, 130, 131, 132, 134, 137, 139, 141, 184
Anglesey, 142
Anson, 17, 88, 108, 114
Ardour, 86, 92
Artillery, 28, 35, 62, 67, 79, 81, 86, 88, 89, 100, 106, 107, 110, 111, 122, 175, 177

Bachelu, 158
Badajoz, 5, 6, 7, 9, 10, 11, 16, 17, 180, 183, 184, 185, 186, 188, 203
Barcelona, 16, 17, 99, 204
Bayonne, 17, 33, 55, 57, 62, 64, 65, 79, 80, 84, 86, 88, 92, 93, 96, 126
Belgians, 137, 178
Bentinck, 13, 17, 29
Beresford, 5, 6, 86, 103, 108, 182, 184, 202
Bermuda, 135, 136, 137
Biar, 13, 14, 16
Blücher, 142, 152, 164, 177
Bordeaux, 126, 130, 132, 135
Boulogne, 47
Braine L'Alleud, 166
Browne, 116, 157, 176
Bruges, 177

Brussels, 142, 144, 146, 151, 154, 161, 165, 172, 177, 178
Burgoyne, 5, 202
Busaco, 4, 181, 183
Bylandt, 178

Cadiz, 4
Calabrese Free Corps, 14
Cambo, 57
Canada, 132, 133, 134, 186, 188, 209
Castalla, 13, 15, 16, 184, 186, 188, 204
Charleroi, 146, 166, 177, 179
Chitty, 41, 72, 91, 92, 97, 99, 110, 112, 114, 115, 116, 122, 123, 131
Citadel, 36, 37
Ciudad Rodrigo, 7
Clinton, 57, 59, 86, 108, 120
Colchester, 61
Cole, 4, 5, 26, 27, 42, 53, 69, 83, 91, 108, 111, 141, 199, 201
Commissariat, 42, 70, 73, 76, 82, 84
Convent, 36, 38, 48, 54, 67
Corunna, 4, 182, 201, 206
Coup de Soleil, 22, 46
Court Martial, 32, 72, 73, 74, 75, 103, 125, 127, 207
Cradock, 4, 201
Crowe, 19, 21, 29, 35, 37, 51, 53, 54, 57, 65, 71, 80, 84, 103, 119, 121, 127, 129, 130, 135, 137, 139, 171, 172, 193, 199, 204

Cuba, 136
Cuirassiers, 173, 179
Curragh, 2

Doctors, 10, 49, 53
Donkin, 13, 201
Donzelot, 151, 178
Dragoons, 50, 75, 82, 142, 176,
    177, 178, 179, 181, 182, 201,
    210
Dutch, 137, 178
Dutch-Belgians, 150, 153, 178

Elba, 124, 136
England, 2, 26, 32, 34, 36, 38, 43,
    45, 47, 48, 50, 51, 52, 53, 57,
    61, 62, 65, 68, 69, 73, 75, 77,
    81, 84, 100, 122, 125, 135,
    139, 141, 172, 184, 202, 208
Enniskillen, 2, 138, 201
Erie, 134

Falmouth, 2
Forlorn Hope, 27, 38, 205
Foy, 158, 165, 167, 194, 210
France, 1, 2, 17, 33, 41, 50, 79, 82,
    92, 124, 136, 137, 138, 139,
    141, 166, 186, 201, 202, 208,
    209

Garonne, 102, 105, 106, 107, 108,
    125
Genappe, 144, 146, 161, 177
George III, 1
Ghent, 141, 144
Gosport, 96, 135
Grammont, 177
Grenada, 90, 105
Grenadier, 46, 55, 106, 112, 120
Grouchy, 164, 209
Guadiana, 5, 6

Halkett, 150, 159, 209
Hanoverians, 137, 160, 169

Hare, 83, 114, 161, 187, 195, 196,
    204
Hay, 57
Heavy Cavalry, 107, 177, 178,
    179, 199
Hougoumont, 165, 167
Hussars, 22, 107, 108, 142, 172,
    178

Inniskilling Dragoon, 153, 166,
    176, 177, 178, 179, 199
Inniskillings, 1, 4, 5, 6, 7, 8, 9, 10,
    11, 12, 13, 14, 15, 16, 17, 29,
    30, 31, 69, 108, 132, 134,
    137, 138, 141, 144, 145, 147,
    149, 154, 155, 156, 157, 158,
    159, 160, 161, 163, 166, 168,
    169, 171, 172, 173, 174, 178,
    180, 187, 188, 199, 201, 204,
    207, 208, 210
Ireland, 2, 51, 53, 123, 135, 139,
    171, 182, 186, 189, 202, 208
Italian Legion, 14

Jamaica, 72, 136
Junot, 2

Kempt, 150, 153, 154, 158, 178,
    210
Kielmansegge, 150

La Belle Alliance, 166
Lake Champlain, 134
Lambert, 141, 144, 146, 149, 154,
    156, 158, 160, 161, 162, 166,
    170, 209
Languedoc, 102, 103, 114, 184
Light Division, 7, 9, 12, 40, 57, 58,
    86, 89, 103, 106, 107, 108,
    120
Ligny, 142, 148
Lisbon, 4, 48, 77, 91, 124

Madox, 176, 177, 179

214

Madrid, 17, 76, 209
Marcognet, 178
Marmont, 10, 11, 12
Massena, 181, 202, 203
Merbe Braine, 166
Middle Guard, 165
Militia, 52, 60, 132, 180
Miller, 171, 176, 177, 179, 188,
    191
Mont St. Jean, 145, 146, 154, 178
Montreal, 132, 134, 135, 138
Moore, 4, 47, 82, 89, 192, 201,
    206, 208
Murray, 14, 15, 16, 18, 196
Murter, 178

Napoleon, 2, 13, 122, 124, 132,
    136, 137, 141, 142, 148, 151,
    152, 156, 160, 162, 163, 164,
    166, 167, 178, 199, 201, 209,
    210
Nassauers, 137
Neynoe, 138, 139, 209
Nive, 57, 183, 184, 185, 207
Nivelle, 51, 57, 81, 183, 184, 185,
    186, 207

Ompteda, 150, 160, 210
Ontario, 132, 134
Oostaker, 177
Ordal, 29, 30, 31, 184, 189, 204
Orthes, 86, 88, 89, 183, 185
Ostend, 137, 177

Pack, 69, 113, 150, 153
Pamplona, 23, 45, 73
Papelotte, 146
Passages, 38, 43, 44, 45, 46, 48,
    50, 54, 65, 66, 68, 69, 70, 71,
    72, 75, 77, 78, 79
Peninsula, 2, 13, 25, 33, 52, 61,
    102, 124, 130, 132, 133, 136,
    137, 141, 148, 152, 157, 165,
    171, 173, 176, 180, 181, 187,

    188, 189, 201, 202, 204, 207,
    208, 209, 210
Picquet, 59, 66, 93, 98, 103, 104,
    106, 107, 121
Picton, 9, 86, 103, 108, 150, 151,
    152, 153, 154, 169, 178, 203,
    210, 211
Plattsburg, 134, 138, 183, 209
Ponsonby, 108, 153, 154, 177,
    178, 179, 197, 210
Pontoon, 105, 106
Portsmouth, 28, 48, 56, 61, 135,
    137, 172
Portugal, 2, 4, 5, 13, 19, 41, 74,
    76, 84, 126, 176, 182, 203,
    205, 208, 210
Prevost, 132, 133, 134, 135
Prince of Wales, 46, 69, 173
Prussian, 166

Quatre Bras, 142, 144, 148, 153,
    173, 177
Quebec, 132, 188

Redoubt, 42, 110, 117, 120
Reeves, 30, 203, 204
Reille, 151, 152, 210
Renteirea, 36
Rifle Brigade, 162, 210
Rio Grande, 103
Rocket Brigade, 62
Roman Catholic, 20, 21, 25, 76
Royal Navy, 2, 46, 145, 209
Royals, 72, 153, 177, 178, 210

Sabbath, 21, 22, 25
Saint Cyprien, 102, 103
Salamanca, 10, 11, 183, 184, 185,
    209
San Cristobal, 5
San Sebastian, 27, 36, 37, 38, 70,
    126, 186
San Vincente, 7
Santa Maria, 8, 9

Scots Greys, 153, 177, 178, 210
Sharpe, 54
Sicily, 13, 17, 185, 187, 188, 207
Smohain, 146
Soult, 57, 58, 59, 64, 68, 86, 87,
    88, 89, 102, 103, 107, 113,
    121, 122, 123, 124, 129, 202
Spain, 2, 4, 5, 13, 19, 42, 74, 76,
    176, 182, 188, 199, 202, 203,
    204, 209
Suchet, 14, 15, 16, 17, 203
Surgeons, 22, 23

Talavera, 4, 201, 206
Tarragona, 16, 17, 29, 188, 204,
    206
Toulouse, 89, 100, 101, 102, 103,
    107, 120, 121, 122, 123, 125,
    126, 180, 185, 186, 207

Valencia, 13, 41
Vandeleur, 150, 177, 179
Vician, 150
Villafranca, 17, 29

Vittoria, 17, 28, 180, 181, 183,
    185, 186
Vivien, 107

Waterloo, 13, 19, 54, 135, 136,
    138, 139, 141, 142, 144, 146,
    148, 149, 151, 153, 154, 156,
    161, 162, 166, 168, 169, 171,
    172, 173, 174, 176, 177, 178,
    185, 186, 187, 188, 189, 190,
    202, 204, 209, 210, 211
Wellington, 4, 5, 6, 7, 8, 10, 11,
    12, 13, 16, 17, 26, 50, 57, 58,
    59, 62, 64, 68, 75, 76, 80, 83,
    88, 89, 91, 94, 100, 102, 107,
    108, 113, 122, 125, 132, 133,
    136, 137, 142, 144, 146, 148,
    149, 150, 151, 152, 153, 156,
    158, 159, 160, 162, 163, 164,
    165, 166, 171, 174, 177, 178,
    182, 184, 199, 202, 205